CASE-LAW OF THE WORLD BANK ADMINISTRATIVE TRIBUNAL

An Analytical Digest

Volume II

by

C. F. AMERASINGHE

CLARENDON PRESS · OXFORD

This book has been printed digitally and produced in a standard design in order to ensure its continuing availability

OXFORD
UNIVERSITY PRESS

Great Clarendon Street, Oxford OX2 6DP
Oxford University Press is a department of the University of Oxford.
It furthers the University's objective of excellence in research, scholarship,
and education by publishing worldwide in

Oxford New York

Athens Auckland Bangkok Bogotá Buenos Aires Cape Town
Chennai Dar es Salaam Delhi Florence Hong Kong Istanbul Karachi
Kolkata Kuala Lumpur Madrid Melbourne Mexico City Mumbai Nairobi
Paris São Paulo Singapore Taipei Tokyo Toronto Warsaw

with associated companies in Berlin Ibadan

Oxford is a registered trade mark of Oxford University Press
in the UK and in certain other countries

Published in the United States
by Oxford University Press Inc., New York

Reprinted 2001

ISBN 0-19-825819-4

PREFACE

In this second volume I have set out to analyse the judgments and Orders by the World Bank Administrative Tribunal which were handed down between the beginning of 1988 and 30 June 1991. This volume includes Decisions Nos. 55 to 104 and any Orders made during that period. It follows the first one in keeping with the hope expressed in the preface to the latter. The same methodology adopted in the first volume has been adopted in this one. Needless to say, like the first volume, this is intended to be a companion to my two-volume treatise entitled *The Law of the International Civil Service*, which will hopefully soon be published in its second edition, and to my subsequent publication, *Documents on International Administrative Tribunals*.

My thanks are due to those who worked on the typing of the manuscript, Pamela Fraser, Eugenia Alvarez, and Alicia Gormont, especially the first. Above all I must express my deep-felt gratitude to my associate Sophia Hatziconstanti, who not only arduously and with dedication performed many tasks connected with the production of the book, but also gave me invaluable assistance with the analysis. Her contribution has been most welcome and useful and is greatly appreciated. The responsibility for the analysis, however, lies with me.

Any views expressed in this work are not necessarily the views of the World Bank Administrative Tribunal or the World Bank.

C.F.A.

Washington, DC
March 1992

CONTENTS

THE TRIBUNAL

1 January 1988–30 June 1991

Judges

Ahmad Kamal Abul-Magd
Vice-President

Fred K. Apaloo
(from January 1990)

Robert A. Gorman

Eduardo Jiménez de Aréchaga
President (till May 1990)

Elihu Lauterpacht
Vice-President (from May 1990)

Charles Dadi Onyeama
(till January 1990)

Tun Mohamed Suffian

Prosper Weil
Vice-President (till May 1990)
President (from May 1990)

Executive Secretary

Chittharanjan F. Amerasinghe

TABLE OF CASES

ABBREVIATIONS

AGREP	Agriculture and Rural Development Department
APR	Annual Performance Review
EAP	East Asia Projects Department
EDP	Electronic Data Processing Unit
EMENA	Europe, Middle East, and North Africa Region
EM4IE	Europe, Middle East and North Africa, Country Department IV, Industry and Energy Division
ERS	Economics and Research Department
IAD	Internal Auditing Department
IFC	International Finance Corporation
JEU	Job Evaluation Unit
JGAB	Job Grading Appeals Board
PA	Personnel and Administration
PERPD	Personnel Policy Division
PMD	Personnel Management Department
PMS	Personnel Manual Statement
PPR	Performance Planning and Review
PRJ—C	Project Officer—C
PTCO	Principal Technical Co-operation Officer
SAR	South Asia Region
SCPO	Senior Country Program Officer
TAP	Temporary Assignment Program
TCU	Technical Co-operation Unit
UN	United Nations
VIS	Vacancy Information Service
VPCOF	Vice-President Co-financing
VPCTR	Vice-President and Controller
VPP	Vice-President Personnel

1. JURISDICTION

1. Basic provisions

(*a*) *Article II para. 2*

[See also Sect. 3, 'Inadmissibility for Other Reasons', 1.iii and iv.]

i. 32. On the third issue concerning the reservation of the right of appeal to the Tribunal from the decision of February 26, 1987 of the VPCTR until 90 days after the date of the release of the job audit findings by reason of the existence of exceptional circumstances under Article II, para. 2 of the Statute, the Tribunal holds that it is inappropriate for it to decide at the present time on the conditions or requirements of an application which is not before it. (*Breton*, Decision No. 69 [1988], para. 32)

(*b*) *Nature of jurisdiction*

[See also Sect. 9, 'Discretionary Power', 1.iv; Sect. 12, 'Substantive Irregularity', 1.iii, xii, and xiii; Sect. 13, 'Procedural Irregularity', 1.iv; Sect. 16, 'Classification', 1.ii, 13.iii; Sect. 20, 'Fixed-Term Contracts', 2.i; Sect. 30, 'Procedure before Tribunal', 3 (*a*) iii and vi.]

i. 34. The Respondent pointed out that these grievances were addressed to the design of the new grading and salary structure itself, rather than specifically to the correctness of the grading decision with respect to the Applicant's position. On these grounds, the Job Grading Appeals Board concluded that it was not competent to judge the adequacy or otherwise of the new grading system and methodology, but only their application to specific cases. The grounds for appeal enumerated in para. 3.01 of Staff Rule 9.04 obviously do not apply to this Tribunal, whose competence is governed by its Statute, which confers jurisdiction with respect to 'any application by which a member of the staff of the bank group alleges non-observance of the contract of employment or terms of appointment of such staff member.' (*Pinto*, Decision No. 56 [1988], para. 34)

ii. 44. Although the Tribunal does not subscribe to the sweeping statement made by the Respondent to the effect that the '*correctness* of the grading decision is not before the Tribunal at all', it is now well established that this Tribunal will not substitute its own judgement for that of the Respondent as to the merits of an exercise of discretionary power. The reviewing power of this Tribunal, however, extends to a decision taken in exercise of discretionary power by the Respondent to ensure that such exercise is not vitiated by an abuse of discretion, by reason of the action taken in a concrete case 'being arbitrary, discriminatory, improperly motivated or carried out in violation of a fair and reasonable procedure'. (*Saberi*, Decision No. 5 [1982], para. 24 and *Pinto*, Decision No. 56 [1988], para. 36). The Tribunal, therefore, is not in a position to take sides in the dispute between the JEU and the Vice President, on the one hand, and the Applicant and the JGAB, on the other, concerning the proper grade to be assigned to the Applicant's position. Whereas both the Applicant and the JGAB maintain that the grading of the Applicant's position had involved an erroneous application of the grading methodology, the Vice President and Controller insists that the grading of the Applicant's position was the result of the application of the Hay methodology in a technically correct manner. All that the Tribunal has to determine is whether the decision of the Respondent taken by the Vice President and controller reveals an abuse of discretion. (*Rae*, Decision No. 74 [1988], para. 44)

iii. 36. Although, as the Tribunal will note shortly, its own jurisdiction is not limited to review of affirmative administrative decisions but can encompass as well certain omissions or failures to act, the reference in Staff Rule 9.01 to review of an administrative decision' can obviously give rise to uncertainties on the part of staff members.

In the circumstances of this case in particular, it is difficult to say what kind of specific relief or decision the Applicant could have expected from the Pension Information Assistant, in view of the fact that the revised U.S. tax law was indisputably applicable to her late-1986 commuted pension payments; she was indeed informed by him that there was nothing that the Bank could do for her. If, as the Respondent sometimes argues in this case, this did not amount to an 'administrative decision' that this Tribunal can review, it is understandable that there could be uncertainty on the part of the Applicant as to whether the Bank's internal administrative review provisions in Staff Rule 9.01 were applicable and as to whom the Applicant should turn to for recourse. She was therefore not unreasonable when she moved promptly to seek the advice of the Staff Association and then of the Ombudsman. The Applicant might well have moved equally promptly to file an appeal with the Appeals Committee had she not been accurately advised by the Ombudsman that she need not do so because of a pending appeal that the Bank had agreed to apply to her should the outcome favor the staff member. It is noteworthy, in any event, that when the Applicant did take her case to the Appeals Committee, the Bank challenged the Committee's jurisdiction for lack of an 'administrative decision' from which administrative review and ultimately appeal could be taken.

37. The Tribunal is of the view that Staff Rule 9.01 and its provisions for administrative review should not be construed in an overly technical manner. Those provisions are designed to rectify misunderstandings and to resolve a wide range of claims by staff members in an expeditious but essentially informal manner. Between the Bank and its staff members, there are often ongoing communications and exchanged letters and memoranda that sometimes render it unclear whether firm decisions have been made and time periods crystallized. As this case shows, there may be ambiguities about whether the administrative review procedures are intended to apply at all. Given the fact that these procedures were designed

to be utilized by all categories of staff members, most of them lacking legal expertise and most of them presumably acting without the aid of counsel at this relatively early dispute stage, the Tribunal concludes that they should be applied flexibly in accordance with their terms and their spirit.

38. It is perhaps for these reasons that the Appeals Committee, despite the Respondent's challenge to its jurisdiction for reasons similar to those raised here, decided to rule upon the Applicant's appeal on the merits. The Tribunal also concludes that Staff Rule 9.01 should not provide a bar to the application in the circumstances of this case.

39. Not only does the Respondent contend that the Tribunal is without jurisdiction by virtue of the Applicant's untimeliness and her failure to exhaust administrative review, but it also argues that this case is 'moot' because there has been no 'administrative decision' that the Tribunal has jurisdiction to review. The Statute of the Tribunal, however, does not limit its jurisdiction to the review of only affirmative decisions by the Bank. Article II, para. 1, of the Statute provides in part: 'The Tribunal shall hear and pass judgment upon any application by which a member of the staff of the Bank Group alleges non-observance of the contract of employment or terms of appointment of such staff member.' Article XII, para. 1, of the Statute provides in part: 'If the Tribunal finds that the application is well-founded, it shall order the rescission of the decision contested or the specific performance of the obligation invoked.' It appears clear that claims of nonfeasance are as much within the Tribunal's jurisdiction as claims of improper affirmative decisions. Indeed, it is frequently illusory to make such a distinction, as the Bank's action in failing to give a staff member a greater salary increase or in failing to grade a position at a higher level can be viewed either as an affirmative decision or as a failure to decide. If the contract of employment or terms of appointment of a staff member impose an obligation upon the Bank to act, and an improper failure to act results in injury to a staff

member, the Tribunal is given the power to redress that injury.

40. The Tribunal concludes that the Applicant has adequately framed her claim as one for the 'non-observance of [her] contract of employment or terms of appointment.' Her claim is that the Respondent undertook to provide accurate tax advice to its retiring staff members, that she reasonably relied on this undertaking, and that the Respondent neglected to inform her in a timely manner of the retroactive change in U.S. tax law so that she could accordingly conform her decisions regarding the commutation of her pension payments. These claims fall within the jurisdiction of the Tribunal to decide on the merits. (*Robinson*, Decision No. 78 [1989], paras. 36–40)

iv. 43. The Applicant was not selected in Round 1 of the Reorganization Program. She complains that she was entitled to 'intra-departmental' preference for positions and that the Respondent failed to protect that priority during Round 1. However the 'Guide to Staffing Policies' of May 1987 provides that, while incumbency would be an underlying factor for Round 1 selection, incumbency alone would not be given precedence over needed skills as a selection criterion. The Appeals Committee found that in the selection process in Round 1 'there does not seem to have been an effort to inform the Appellant of' the conversion of a position of Research Assistant to Operations Assistant (for which she was one of the top candidates) and that she was not interviewed for that position. The Tribunal, however, cannot go into this question, because, among other reasons, the Applicant has declared repeatedly that this application is not an appeal against non-selection during the 1987 Reorganization. (*Sukkar*, Decision No. 84 [1989], para. 43)

v. 56. (2) The second point which the Tribunal has made repeatedly before is that in matters involving the exercise of discretion by the Bank, the Tribunal is not charged with the task of re-examining the substance of the

Bank's decision with a view to substituting the Tribunal's decision for the Bank's. The duty of the Tribunal is to assess the Bank's decision—as to both its content and the manner in which it has been made—to determine whether it constitutes an abuse of discretion, being arbitrary, discriminatory, improperly motivated or carried out in violation of a fair and reasonable procedure. . . .

68. The Applicant maintains that these requirements were not met because appropriate procedures were not followed nor were appropriate standards applied. Moreover, he charges that the Vice President of his Region was biased or prejudiced against him. . . .

72. In his application the Applicant provides a detailed analysis on a country by country basis of how he dealt with the 'strategic' aspects of his work in respect of which he had received adverse comments in his APR. This approach assumes, however, either that the Tribunal is entitled to review the substance of the Bank's assessment of the quality of the Applicant's work or that the Bank's assessment is so manifestly unreasonable that it cannot possibly be accepted. However, it is common ground that it is not for the Tribunal to substitute its own assessment for that of the Bank. Nor, in the light of the documents before the Tribunal, especially those reflecting the discussions that took place between the Applicant and his Division Chief and Director, can it be said that the bank's assessment is so manifestly unreasonable that it may be invalidated . . . (*de Raet*, Decision No. 85 [1989], paras. 56, 68, 72)

vi. 43. . . . The Applicant, in effect, invites the Tribunal to substitute its discretion for that of the Bank. According to well-established jurisprudence this is not permissible save in certain very limited cases. In *Broemser*, Decision No. 27 [1985], para. 31, this Tribunal gave clear expression to this principle with the following words:

The essence of the present case is a challenge by the Applicant to the validity of the decision terminating her employment with the Bank. That the Bank has the power to terminate a staff member's employment for unsatisfactory performance, there is no doubt. The exercise of this power is a matter within the Bank's discretion and its appraisal in this respect is final unless the decision constitutes an abuse of discretion being arbitrary, discriminatory, improperly motivated or carried out in violation of a fair and reasonable procedure . . .

The Tribunal's earlier decisions in *Saberi*, Decision No. 5 [1981], para. 24; *Suntharalingam*, Decision No. 6 [1981], para. 27, reiterate the same principles. (*Georgiev*, Decision No. 96 [1990], para. 43)

vii. 45. The Tribunal has jurisdiction to determine applications by which a staff member alleges non-observance of the terms of his appointment. But no application is admissible unless the Applicant has exhausted all other remedies available to him within the Bank. . . .

51. The Tribunal has ruled in *de Raet*, Decision No. 85 [1989], para. 56, that:

[I]n matters involving the exercise of [managerial] discretion by the Bank, the Tribunal is not charged with the task of re-examining the substance of the Bank's decision with a view to substituting the Tribunal's decision for the Bank's. The duty of the Tribunal is to assess the Bank's decision—as to both its content and the manner in which it has been made—to determine whether it constitutes an abuse of discretion, being arbitrary, discriminatory, improperly motivated or carried out in violation of a fair and reasonable procedure. . . .

58. In view of the Applicant's unsuitability for the evolving needs of the growing Bank, as evidenced by the PPR's for 1985/1986 and 1986/1987, the Tribunal considers that the Respondent has lawfully exercised its administrative discretion. The Tribunal may not substitute its own judgement for that of the Respondent. This claim is therefore dismissed. (*Kassab*, Decision No. 97 [1990], paras. 45, 51, 58)

2. INADMISSIBILITY *RATIONE TEMPORIS*

1. Time limits

[See Sect. 3, 'Inadmissibility for Other Reasons', 1.iii.]

2. Extension of time limits

[See Sect. 3, 'Inadmissibility for Other Reasons', 1.iii and iv.]

3. INADMISSIBILITY FOR OTHER REASONS

1. Exhaustion of internal remedies

[See also Sect. 25, 'Salary', 4.iii.]

i. 22. The Tribunal has stated, with reference to this provision, that the 'statutory exhaustion requirement is of the utmost importance. It ensures that the management of the Bank shall be afforded an opportunity to redress any alleged violation by its own action, short of possibly protracted and expensive litigation before this Tribunal. In addition, the pursuit of internal remedies, in particular the findings and recommendations of the Appeals Committee, greatly assists the Tribunal in promptly and fairly disposing of the cases before it. The Appeals Committee permits a full and expeditious development of the parties' position, including the testimony of witnesses, that often results in the announcement of recommendations that are satisfactory to both the Bank and to the aggrieved staff member'. (*Klaus Berg*, Decision No. 51, para. 30)

23. The record of this case shows that the Applicant filed his appeal to the Appeals Committee on April 1, 1988, contesting a decision which had been taken by the Acting Vice President of Personnel on October 21, 1987; that is to say, the appeal was submitted more than four months late. The Appeals Committee regulations (Article 9.03, para. 5.01) allow a term of 30 days, which upon request may be extended for 30 days more, in order to file appeals. Consequently, the Appeals Committee rejected this appeal as time-barred.

24. The Tribunal does not find in this case exceptional circumstances justifying such a delay in appealing. Furthermore, the Respondent has not agreed to direct submission of the application to the Tribunal.

25. In these circumstances the Tribunal concludes that the Applicant has failed to exhaust properly the internal remedies available to him. (*Dhillon*, Decision No. 75 [1989], paras. 22–5)

ii. 16. In order to challenge the decision of January 21, 1988, the Applicant, in order to comply with Article II, para. 2 of the Statute, should have exhausted all internal remedies available within the Bank Group. Therefore, the Applicant should have appealed the Respondent's decision to the Appeals Committee before filing his application with the Tribunal. Staff Rule 9.03, paragraph 5.01, required that the Applicant have filed such an appeal within thirty-days of his receipt of the Respondent's decision of January 21, 1988. He did not do so, and the Appeals Committee, in its report of November 1, 1988 declared his appeal of July 1, 1988 to be time barred and inadmissible.

17. The Tribunal concludes, therefore, that the Applicant did not exhaust internal remedies within the Bank Group in a timely manner. Consequently, his application to the Tribunal is inadmissible. (*Steinke*, Decision No. 79 [1989], paras. 16, 17)

iii. 29. According to Article II, para. 2 of the Statute of the Tribunal:

> No . . . application shall be admissible, except under exceptional circumstances as decided by the Tribunal, unless:
>
> (i) the applicant has exhausted all other remedies available within the Bank Group, except if the applicant and respondent institution have agreed to submit the application directly to the Tribunal; and
>
> (ii) the application is filed within ninety days after . . .
>
> (*b*) receipt of notice, after the applicant has exhausted all other remedies available within the Bank Group, that the relief asked for or recommended will not be granted . . .

30. As already noted, the application was received by the Tribunal on January 30, 1989. Whether the time limit of ninety days is computed from November 8, 1988, when the Applicant received the Appeals Committee's decision rejecting his appeal, or from January 25, 1989, when the Applicant was advised of the rejection by the Appeals Committee of his request for reconsideration of the Committee's decision, the application has been filed within ninety days of 'receipt of notice . . . that the relief asked for . . . will not be granted'. The timeliness of the application to the Tribunal, therefore, is beyond question.

31. The jurisdictional issue raised by the Respondent relates to the other condition of admissibility laid down by Article II, para. 2, i.e., the exhaustion of 'all other remedies available within the Bank Group'. The Respondent objects to the admissibility of the application on the ground that, since the Applicant failed to observe the time limits for seeking administrative review, his appeal to the Appeals Committee was rejected as time-barred and that, consequently, the statutory requirement of exhaustion of internal remedies is not met.

32. The importance attached by the Statute of the Tribunal to the exhaustion of 'all other remedies available within the Bank Group' prior to filing an application before the Tribunal is highlighted by the fact that, having been laid down in sub-paragraph (i), this condition is again referred to in sub-paragraph (ii) in relation to the determination of the *dies a quo* of the ninety day time-limit. The Tribunal has declared:

(The) statutory exhaustion requirement is of utmost importance. It ensures that the management of the Bank shall be afforded an opportunity to redress any alleged violation by its own action, short of possibly protracted and expensive litigation before this Tribunal. In addition, the pursuit of internal remedies, in particular the findings and recommendations of the Appeals Committee, greatly assists the Tribunal in promptly and fairly disposing of the cases before it. The Appeals Committee permits a full and expeditious development of the parties' positions, including the testimony of witnesses, and often results in the announcement of recommendations that are satisfactory to both the Bank and to the aggrieved staff members (*Klaus Berg*, Decision No. 51 [1987], para. 30; *Dhillon*, Decision No. 75 [1989], para. 22).

33. On this basis the Tribunal has concluded that, where an Applicant has failed to observe the time limits for the submission of an internal complaint or appeal, with the result that his complaint or appeal had to be rejected as untimely, he must be regarded as not having complied with the statutory requirement of exhaustion of internal remedies (*Dhillon*, Decision No. 75 [1989], paras. 23–5; *Steinke*, Decision No. 79 [1989], paras. 16–17). . . .

36. Insofar as Rule 9.03, para. 5.01 is concerned, the Tribunal is unable to share the Appeals Committee's view. Rule 9.03 governs the appeals to the Appeals Committee. Paragraph 5.01 provides as follows:

> After the Administrative Review has been completed, a staff member who wishes to appeal the decision to the Appeals Committee must submit the appeal in writing . . . within 30 calendar days following receipt by the staff member of the written decision from the highest level in the applicable administrative channel. . . .

The record shows that the Applicant's formal request for administrative review had been rejected on May 9, 1988. So, in filing his appeal before the Appeals Committee on June 8, the Applicant clearly complied with the provisions of Rule 9.03, para. 5.01, and his appeal should not have been held inadmissible by the Appeals Committee on that ground. Had the alleged non-observance of Rule 9.03 been the only ground on which the Appeals Committee's decision rested, the Tribunal would have concluded that the Applicant cannot be regarded as not having exhausted internal remedies.

37. But the Appeals Committee's decision rests on yet another ground. The appeal before the Appeals Committee was rejected not only because it was held untimely in itself but also because it followed upon an administrative review which had itself ended in a decision dated May 9, 1988, rejecting the applicant's request for administrative review as time-barred because of non-compliance with Rule 9.01 governing 'Administrative Review'. The legal situation is, therefore the following. If the decision of May 9, 1988 was correct, then there existed a legal basis for the Appeals Committee's decision based on non-compliance with Rule 9.01, 'Administrative Review'; the Applicant should then be regarded as not having exhausted all internal remedies available to him prior to his application before the Tribunal. If, on the other hand, the May 9, 1988 decision rejecting the Applicant's request for administrative review as time-barred was wrong, then the Applicant should be deemed to have complied with the requirement of exhausting internal remedies. The question before the Tribunal thus boils down to whether the Applicant's request of April 25, 1988 for administrative review was timely or not. . . .

44. In the light of the preceding, the Tribunal determines that end June–beginning July 1987 is the latest date conceivably to be taken as the *dies a quo* for the purpose of compliance with Rule 9.01, para. 2.01. It remains, therefore, to be seen whether the administrative review has been requested within the time limits prescribed by this Rule.

45. Even assuming that the Applicant's discussions with his supervisors in 1987 are to be regarded as complying with the provisions of paragraph 2.02 defining 'step 1' of the administrative review procedure, the fact of the matter is that the formal written request for administrative review was filed only on April 25, 1988,

i.e., 9 months after the *dies a quo* defined in the most liberal way. Rule 9.01, para. 2.01, it may be recalled, provides for a maximum of 132 days, i.e. less than 5 months from the date of the decision the administrative review of which the Applicant requests.

46. In any event, the record does not substantiate any claim for exceptional circumstances which might condone the Applicant's request for administrative review not within 5 months but more than 9 months after the moment he most certainly became aware of the low level of his merit increases and the reasons therefor. The Tribunal concludes that, even conceding to the Applicant his most optimistic views or arguments, his request for administrative review of April 25, 1988 can by no stretch of imagination be held as having been filed within the prescribed time limits. It follows that the Appeals Committee was right in deciding that it lacked jurisdiction because of non-compliance with Staff Rule 9.01 at the administrative review stage. It follows also that the Applicant did not exhaust 'all other remedies available within the Bank group' before applying to the Tribunal. Hence, the application is not admissible. (*de Jong*, Decision No. 89 [1990], paras. 29–33, 36–7, 44–6)

iv. 24. Against this application the Respondent has raised a jurisdictional issue, based on the alleged non-compliance by the Applicant with the statutory requirement of exhaustion of internal remedies. The Respondent's request to separate the jurisdictional issue from the merits having been granted, the present judgement will address this issue without going into the merits.

25. According to Article II, para. 2 of the Statute of the Tribunal:

> No . . . application shall be admissible, except under exceptional circumstances as decided by the Tribunal, unless:
>
> (i) the applicant has exhausted all other remedies available within the Bank Group, except if the applicant and respondent institution have agreed to submit the application directly to the Tribunal; and

> (ii) the application is filed within ninety days after . . .
>
> (*b*) receipt of notice, after the applicant has exhausted all other remedies available within the Bank Group, that the relief asked for or recommended will not be granted . . .

26. The jurisdictional issue raised by the Respondent relates to the condition of admissibility laid down by Article II para. 2, i.e. the exhaustion of 'all other remedies available within the Bank Group.' The Respondent objects to the admissibility of the application on the ground that, since the Applicant failed to observe the time limits for seeking administrative review, the statutory requirements of exhaustion of internal remedies is not met.

27. As the Tribunal stated in *de Jong*, Decision No. 89 [1990], para. 32:

> The importance attached by the Statute of the Tribunal to the exhaustion of 'all other remedies available within the Bank Group' prior to filing an application before the Tribunal is highlighted by the fact that, having been laid down in sub-paragraph (i), this condition is again referred to in sub-paragraph (ii) in relation to the determination of the *dies a quo* of the ninety day time limit.

The Tribunal declared in *Klaus Berg*, Decision No. 51 [1987], para. 30:

> [The] statutory exhaustion requirement is of utmost importance. It ensures that the management of the Bank shall be afforded an opportunity to redress any alleged violation by its own action, short of possibly protracted and expensive litigation before this Tribunal.

28. On this basis the Tribunal has concluded that, where an Applicant has failed to observe the time limits for the submission of an internal complaint or appeal, with the result that his complaint or appeal had to be rejected as untimely, he must be regarded as not having complied with the statutory requirement of exhaustion of internal remedies (*Dhillon*, Decision No. 75 [1989], paras. 23–25; *Steinke*, Decision No. 79 [1989], paras. 16–17, *de Jong*, Decision No. 89 [1990], paras. 43). . . .

33. In the light of the above the Tribunal concludes that the administrative review process, despite its timely invocation by the applicant, as well as the subsequent internal remedies, has not yet been completed. However, having been initiated by the Applicant in time, the now suspended internal remedies should continue in accordance with the applicable provision, so that the case might, if necessary, eventually come back before this Tribunal for a decision on the merits. (*Ramorasoavina*, No. 95 [1990], paras. 24–8, 33)

v. 47. Nor did the Applicant when he complained to the Appeals Committee on December 31, 1987 ask for rescission of the redundancy decision. Thus he has not exhausted all the internal remedies available to him; this claim before the Tribunal must therefore be declared inadmissible. (*Kassab*, Decision No. 97 [1990], para. 47)

4. RELEASE AGREEMENTS

1. General

i. 22. . . . Although the Respondent did not find that the Applicant's . . . claims were well-founded, it offered the Applicant an *ex gratia* payment in the sum of Rs. 13, 200, . . . equal to four months' salary in 'full and final settlement of his claim against the World Bank. . . .' . . .

24. On May 7, 1986 seven months after the offer of the *ex gratia* payment was made, the Applicant wrote a letter to the Respondent, saying *inter alia*:

> Since I am leaving for America to live with my son, your check for an equivalent amount in dollar currency may please be sent to me to reach me there after May 12 addressed care R. K. Pruthi, 25 Sunset Court, Montville, N.J. 07045, and *this letter may be taken as receipt in full and final settlement.* (Emphasis added)

25. Two days after this letter, the Applicant sought to resile from his acceptance of the *ex gratia* offer by alleging

that he had accepted the offer under duress. There is no indication what constituted this duress, nor is there anything in the Applicant's letter of May 7, 1986 to suggest that the Applicant was under the constraint of any illegal or improper compulsion in accepting after seven months of reflection the *ex gratia* payment 'in full and final settlement' of his claim.

26. As the Tribunal stated in paragraph 26 of the decision in *Mr. Y* (Decision No. 25 [1985]):

> It would unduly interfere with the constructive and efficient resolution of (a staff member's claim of improper treatment) if the Bank could not negotiate—in exchange for concessions on its part—for a return promise from the staff member not to press his or her claim further. If such an agreed settlement were not binding upon the affected staff member, there would be little incentive for the Bank to enter into compromise arrangements, and there might instead be an inducement to be unyielding and to defend each claim through the process of administrative and judicial review. It is therefore in the interest not only of the Bank but also of the staff that effect should be given to such settlements.

27. The Tribunal concludes that there is no evidence of duress that might affect the validity of the Applicant's acceptance of the *ex gratia* payment as a full and final settlement of his claim. (*Pruthi*, Decision No. 55 [1988], paras. 22, 24–7)

2. Settlement/separation agreement

[See also Sect. 4, 'Release Agreements', 1.i; Sect. 8, 'Sources of Law', 2 (*a*)i; Sect. 28, 'Reorganization', 2.v, 3.v, viii, and ix.]

i. 48. By a memorandum dated August 21, 1987 the Vice President, Personnel, denied the Applicant's request for Package A for the following reasons:

> Staff Rule 5.09 provides that applications for voluntary separation may be denied, among other reasons, if approval of the application would cause the number of voluntary separations added to the expected number of separations under the Enhanced Separation Package to exceed the aggregate budgetary

provision for such separations or the related number of such separations. As was to be done in such an eventuality, I have proceeded with the award of Package A, giving priority to applications by staff who have not been offered a position to date. I regret to advise you that it currently appears that the granting of further Package A at this time to staff who have been offered positions will result in both the budget for and total number of separations being exceeded. Accordingly, I have decided that your application for Package A cannot be approved at this time. . . .

58. On September 30, 1987 the Applicant was informed of the terms proposed by the Respondent for an agreed separation from the service of the Bank. These terms included special leave through November 30, 1987, the lump sum equivalent of six months net pay, and a release of claims provision. On October 9, 1987 the Applicant maintained his claim to a Standard Separation Package or alternatively to reach an agreement under the terms of an Enhanced Separation package, on the ground that he had not been offered a position comparable to his former position. He proposed certain amendments to the separation terms concerning educational benefits and medical insurance. The Respondent did not accept these amendments.

59. On November 16, 1987 the Applicant filed an appeal with the Appeals Committee requesting as relief (*a*) Package B or (*b*) Package A or (*c*) the opportunity to negotiate the terms of a separation package 'appropriate to the circumstances of his own case'.

60. The Appeals Committee dismissed the appeal in respect of (*a*) and (*b*) and in respect of (*c*) recommended that the Bank make a more generous offer than those made to the Applicant on September 30, 1987. The Senior Vice President, External Affairs and Administration, indicated that he could not accept the Appeal Committee's recommendation on a more generous offer, since the Applicant had already been offered negotiated terms of separation but chose to resign and retain his rights of appeal.

61. The decision of the Respondent to deny the

Applicant's request for Package A was, for the reasons given, consistent with the provisions of Staff Rule 5.09.

62. As the Applicant had unsuccessfully applied for Package A and had been offered two positions at his current level, he could not subsequently apply for Package B, and it is, therefore, difficult to see how he can base his claim for compensation on Package B. As he had rejected the terms of the separation agreement he was offered by the Bank on September 30, 1987, he cannot now get the Tribunal to order the Bank to accept amended terms put forward by him. (*Apergis*, Decision No. 83 [1989], paras. 48, 58–62)

ii. 33. Lastly, the Applicant makes an issue of the manner in which his Separation Agreement was concluded, saying that he was tendered a memorandum the contents of which he was not permitted to negotiate and that he had no viable choice but to accept its terms. However, provided that the consensual will is present (as it was here), an agreement is no less an agreement because it follows a form established and even insisted on by one of the parties. The adverb 'mutually' that qualifies the verb 'agreed', and to which the Applicant appears to attach importance, really adds nothing to the verb. Every agreement is 'mutually' agreed. A non-mutually agreed agreement is a juridical impossibility. The Applicant does not, it may be noted, argue that he was subjected to any duress in the conclusion of the separation agreement; any such argument could not, on the facts of this case, have been supported. (*Lindsay*, Decision No. 92 [1990], para. 33)

iii. 44. In explaining his reasons for rejecting the offer the Applicant asserted that the new Section Chief 'and I have not seen eye to eye on things over the years, which suggests future conflicts in our relationship'. On the other hand, he recognized that her selection was 'a logical one'. But his disagreements with the new Chief and his preference for the former supervisor are not grounds for making the offer not bona fide or justifying his refusal to continue in his current position. Likewise, it is not a valid ground for justifying the Applicant's refusal or altering the bona fide nature of the offer that he was concerned that 'the doubling of the Region size, as well as changes in its institutional structure and functions, would impose unprecedented operational problems' for which he would be almost solely responsible. Nor is it a valid ground for his concern that, as a consequence, 'his experience and technical skills might be exploited without proper compensation'. These fears and concerns might be justifiable grounds for declining the job offered, but not for claiming additional compensation after having refused to perform the additional tasks. . . .

51. Despite not being required by Rule 7.01, the Bank subsequently decided to offer six months compensation to staff in the Applicant's situation. Those were the conditions offered to the Applicant by close of business on September 30 and he accepted the offer, signing the Separation Agreement in October 1987. There was no duress in that mutual separation agreement, because the situation in which the Applicant found himself was of his own choosing. (*Pavesich*, Decision No. 94 [1990], paras. 44, 51)

3. Duress

[See Sect. 4, 'Release Agreements', 2.ii and iii.]

5. REVIEW OF JUDGMENTS

1. Article XI: Finality of judgments

[See also Sect. 5, 'Review of Judgments', 3.i; Sect. 29, 'Remedies', 10.v.]

i. 15. The Applicant has misunderstood the nature of the Tribunal's observation. The Applicant made a request for costs and the Tribunal did not make an interim decision on his request, postponing a final decision and inviting him to submit further particulars to enable it to make a final decision. On the contrary the Tribunal did make a final decision—awarding him costs in the amount of $1,000 which was intended to include attorney's fees. This decision makes the award *res judicata*, as is confirmed by Article XI (1) of the Tribunal's Statute, which declares its judgments 'final and without appeal'. Thus, clearly the Tribunal cannot reopen Decision No. 73 by way of appeal. As was stated in *Van Gent (No. 2)*, Decision No. 13 [1983], para. 21:

> No party to a dispute before the Tribunal may bring his case back to the Tribunal for a second round of litigation, no matter how dissatisfied he may be with the pronouncement of the Tribunal or its considerations. The Tribunal's judgment is meant to be the last step along the path of settling disputes arising between the Bank and the members of its staff.

(*Alan Berg (No. 2)*, Decision No. 87 [1990], para. 15)

2. *Res Judicata*

[See Sect. 5, 'Review of Judgments', 1.i.]

3. Article XIII: General rule of revision

i. 16. The Tribunal may however revise a judgment; revision is governed by Article XIII (1) which reads:

> A party to a case in which a judgment has been delivered may, in the event of the discovery of a fact which by its nature might have had a decisive influence on the judgment of the Tribunal which at the time judgment was delivered was unknown both to the Tribunal and that party, request the Tribunal . . . to revise the judgment.

As the Tribunal observed in *Skandera*, Decision No. 9 [1982], para. 7:

> This Article, as well as Article XI (1) providing for finality of the judgments of the Tribunal, compel the conclusion that the powers of revision of a judgment are strictly limited and may be

exercised only upon compliance with the conditions set forth in Article XIII.

One of the conditions is that the facts in support of revision applied for were, at the time judgment was delivered, unknown to both the Tribunal and the Applicant. Here there is no question of the facts set out in support of the application being at the time of judgment unknown to the Applicant; most of them were then known to him or his attorney and should have properly been brought to the notice of the Tribunal before delivery of judgment. In any event it cannot be said that they were then completely unknown to the Tribunal. (*Alan Berg (No. 2)*, Decision No. 87 [1990], para. 16)

4. New facts

[See also Sect. 5, 'Review of Judgments', 3.i.]

i. 17. Besides, the extra amount ($6,121) sought by the Applicant and reasons advanced by him are not facts which by their nature might have had a decisive influence on the judgment of the Tribunal. (*Alan Berg (No. 2)*, Decision No. 87 [1990], para. 17)

5. Interpretation

[See Sect. 8, 'Sources of Law', 5 (*b*) i.]

6. ADMINISTRATIVE REVIEW

1. General

[See also Sect. 3, 'Inadmissibility for Other Reasons', 1.iv; Sect. 12, 'Substantive Irregularity', 1.xi; Sect. 13, 'Procedural Irregularity', 1.i, 5.ii; Sect. 16, 'Classification', 1.ii, 13.i; Sect. 25, 'Salary', 4.iii; Sect. 26, 'Taxation', 1.i; Sect. 28, 'Reorganization', 2.v.]

i. 45. The Tribunal notes that from the time the Applicant expressed her dissatisfaction with the grading of her position by the JEU, the Respondent took a series of measures aimed at confirming and consolidating the decision to grade the Applicant's position at level 17. Many of these measures fell short of meeting the requirements of due process and a fair and reasonable procedure.

46. At the stage of administrative review corrections had been made to the Applicant's submission without prior involvement or knowledge of the Applicant, thereby unduly depriving the Applicant of an opportunity to comment on the intended revision . . . (*Rae*, Decision No. 74 [1988], paras. 45, 46)

ii. 32. It is true that the request for administrative review was not directly and expressly addressed to his immediate supervisor, the Resident Representative, but to several officers of the Bank in its main offices in Washington, D.C., including high officials in charge of personnel matters and others competent to review the decisions taken on his own by the Resident Representative. However, taking into account all the circumstances of the present case, it would be an excess of formalism to reject the request for administrative review as time-barred because it was not directly and expressly addressed to the Resident Representative in Madagascar, who, after extensive discussions with the Applicant during two days, had communicated to him the confirmation of his decision in writing. It would have been very easy for the local authorities in Antananarivo to ensure that the proceedings for administrative review were addressed and developed in proper sequence.

33. In the light of the above the Tribunal concludes that the administrative review process, despite its timely invocation by the applicant, as well as the subsequent internal remedies, has not yet been completed. However, having been initiated by the Applicant in time, the now suspended internal remedies should continue in accordance with the applicable provision, so that the case

might, if necessary, eventually come back before this Tribunal for a decision on the merits.

Decision:
For these reasons the Tribunal unanimously decides that the case is remanded to the Respondent for pursuit of the internal procedure validly initiated by the Applicant's request for administrative review. (*Ramorasoavina*, Decision No. 95 [1990], paras. 32, 33, Decision)

iii. 57. The Tribunal considers that in the present case the administrative review conducted by the Assistant Director did not seriously impair the Applicant's ability to defend himself. The documentation submitted to the Assistant Director in charge of the review was also made available to the Applicant; he was invited by the Assistant Director to submit additional material that he might deem relevant and he did submit a folder; finally, the Assistant Director met with him on November 18, 1986 to complete the factual information. The memorandum or report which was not communicated to him is only a review of documents concerning the Applicant's performance in the preparation of a Special Appraisal Report for the Zaire Navigation Improvement Project. No additional facts unknown to the Applicant were included in that Memorandum and consequently the Applicant 'had full knowledge of the facts necessary to argue his case properly.' (*Suntharalingam*, Decision No. 6 [1981], para. 38). (*Kassab*, Decision No. 97 [1990], para. 57)

7. APPEALS COMMITTEE

1. General

[See also Sect. 1, 'Jurisdiction', 1 (*b*) i; Sect. 3, 'Inadmissibility for Other Reasons', 1.i–iii and v; Sect. 4, 'Release Agreements', 2.i; Sect. 11, 'Prejudice/Discrimination', 1.i; Sect. 13, 'Procedural

Irregularity', 6.iv; Sect. 28, 'Reorganization', 2.v, 3.v; Sect. 30, 'Procedure before Tribunal', 3 (*a*) i; Sect. 32, 'Miscellaneous', 6.iii.]

i. 54. (1) The first is that the relationship of the Appeals Committee to the Tribunal is not of an inferior to a superior court. The Tribunal is not a court of appeal from the Appeals Committee and does not review the manner in which the Appeals Committee has dealt with a case before it. The proceedings before the Tribunal are entirely separate and independent despite the fact that recourse to the Appeals Committee is a condition precedent to the commencement of proceedings before the Tribunal. The function of the Appeals Committee is to assist the management of the Bank to determine for itself whether there has been a failure on the part of the Bank. The function of the Appeals Committee ends with its recommendation, which the Bank may or may not accept. It is a complete misunderstanding of the situation to aver, as does the Applicant, after complaining of certain aspects of the Appeals Committee's procedure, that 'consequently, the Report of the Committee does not provide a basis upon which the Tribunal can deal with the questions raised in this application.' The report of the Committee is never regarded as 'the basis' upon which this Tribunal deals with cases and is in no way binding upon it. The Tribunal is the only body within the Bank that deals with complaints judicially and it does so only on the basis of the evidence before it.

55. The Applicant has complained of certain inherent limitations in the operation of the Committee as well as procedural and substantive flaws in its conduct in this case. The Tribunal has found itself able to review these complaints without entering further into the question of the powers of the Appeals Committee or its relation to the Tribunal. It has concluded that the complaints cannot be sustained. (*de Raet*, Decision No. 85 [1989], paras. 54–5)

ii. 42. The Applicant also contends that she did not receive a fair trial before the Appeals Committee. For this reason she requests the Tribunal to order that the case be remanded to the Bank's Administration in accordance with Article XII (2) of the Statute of the Tribunal. In support of that request the Applicant refers to what she considers to be three procedural defects: (*a*) that she did not get adequate expert assistance before and during the hearing; (*b*) that the hearing panel was weighted in favor of Management; and (*c*) that the Respondent made certain unfair and prejudicial attacks against her motive in acquiring U.S. citizenship and in eventually considering renouncing it. The Tribunal cannot find any ground for these contentions. The principles contained in Staff Rule 9.03 on the Appeals Committee have been respected by the Respondent and none of the Applicant's procedural guarantees under this rule or the general principles of law has been violated. (*Wahie*, Decision No. 93 [1990], para. 42)

8. SOURCES OF LAW

1. General principles of law

(*a*) *General*

[See also Sect. 25, 'Salary', 3 (*a*) i.]

i. 30. The Tribunal, as an international tribunal has the inherent power to interpret its own decisions in case of dispute between the parties as to their meaning or scope, even if its Statute contains no provision to that effect. The Hague Convention on Pacific Settlement of Disputes of 1907 gives expression to this general principle, when it provides in Article 82 that:

> Any dispute arising between the parties as to the interpretation and execution of the award shall, in the absence of an agreement to the contrary, be submitted to the decision of the tribunal which pronounced it.

(*Agodo et al.*, Decision No. 76 [1989], para. 30)

(*b*) *Right to counsel*

[See also Sect. 29, 'Remedies', 8.ii.]

i. 42. The Applicant also contends that she did not receive a fair trial before the Appeals Committee. For this reason she requests the Tribunal to order that the case be remanded to the Bank's administration in accordance with Article XII (2) of the Statute of the Tribunal. In support of that request the Applicant refers to what she considers to be three procedural defects: (*a*) that she did not get adequate expert assistance before and during the hearing; (*b*) that the hearing panel was weighted in favor of Management; and (*c*) that the Respondent made certain unfair and prejudicial attacks against her motives in acquiring U.S. citizenship and in eventually considering renouncing it. The Tribunal cannot find any ground for these contentions. The principles contained in Staff Rule 9.03 on the Appeals Committee have been respected by the Respondent and none of the Applicant's procedural guarantees under this rule or the general principles of law has been violated. (*Wahie*, Decision No. 93 [1990], para. 42)

(*c*) *Principle of interpretation*

i. 37. It is a recognized principle of interpretation that different parts of a legal text should be read together. It is also accepted that any reading of the text that results in making one part thereof superfluous or merely repetitive should not be adopted. Applying these principles to para. 2.01 of Rules 6.13 and 6.14, the Tribunal concludes that the two sentences of the paragraph established two interrelated and complementary rules:

(*a*) a staff appointment on or before January 28, 1985 (which is the case of the Applicant) is eligible for expatriate benefits if two conditions are fulfilled, namely:

(i) his or her service has been continuous since that date;

(ii) he or she is not a citizen of the duty station country.

(*b*) eligibility will cease on the staff member's acquisition of the citizenship of the duty station country.

A reading of the second sentence of the paragraph as merely providing for a temporary suspension rather than a permanent cessation of the benefits during the period of citizenship with the possibility of regaining said benefit on the subsequent renunciation of the citizenship would render that second sentence a mere repetition of the first, a conclusion that runs against the accepted rules of interpretation. (*Wahie*, Decision No. 93 [1990], para. 37)

(*d*) *Principle of proportionality*

[See Sect. 14, 'Performance', 1.iv; Sect. 27, 'Termination', 1 (*a*) ii.]

(*e*) *Fairness*

[See also Sect. 14, 'Performance', 1.iv; Sect. 16, 'Classification', 13.iii.]

i. 48. Staff Rule 9.04 dealing with Job Grading Appeals does not stipulate for any such right of the Vice President, PA to refer back to the JGAB or to the Chief of its panel to reconsider the decision taken. The Vice President may be free to seek whatever advice he deems useful or helpful for taking his decision as to whether he should go along with the recommendation of the JGAB. He should not, however, without advising the Applicant, involve the JGAB, which is entrusted with a quasi-judicial mission of deciding on appeals seeking review of the grading decision. Moreover, the Vice President's letter of December 5, 1986 was sent even before the decision of the JGAB itself was communicated to the Applicant. In these circumstances the Tribunal finds the action of the Vice President, in referring back the decision of the JGAB for reconsideration of its substance to be in violation of Principle 2.1 of Staff Employment which states that:

> The Organizations shall at all times act with fairness and impartiality and shall follow a proper process in their relations with staff members.

(*Rae*, Decision No. 74 [1988], para. 48)

ii. 34. The Applicant further contends that, although she had good prospects for satisfactory performance elsewhere in the Bank, these were blocked by the unwarranted intervention of the Personnel Department and this, she argued, 'was unfair and unreasonable.' On the record it is difficult to see that the Respondent took any action that can be said to be either unfair or unreasonable. After her appointment was terminated the Applicant learnt of a vacancy in the post of Administrative Secretary in the Computer Technology Center. At an interview she appeared to have impressed the Acting Manager as well as one of the other senior members of the staff as a suitable candidate. But when the Manager learnt that the Applicant's services had been terminated by another branch of the Bank, he sought the advice of her personnel officer. The advice he received was that the Bank would be willing to reconsider the Applicant if she 'was head and shoulders above all the other candidates.' The Manager could not honestly say that the Applicant was head and shoulders above all the other candidates. So he excluded her from the list of candidates.

35. On these facts, it would be less than accurate to say that there was 'Unwarranted intervention' by the Personnel Department. . . .

37. The Applicant also argues that in the light of the excellent performance record she had prior to joining EM4IE

> It is . . . not consistent with the requirement of fair and reasonable procedure, to have acted as the Respondent has done in March 1988 and thereafter.

Although the Applicant puts her objection in this part of the case to lack of 'fair and reasonable' procedure, actually she is contesting the decision by management to invoke Staff Rule 7.01, para. 11.02, to subject her to a three-month performance evaluation. It is that decision that was taken in March 1988.

38. Accordingly, the question that falls for decision here is whether management acted unfairly or unreasonably in deciding that the Applicant's work should be evaluated during the three-month period. It is clear from the record

that the quality of her work was thought to be unsatisfactory by a number of her supervisors. More important still, her ability to work harmoniously with her peers or supervisors was, to put it mildly, debatable. This was because she took a rather generous view of her own ability and thus disabled herself from appreciating the need for improvement. In those circumstances it was the plain duty of management to appraise her not only of its dissatisfaction with her performance, but to proceed to an evaluation of her work within the true intendment of Staff Rule 7.01, para. 11.02. The Tribunal is unable to accept that there is anything unfair or unreasonable about the Respondent's decision. (*Georgiev*, Decision No. 96 [1990], paras. 34, 35, 37, 38)

2. Contract of employment

(*a*) *Offer*

[See also Sect. 4, 'Release Agreements', 2.iii.]

i. 44. In explaining his reasons for rejecting the offer the Applicant asserted that the new Section Chief 'and I have not seen eye to eye on things over the years, which suggests future conflicts in our relationship'. On the other hand, he recognized that her selection was 'a logical one'. But his disagreements with the new Chief and his preference for the former supervisor are not grounds for making the offer not bona fide or justifying his refusal to continue his current position. Likewise, it is not a valid ground for justifying the Applicant's refusal or altering the bona fide nature of the offer that he was concerned that 'the doubling of the Region size, as well as changes in its institutional structure and functions, would impose unprecedented operational problems' for which he would be almost solely responsible. Nor is it a valid ground for his concern that, as a consequence, 'his experience and technical skills might be exploited without proper compensation'. These fears and concerns might be justifiable grounds for declining the job offered, but not for claiming additional compensation after having refused to perform the additional tasks. . . .

50. Yet, the next day, September 25, the Applicant received from his supervisor, the Section Chief, the offer to retain his prior position at grade 15. The Applicant complains that the offer was communicated to him by the Section Chief and not personally by the Chief Administrative Officer. This is not a valid reason for not having answered. On September 29 the Chief Personnel Officer for the Asia Section called the Applicant by telephone at his home to urge him to accept the position which had been offered to him a second time. The Applicant was advised that in order to avoid being without a job, he should accept that offer even if he chose later to apply for other positions through the Vacancy Listing Service. His answer was to ask about separation benefits, and he was advised that at that time no provision had been made for severance payments to staff members who had been offered but not accepted a position at their level.

51. Despite not being required by Rule 7.01, the Bank subsequently decided to offer six months compensation to staff in the Applicant's situation. Those were the conditions offered to the Applicant by close of business on September 30 and he accepted the offer, signing the Separation Agreement in October 1987. There was no duress in that mutual separation agreement, because the situation in which the Applicant found himself was of his own choosing. (*Pavesich*, Decision No. 94 [1990], paras. 44, 50, 51)

(*b*) *Essential elements*

[See also Sect. 15, 'Terms and Conditions of Employment', 1.iii.]

i. 25. The central issue in this case is whether failure of the Respondents to carry out a comprehensive review of staff compensation in 1987 and 1988 as prescribed by the Kafka Committee, and laid down by the management of the Respondents, constituted a non-observance of the conditions of employment or terms of appointment of the Applicants.

26. The Applicants consider such deviation from the triennial comprehensive review rule to be a unilateral change by the Respondents of an essential element of the contract of employment, violating the rights of the staff as defined by the Tribunal in its decisions in *de Merode* (Decision No. 1 [1981], *von Stauffenberg* (Decision No. 38 [1987]) and *Pinto* Decision No. 56 [1988]).

27. The Respondents, on the other hand, view their postponement of the comprehensive review for two consecutive years, and their reliance, instead, on intervening years review, to be a valid exercise of their discretion in implementing the rule of periodicity of salary adjustment, prescribed by the Kafka System, and sanctioned by the Tribunal in a consistent line of decisions. . . .

33. The Tribunal, in this case, does not find the postponement of the comprehensive review for two years to be, in itself, a violation of an essential element of the conditions of employment of the Applicants. (*Hammond et al.*, Decision No. 86 [1989], paras. 25–27, 33)

ii. 26. The Applicant contends that his non-selection constitutes a violation, or improper unilateral amendment, of an 'essential element' of his conditions of employment. He invokes the Tribunal's decisions in *de Merode*, Decision No. 1 [1981], and *Harrison*, Decision No. 53 [1987], which held that certain elements of a staff member's employment conditions—in those cases, periodic adjustment in salary and access to the Tribunal—are so fundamental as not to permit of unilateral change by the Bank. He asserts that a number of Bank documents and policies, in particular the *Principles of Staff Employment* and Staff Rule 5.09, create for staff members a right to selection for positions at their grade level that they are qualified to perform in preference to a promoted lower-level staff member. He then goes on to claim that this right is of so fundamental a character, comparable to the rights in *de Merode* and *Harrison*, that it too should be held by the Tribunal to be an essential element of employment for all staff members.

27. Upon an examination of the documents and policies

invoked by the Applicant, the Tribunal concludes that they do not warrant the inference of any such right. It is therefore not necessary to consider whether any such right, if found, should properly be regarded as an 'essential element' of employment . . .

40. Decisions such as these are within the Bank's discretion and may not be nullified, 'unless the decision constitutes an abuse of discretion, being arbitrary, discriminatory, improperly motivated or carried out in violation of a fair and reasonable procedure.' (*Saberi*, Decision No. 5 [1982], para. 24.)

41. There is no evidence before the Tribunal to substantiate any such finding in this case. Indeed, the Applicant's challenge to the Bank's selection of level 25 staff members to level 26 positions is based not on the particular qualifications of the former group of employees but rather upon a claim that 'the selection of a lower level staff member into positions for which Applicant was qualified is *per se* violation of his essential employment rights.' (*Fernandes*, Decision No. 90 [1990], paras. 26–7, 40–1]

(*c*) *Obligations of respondent/breach*

[See also Sect. 16, 'Classification', 13.iv; Sect. 18, 'Benefits', 3.i; Sect. 22, 'Transfer and Reassignment', 1.iii; Sect. 26, 'Taxation', 1.i; Sect. 28,'Reorganization', 3.iv; Sect. 29, 'Remedies', 6.i; Sect. 32, 'Miscellaneous', 2.i, 5.i, 6.i.]

i. 41. The Bank, commendably, has undertaken—through general informational seminars and through individualized counseling of staff members by Pension Information Assistants—to keep its staff members abreast of pertinent legal developments that bear upon their compensation and other terms of employment. By doing so, the Bank can properly be expected—using the language from its answer in this proceeding—'to act reasonably in the circumstances.' The Bank, therefore, may not intentionally or recklessly or carelessly give inaccurate information to its staff members, knowing that

that information will be utilized by staff members in making important decisions regarding their employment. Neither, however, must the Bank be held to the standard of a guarantor of the unfailing accuracy of its advice or its predictions; it is expected only to act reasonably, and even reasonably offered advice will sometimes prove ultimately to be wrong.

42. The Tribunal therefore shares the view of the Appeals Committee that the comments and advice provided at the April 1986 seminar were reasonable; the lecturers informed the staff members in attendance of the possibility of legislative modification of the 'cost recovery method' for taxing pension payments and of the uncertainty and unpredictability of that modification. But the Appeals Committee failed to consider the conduct of the Respondent after the April 1986 seminars.

46. For these reasons, and on the particular facts of this case, the Tribunal concludes that the failure to inform the Applicant of the adverse tax consequences of her pension payments until December 1986 (and possibly, as the Applicant claims, even later, in February 1987) was a violation of the Respondent's duty to act reasonably in all the circumstances. (*Robinson*, Decision No. 78 [1989], paras. 41, 42, 46)

ii. 36. It is the conclusion of the Tribunal that the above-quoted language of Rule 5.09, para. 7.06 is not ambiguous as pertains to this case, and by its terms the Applicant is not eligible for the Enhanced Separation Package. During the reorganization, the Staff Assistant position offered to her in the Latin America Technical Department, Human Resources Division, was graded at level 15. We therefore conclude that under para. 7.06 the Applicant has been 'selected for a position at [her] current or higher grade level.' Having being offered this position, the Applicant was no longer eligible for the Enhanced Separation Package, so that the Respondent's insistence upon standard separation terms did not constitute a violation of the Applicant's contract of employment. (*Montesa*, Decision No. 82 [1989], para. 36)

iii. 39. The Applicant asserts that an implied obligation on the part of the Respondent results from the fact that she had assumed, on her part, the obligation to stay with the Bank for a specified period of time. This, in the Applicant's contention, created a bilateral contract establishing mutual obligations regarding service to the Bank. This argument refers to the fact that the Bank, in subsidizing full-time external training, requires from the staff member the undertaking to remain in the service of the Bank for at least three years upon completion of the full-time study program. If the beneficiary leaves the Bank within three years for any reason, he is required to repay the Bank a prorated portion of the costs it incurred. Such a commitment was obtained from the Applicant, although she continued working in the Bank on a part time basis. However, this 'bonding', as it is called, does not signify the existence of a corresponding, mutual obligation on the part of the Bank to retain for a period of time the services of the beneficiary of a full time external program. There is no indication that the Bank has given up its power of declaring a position redundant. This is confirmed by the letter of September 23, 1985 approving the Applicant's study program, where reference is made to the possibility of a termination grant and of resettlement upon termination. In any event, the 'mutuality' sought by the Applicant in her bilateral contract was already amply provided when the Bank paid a substantial portion of her educational expenses.

40. The Applicant further contends that by inducing her to enter on a prolonged training program, partially paid for by the Respondent and supervised by its Training Division, the Bank assumed an implied obligation, resulting from the reasonable expectations of the parties, to the effect that she would be entitled to return to full time work to use and demonstrate her newly acquired skills. However, the record of the case shows that there was no exact correspondence between the expectations of the parties. While the Applicant intended to pursue a Master's degree in the School of Advanced International Studies at Johns Hopkins University, so as to qualify for

a post as Project Economist/Operations Officer, her supervisors insisted that the acceptance of her educational program did not imply any commitment or encouragement for promotion or reassignment, and made clear that she would be returning to work at her previous level as Operations Assistant. (*Sukkar*, Decision No. 84 [1989], paras. 39, 40)

iv. 41. The Tribunal concludes that, by denying the Applicant's request to regain expatriate benefits on her renunciation of U.S. citizenship, the Respondent has not violated any element of the Applicant's right under her contract of employment or terms of appointment. (*Wahie*, Decision No. 93 [1990], para. 41)

v. 37. The attempt by the Bank to support its approach by saying that no purpose would have been served by an examination 'in the case of candidates that are otherwise unfit, as in the Applicant's case, due to an uncontested prior illness' is not convincing. What matters is not whether in the particular case an examination may medically 'serve any purpose' but the fact that the relevant Staff Rule prescribes that there shall be a complete medical examination. The requirement is mandatory. If the Bank had intended that the conduct of an examination should be a matter for the discretion of the medical staff in the light of the medical history of any candidate for employment it could have expressed Section 4.04 of Staff Rule 4.01 in terms which would have permitted the medical staff to base their clearance 'either on the results of a complete medical examination or their assessment of the candidate's medical history'. But the Staff Rule does not say this and it is not open to the Bank to interpret the existing words in this way. (*Arellano*, Decision No. 98 [1990], para. 37)

3. Articles of agreement, by-laws, manuals, circulars

(*a*) *Memoranda*

[See also Sect. 13, 'Procedural Irregularity', 5.i and iv; Sect. 17, 'Recruitment', 2.i; Sect. 28, 'Reorganization', 2.vii, 3.iv.]

i. 41. Although the Applicant relies upon some colorably supportive language in a document dated February 10, 1986, from the Assistant Director, PMD, to another supervisor in the department, that is too slender a reed upon which to rest the Applicant's claim. First, it is not explained how this memorandum could supersede the clear language of Pers./11/81. Nor is there any evidence that the memorandum or the personnel manual circular was applied with respect to any other staff member so as to vary the grade level of TAP positions from time to time. Finally, the memorandum of the Assistant Director, PMD, continued as follows: 'In future the following provisions apply: a staff member who joins TAP will carry the grade of their [*sic*] previous regular assignment on a personal basis for up to two years and will be given assignments appropriate to their grade to the extent possible.' In other words, staff members in TAP were to have their grade level fixed, with temporary assignments to be made consistently therewith—not, as the Applicant contends, the other way around, with grade level being temporarily determined by work assignments. (*Montesa*, Decision No. 82 [1989], para. 41)

ii. 46. With respect to Round 2 procedures, the Applicant alleges that he was deprived of opportunities to find a suitable position by reason of the failure of the Respondent to furnish him the assistance required by the applicable provisions concerning alternative placements in Round 2, in particular, the alleged failure to communicate vacancies for which he was eligible. The Applicant asserts that he 'was never personally contacted by any member of the Personnel team from August 10 to September 29'. However, the record shows that he had a meeting with the Chief Personnel Officer for Asia on September 22. Besides, obtaining new placements in the Bank-wide roster for Round 2 did not depend exclusively on the initiative of Personnel Officers. It has to be seen as a two way effort, in which the staff member was expected to take a leading role. In a Model Memorandum addressed by the Bank to members participating in Round 2 they were advised as follows:

> When you identify a position or positions in which you are interested and for which you are qualified or could become qualified with training, you should check with the personnel team for the appropriate vice-presidential unit to verify that they are aware of your interest and potential candidacy . . .

49. Each staff member participating in Round 2 was advised in the above referred Model Memorandum that if he refused

> . . . to accept the offer of a position at your current grade or above, you will be ineligible for Package B and you would have to resign from the Bank or your employment could be terminated.

This formal advice was followed by a direct warning personally addressed to the Applicant by the Vice President, Personnel, on September 24, reminding him that:

> . . . unless you accept an outstanding job offer, or agree to be placed in some other position, you will be subject to the relevant provisions of Staff Rule 7.01, related to termination of employment.

In that same letter the Applicant was asked to contact his Personnel Officer without delay. There is no record that the Applicant followed this advice. (*Pavesich*, Decision No. 94 [1990], paras. 46, 49)

(*b*) *Guidelines/policy*

[See also Sect. 16, 'Classification', 15.i; Sect. 28, 'Reorganization', 2.i, 3.v and vi; Sect. 32, 'Miscellaneous', 2.i.]

i. 39. The first objection is that an 'established policy' is something which should be capable of identification by the persons affected prior to any occasion on which it is to be applied. But in the present case no such identification was possible. At no point in its pleadings does the Bank suggest that 'the established policy' was a generally known one. The closest that the Bank comes to the point is in the following statement:

> The policy that resulted in Applicant's being found medically unfit rests at bottom on a medical judgment. The medical judgment was made with reference to the Guide to Medical Fitness Standards for Application by the International Organization in the United Nations when Awarding Regular Contracts (the 'UN Guide lines'). The judgment was based on the UN Guidelines as well as the Medical Department's own assessment of all the facts and circumstances presented by Applicant's case. . . .

By implication, perhaps, the Bank is saying that the policy is to be found stated in the UN Guidelines. If that is the Bank's argument it is defective. There is no reference to the role that the Bank attributes to those Guidelines in anything that can be regarded as forming part of the applicable terms and conditions of service. The Applicant was unable to obtain the Guidelines from the Bank and only after considerable effort and delay was she able to obtain them from the United Nations. In short the 'policy' was not published in any manner sufficient to vest it with the status of a rule governing an important aspect of the relationship between the Bank and the Applicant.

40. It is a mistake to introduce as a defence to a complaint an argument based upon a dictate of policy if that policy has not previously been identified in a clear and comprehensible manner as part of the system of rules applicable between the Bank and its staff. If the Bank insists that medical assessment should remain within the realm of unreviewable medical discretion then it must not tie that assessment to guidelines that are claimed to be controlling. If, on the other hand, it wishes to reduce the risk of any arbitrariness or unfairness in medical judgment by requiring medical staff to adhere to pre-established guidelines then the role of those guidelines must be specified, they must be made readily available for inspection and the manner of the application to any particular case must be clear.

41. The Tribunal sees a second objection to the Bank's invocation of the 'application of an established policy' of which the UN Guidelines appear to form a significant part. While, in principle, the adoption by the Bank medical

cal staff to adhere to pre-established guidelines then the role of those guidelines must be specified, they must be made readily available for inspection and the manner of the application to any particular case must be clear.

41. The Tribunal sees a second objection to the Bank's invocation of the 'application of an established policy' of which the UN Guidelines appear to form a significant part. While, in principle, the adoption by the Bank medical staff of a policy contained in the UN Guidelines or any other internal guidelines, cannot be questioned, it is essential that the application of the policy should be fully consistent with the provisions of the Staff Regulations which require a complete medical examination. (*Arellano*, Decision No. 98 [1990], paras. 39–41)

(*c*) *Circulars, etc.*

[See Sect. 8, 'Sources of Law', 3 (*a*) i; Sect. 30, 'Procedure before Tribunal', 3 (*a*) i.]

4. Staff rules/principles of staff employment

(*a*) *Staff rules and regulations*

[See under the following sections for references:

Staff Rule 4.1: Sect. 8, 'Sources of Law', 2 (*c*) v; Sect. 32, 'Miscellaneous', 2.i

Staff Rule 5.03: Sect. 14, 'Performance', 1.iii

Staff Rule 5.06: Sect. 15, 'Terms and Conditions of Employment', 1.i and iii; Sect. 16, 'Classification', 1.i and ii; Sect. 25, 'Salary', 2.i; Sect. 29, 'Remedies', 8.i

Staff Rule 5.09: Sect. 4, 'Release Agreements', 2.i; Sect. 8, 'Sources of Law', 2 (*b*) ii and 2 (*c*) ii; Sect. 15, 'Terms and Conditions of Employment', 1.v and vi; Sect. 16, 'Classification', 8.i, 17.i; Sect. 28, 'Reorganization', 2.iv, vii and ix, 3.iv and v; Sect. 29, 'Remedies', 2.iv, 4.ii, 9.i; Sect. 30, 'Procedure before Tribunal', 11.i; Sect. 32, 'Miscellaneous', 5.i, 6.ii

Staff Rule 6.13: Sect. 8, 'Sources of Law', 1 (*c*) i; Sect. 32, 'Miscellaneous', 3.i

Staff Rule 6.14: Sect. 8, 'Sources of Law', 1 (*c*) i; Sect. 32, 'Miscellaneous', 3.i

Staff Rule 7.01: Sect. 4 'Release Agreements', 2.iii; Sect. 8, 'Sources of Law', 1 (*c*) ii and 2 (*a*) i; Sect. 10, '*Détournement de Pouvoir*', 1.i; Sect. 14, 'Performance', 1.iv

Staff Rule 9.01: Sect. 1, 'Jurisdiction', 1 (*b*) iii; Sect. 3, 'Inadmissibility for Other Reasons', 1.iii; Sect. 13, 'Procedural Irregularity', 5.ii; Sect. 26, 'Taxation', 1.i

Staff Rule 9.03: Sect. 3, 'Inadmissibility for Other Reasons', 1.ii and iii; Sect. 7, 'Appeals Committee', 1.ii; Sect. 8, 'Sources of Law', 1 (*b*)i

Staff Rule 9.04: Sect. 1, 'Jurisdiction', 1 (*b*) i; Sect. 8, 'Sources of Law', 1 (*e*) i; Sect. 13, 'Procedural Irregularity', 6.iii; Sect. 16, 'Classification', 7.i, 8.i, 10.i and ii, 13.ii and iii.]

(*b*) *Principles of staff employment*

[See under the following sections for references:

Principle 2.1: Sect. 13, 'Procedural Irregularity', 5.i; Sect. 16, 'Classification', 13.iii

Principle 2.1 (*d*): Sect. 15, 'Terms and Conditions of Employment', 1.vi; Sect. 28, 'Reorganization', 1.ii, 2.ix

Principle 5.1 (*d*): Sect. 22, 'Transfer and Reassignment', 1.iii; Sect. 32, 'Miscellaneous', 6.1

Principle 5.1 (*f*): Sect. 15, 'Terms and Conditions of Employment', 1.i, ii, and iii; Sect. 16, 'Classification', 1.i and ii; Sect. 25, 'Salary', 1.i; Sect. 29, 'Remedies', 8.i

Principle 6.1: Sect. 15, 'Terms and Conditions of Employment', 1.vi

Principle 6.2 (*b*): Sect. 9, 'Discretionary Power', 1.ii; Sect. 12, 'Substantive Irregularity', 2.i; Sect. 16, 'Classification', 11.i; Sect. 25, 'Salary', 4.ii

Principle 7.1 (*b*): Sect. 28, 'Reorganization', 1.ii, 2.iv, 3.vii.]

5. Judicial precedents

(*a*) *Of the same tribunal*

[See under the following sections for references: Sect. 1, 'Jurisdiction', 1 (*b*) ii, vi, and vii; Sect. 3, 'Inadmissibility for Other Reasons', 1.iii and iv; Sect. 4, 'Release Agreements', 1.i; Sect. 5, 'Review of Judgments', 1.i, 3.i; Sect. 6, 'Administrative Review', 1.iii; Sect. 8, 'Sources of Law', 2 (*b*) i and ii; Sect. 9, 'Discretionary Power', 1.i and ii; Sect. 11, 'Prejudice/Discrimination, 2.i and ii; Sect. 12, 'Substantive Irregularity', 1.i, iii, iv, v, vii, viii, xii, and xiii, 2.i; Sect. 13, 'Procedural Irregularity', 1.i, 6.iv; Sect. 14, 'Performance', 1.iv; Sect. 15, 'Terms and Conditions of Employment', 1.i, ii, iii, v, and vi; Sect. 16, 'Classification', 1.i and ii, 2.ii, 3.i, 7.1, 8.i, 14.i, 16. iii; Sect. 20, 'Fixed-Term Contracts', 2.i; Sect. 22, 'Transfer and Reassignment', 1.iii; Sect. 25. 'Salary', 2.i, 3 (*a*) i; Sect. 27. 'Termination', 1 (*a*) ii; Sect. 28, 'Reorganization', 1.iii, 2.v, viii, ix, x and xi, 3.iii, and 5.i; Sect. 29, 'Remedies', 1.vii, 3.iii, 8.i, 9.i, 10.v; Sect. 30, 'Procedure before Tribunal', 3 (*a*) iii, 12. iii; Sect. 32, 'Miscellaneous', 6.i.]

(*b*) *Of other tribunals*

i. 31. The Permanent Court of International Justice has recognized that disputes concerning the meaning or scope of a judgment include disputes 'as to whether a particular point has or has not been decided with binding force' (*Chorzów Factory Case* (Request for Interpretation), PCIJ, Series A, No. 13, pp. 11–12). And this is precisely the case here. (*Agodo et al.*, Decision No. 76 [1989], para. 31)

ii. 32. When the Tribunal decided to dismiss the application in Decisions 41–54, it also decided to dismiss by implication all the pleas contained in each application, including the claim for costs. If the Tribunal had wanted to adopt the unusual course of awarding costs to the losing parties it would have expressly so stated. In the jurisprudence of the Tribunal, only those claims for costs or attorneys' fees which are accepted by the Tribunal are expressly mentioned in the judgement; and silence means rejection. In so acting the Tribunal has followed a dictum of the International Court of Justice in its advisory opinion of July 12, 1973, concerning the review of Judgement No. 158 of the United Nations Administrative Tribunal. In that case the Court said:

> Account must also be taken of the basic principle regarding the question of costs in contentious proceedings before international tribunals, to the effect that each party shall bear its own in the absence of a specific decision of the tribunal awarding

costs (cf. Article 64 of the Statue of the Court) . . . The decision merely to allow the general principle to apply does not necessarily require detailed reasoning, and may even be adopted by implication. (1973 ICJ Reports, para. 98, p. 212)

(*Agodo et al.*, Decision No. 76 [1989], para. 32)

9. DISCRETIONARY POWER

1. General

[See also Sect. 1, 'Jurisdiction', 1 (*b*) vii; Sect. 8, 'Sources of Law', 2 (*b*) i, ii; Sect. 12, 'Substantive Irregularity', 1.vii; Sect. 16, 'Classification', 1.i and ii, 2.i, 3.i, 8.i, 11.i, 14.i, Sect. 20, 'Fixed-Term Contracts', 2.i; Sect. 25, 'Salary', 3 (*a*) i, 4.i, ii; Sect. 27, 'Termination', 1 (*b*) ii; Sect. 28, 'Reorganization', 2.ix.]

i. 35. According to the Respondent, the actions taken in this case were an integral part of the Bank-wide Job Grading Program and constituted a reasonable and non-discriminatory exercise of its discretionary authority. The Respondent claims that, in such cases, 'it is not for this Tribunal to substitute its own judgment for that of the Bank.' (*de Merode*, Decision No. 1 [1981], para. 45)

36. The Tribunal agrees that the Job Grading program. . . . constitutes an exercise of discretionary authority by the Respondent and, as such, is not subject to review by this Tribunal, unless it is shown that there has been an abuse of discretion, by reason of the action taken in a concrete case 'being arbitrary, discriminatory, improperly motivated or carried out in violation of a fair and reasonable procedure.' (*Saberi*, Decision No. 5 [1982], para. 24). No such abuse of discretion has been shown. [*Pinto*, Decision No. 56 [1988], paras. 35, 36)

ii. 21. Staff Principle 6.2 (*b*) directs the Respondent to 'institute and maintain programs of systematic job evaluation, the purpose of which is to grade jobs according to their purpose, function, and level of responsibility so as to provide a sound and equitable basis for remuneration of staff members'. The Applicant contends that the generic evaluation criteria for . . . (grade 24) do not meet the standard of objectivity and fairness required by Staff Principle 6.2 (*b*). According to her each element of the criteria leaves wide room for discretion and judgment, and hence for abuse by managers.

22. The Tribunal does not agree with the Applicant's criticism of the generic criteria for grade 24. The discretion given to the grading individuals and committees . . . does not differ in nature or scope from the discretion possessed by management in other areas relating to the conditions of employment. In all cases of discretion, unless otherwise proven, it is assumed that the administrative authority will exercise its discretion in an objective and non-discriminatory manner. . . . Such an exercise can be invalidated only if it is shown that there has been an abuse of discretion, the action taken in a concrete case 'being arbitrary, discriminatory, improperly motivated or carried out in violation of a fair and reasonable procedure' (*Saberi*, Decision No. 5 [1982], para. 24). (*Sebastian (No. 2)*, Decision No. 57 [1988], paras. 21, 22)

iii. 27. The Respondents, on the other hand, view their postponement of the comprehensive review for two consecutive years, and their reliance, instead, on intervening years review, to be a valid exercise of their discretion in implementing the rule of periodicity of salary adjustment, prescribed by the Kafka System, and sanctioned by the Tribunal in a consistent line of decisions.

28. In order to dispose of the applications, the Tribunal will have to answer several interrelated questions concerning the proper application of the Kafka System: particularly, whether by postponing the Comprehensive Review the Respondents meant to amend that system, and whether such postponement constituted a reasonable exercise of the discretionary powers of the Respondents. . . .

34. The Tribunal finds, however, that the discretion

enjoyed by the Respondents in implementing the principle of periodicity of salary adjustments is not without limitations. Under the Kafka System, the Respondents are undoubtedly required, as a general rule, to carry out comprehensive reviews every three years. If for valid reasons and in good faith they decide to postpone the conducting of such comprehensive review, the postponement should meet two conditions:

(i) It should rest on a reasonable basis justifying the departure from the strict observance of the three year rule.

(ii) It should not lead to exceeding the five year limit prescribed by the Kafka Committee in 1979 . . .

37. The Tribunal finds the explanation given by the Respondents for their decisions to postpone the comprehensive review for two consecutive years to be reasonable enough to bring those decisions within the margin of discretion left to them. (*Hammond et al.*, Decision No. 86 [1989], paras. 27, 28, 34, 37)

iv. 29. That the PTCO position was tailored for the Applicant is admitted by the Bank. But this fact does not by itself mean that the position was wrongly graded. The grading of positions is a matter of Bank management in which the Bank exercises a discretion. The Tribunal will review such matters only for the purpose of ensuring that the Administration has behaved in a procedurally correct way and that it has not reached a substantive conclusion that is not reasonably sustainable. It is not the task of the Tribunal to substitute its own assessment for that of the Bank. (*Lindsay*, Decision No. 92 [1990], para. 29)

2. Arbitrariness

[See also Sect. 16, 'Classification', 2.ii and iii, 13.iii, 15.i; Sect. 27, 'Termination', 1 (*a*) ii; Sect. 28, 'Reorganization', 2.i and x; Sect. 32, 'Miscellaneous', 2.i, 6.iii and iv.]

i. 35. In the present case, the Tribunal can find no basis on which to say that the Applicant was unjustly or harshly treated. The Tribunal notes that the Applicant was, in fact, originally offered in Round 1 the position of Chief of the Technical Cooperation Unit, a post immediately above that of PTCO, and declined it; that the Applicant had presumably understood the position description for PTCO before he accepted that position; and that, when the Applicant resigned the position after less than a week, he cited family reasons for wishing to leave the Bank, in addition to his feeling that the job did not meet his interest or professional skills. (*Lindsay*, Decision No. 92 [1990], para. 35)

ii. 40. It is a mistake to introduce as a defence to a complaint an argument based upon a dictate of policy if that policy has not previously been identified in a clear and comprehensible manner as part of the system of rules applicable between the Bank and its staff. If the Bank insists that medical assessment should remain within the realm of unreviewable medical discretion then it must not tie that assessment to guidelines that are claimed to be controlling. If, on the other hand, it wishes to reduce the risk of any arbitrariness or unfairness in medical judgment by requiring medical staff to adhere to pre-established guidelines then the role of those guidelines must be specified, they must be made readily available for inspection and the manner of the application to any particular case must be clear. (*Arellano*, Decision No. 98 [1990], para. 40)

iii. 58. The conclusion of the Selection Committee that any shortfall in the Applicant's qualifications could not be addressed by any additional counseling and training is also arbitrary and manifestly without rational basis. The few references in earlier PPRs to the Applicant's amenability to training all support the conclusion that he was indeed receptive to training. The record before the Selection Committee would have shown that the Applicant's prior experience with the Bank had been characterized by a failure on the part of his supervisors to recommend or provide training opportunities. As the Appeals Committee concluded:

> In spite of favorable performance evaluations, there was reportedly some dissatisfaction with several aspects of his performance, and yet he seems to have received minimal—if any—feedback, counselling, career development assignments, or training. In this situation, it is hard to understand how the Bank could have rejected the training/retraining program for the Appellant.
>
> Moreover, the principal criticism of the applicant that was set forth by the Acting Director in the 1986–87 PPR, prepared by him initially in draft form in the same week as the Reorganization selections were made—that he 'need[s] to sharpen his focus on the broad and important implications of his findings'—is (to the extent it can be understood) of the sort that does not appear to defy correction through counseling and training. (*Jassal*, Decision No. 100 [1991], para. 58)

For a similar statement see *Fabara-Núñez*, Decision No. 101 [1991], para. 45]

10. *DÉTOURNEMENT DE POUVOIR*

1. General

[See also Sect. 27, 'Termination', 1 (*a*) ii and iii; Sect. 28, 'Reorganization', 1. iii, 2. x.]

i. 31. In earlier cases arising from the Reorganization, the Tribunal has been confronted with claims that an applicant was improperly denied selection to a position that the Bank in fact gave to another staff member. This is the first case before the Tribunal in which an applicant claims to be qualified to serve in a post-Reorganization position that was left vacant. In such a case, a finding of redundancy must turn upon a conclusion that the content of the position was so defined as to render its previous occupant no longer qualified to discharge its responsibilities. Unsatisfactory performance by a staff member in his or her position prior to the Reorganization cannot alone furnish a basis for terminating service with the Bank on the ground of redundancy. To do so would be an improper use of the Reorganization procedures in order to avoid the protections otherwise afforded by the Bank's governing documents—Staff Rule 7.01 in particular—for termination of employment, and would therefore constitute *détournement de pouvoir*, subject to reversal by the Tribunal. (*Jassal*, Decision No. 100 [1991], para. 31)

[For a similar statement see *Fabara-Núñez*, Decision No. 101 [1991], para. 32.]

2. Principle of proportionality

[See Sect. 14, 'Performance', 1. iv; Sect, 27, 'Termination', 1 (*a*) ii.]

3. Improper motive

[See Sect. 11, 'Prejudice/Discrimination', 2.iii; Sect. 12, 'Substantive Irregularity', 1.i–xiii; Sect. 13, 'Procedural Irregularity', 1.iv; Sect. 14, 'Performance', 1.iv; Sect. 16, 'Classification', 17.i; Sect. 28, 'Reorganization', 2.vi, 3.i and viii; Sect. 30, 'Procedure before Tribunal', 11.i; Sect. 32, 'Miscellaneous', 5.i.]

11. PREJUDICE/DISCRIMINATION

1. Prejudice

[See also Sect. 7, 'Appeals Committee', 1.i; Sect. 12, 'Substantive Irregularity', 1.xii; Sect. 28, 'Reorganization', 1.iii, 2.x and xi; Sect. 29, 'Remedies', 8.ii.]

i. 55. The Applicant has complained of certain inherent limitations in the operation of the Committee as well as procedural and substantive flaws in its conduct in this case. The Tribunal has found itself able to review these complaints without entering further into the question of the powers of the Appeals Committee or its relation to the Tribunal. It has concluded that the complaints cannot be sustained. . . .

74. The question of the effect of the adverse APR for 1985–86 and of the determination of redundancy upon the Applicant's prospects in the Reorganization involves a degree of speculation into which it is inappropriate for the Tribunal to enter. Even if managers of other divisions were aware of the emerging 1985–86 APR and of the redundancy notice, it does not follow that their rejections of the Applicant's requests were determined by that knowledge. The same goes for the allegation of bias that plays so prominent a role in the Applicant's case. The allegation rests at best on coincidence. There is no direct or circumstantial evidence to support it. (*de Raet*, Decision No. 85 [1989], paras. 55, 74)

2. Discrimination/inequality of treatment

[See also Sect. 14, 'Performance', 1.v; Sect. 16, 'Classification', 2.i, 3.i; Sect. 27, 'Termination', 1 (*b*) ii; Sect. 28, 'Reorganization', 2.i; Sect. 30, 'Procedure before Tribunal', 3 (*a*) iii; Sect. 32, 'Miscellaneous', 6.iv.]

i. 35. According to the Respondent, the actions taken in this case were an integral part of the Bank-wide Job Grading Program and constituted a reasonable and non-discriminatory exercise of its discretionary authority. The Respondent claims that, in such cases, 'it is not for this Tribunal to substitute its own judgment for that of the competent organs of the Bank.' (*de Merode*, Decision No. 1 [1981], para. 45).

36. The Tribunal agrees that the Job Grading program . . . constitutes an exercise of discretionary authority by the Respondent and, as such, is not subject to review by this Tribunal, unless it is shown that there has been an abuse of discretion, by reason of the action taken

in a concrete case 'being arbitrary, discriminatory, improperly motivated or carried out in violation of a fair and reasonable procedure.' (*Saberi*, Decision No. 5 [1982], para. 24). No such abuse of discretion has been shown. (*Pinto*, Decision No. 56, [1988], paras. 35, 36)

ii. 26. In *de Merode* (paras. 111 and 112) the Tribunal found 'that a consistent practice of periodic adjustment has been established, and that the Bank makes these adjustments out of the conviction that it is legally obliged to do so'. The Tribunal concluded:

> '. . . in consequence . . . the Bank is obliged to carry out periodic reviews of salaries, taking into account various relevant factors. . . . the established practice, [has] created a legal obligation to make periodic adjustments reflecting changes in the cost of living and other factors. In the opinion of the Tribunal such an obligation is a fundamental element in the Applicant's conditions of employment which the Bank does not have the right to change unilaterally.'

The Tribunal concludes that the freezing of the Applicant's salary, from September 30, 1987, would deprive her, without justifiable cause, of the right to benefit from periodic adjustments reflecting changes in the cost of living and other factors, which the Tribunal has found to be a fundamental element in the Applicant's conditions of employment which the IFC does not have the right to change unilaterally. This is not to suggest that a staff member may under no circumstances have his or her grade reduced or salary frozen, for example, when this is done for cause as for disciplinary action. In the present case, however, the downgrading of the Applicant and her position was done not because of her misconduct but because of the organizational needs of the IFC; in such circumstance, the staff member is reasonably entitled to more equitable treatment, as appears to be contemplated by Staff Principle 5 (1) f. (*Gavidia*, Decision No. 66 [1988], para. 26)

iii. 57. (3) The third point is that, despite the assertion of the Applicant to the contrary, it is not the obligation of the Bank to demonstrate that there has been no discrimination or abuse of power—not, that is, until an Applicant has made out a *prima facie* case or has pointed to facts that suggest that the Bank is in some relevant way at fault. Then, of course, the burden shifts to the Bank to disprove the facts or to explain its conduct in some legally acceptable manner. (*de Raet*, Decision No. 85 [1989], para. 57)

iv. 47. The Tribunal does not find substantiated in the record the Applicant's charge that the Acting Director discriminated against her because of her knowledge of alleged mismanagement on his part and because she was a vocal critic of him within IAD. But the Tribunal does conclude that it is highly likely that the negative appraisal on the part of the Acting Director was controlling within the Selection Committee, and that neither he nor the Committee gave any weight to the Applicant's amenability to training or to the Bank's own responsibility for retarding the professional development of the Applicant. (*Fabara-Núñez*, Decision No. 101 [1991], para. 47)

v. 32. Although the Applicant challenges the Respondent's evaluation of his performance as being discriminatory and motivated by a general hostile attitude on the part of the VPCOF towards the Applicant, the Tribunal does not find in the record any evidence that substantiates that contention. (*Mathew*, Decision No. 103 [1991], para. 32)

12. SUBSTANTIVE IRREGULARITY

1. Abuse of discretion

[See also Sect. 13, 'Procedural Irregularity', 1.i and iv; Sect. 14, 'Performance', 1.ii; Sect. 16, 'Classification', 1.ii, 2.ii and iii, 3.i, 8.i, 14.i, 15.i, 17.i; Sect. 20, 'Fixed-Term Contracts', 2.i; Sect. 23, 'Promotion and Demotion', 1.i; Sect. 27, 'Termination', 1 (*b*) ii;

Sect. 28, 'Reorganization', 1.ii, 2.i, iv, v, viii, ix, and x, 3.v; Sect. 30, 'Procedure before Tribunal', 3 (*a*) i.]

i. 22. The Tribunal does not agree with the Applicant's criticism of the generic criteria for grade 24. The discretion given to the grading individuals and committees under the mechanism established and applied by the Respondent does not differ in nature or scope from the discretion possessed by management in other areas relating to the conditions of employment. In all cases of discretion, unless otherwise proven, it is assumed that the administrative authority will exercise its discretion in an objective and non-discriminatory manner. The very fact of allowing the grading and reviewing bodies a wide range of discretion does not by itself invalidate the scheme. It is the exercise of discretion by individuals and committees in particular cases that may be challenged and criticized. Such an exercise can be invalidated only if it is shown that there has been an abuse of discretion, the action taken in a concrete case 'being arbitrary, discriminatory, improperly motivated or carried out in violation of a fair and reasonable procedure' (*Saberi*, Decision No. 5 [1982], para. 24). . . .

24. The Applicant contends that, by virtue of certain elements of the criteria, managers may influence the determination of whether the staff member meets the criteria or not, by assigning to or withholding from the staff member those tasks required for a promotion to a higher grade. The Tribunal notes that this possibility is inherent in any system of hierarchy and supervision within the employment unit. For the staff member the safeguard lies in the possibility of administrative and judicial review to determine whether there has been an abuse of discretion. . . .

27. The Tribunal turns next to the Applicant's second criticism of the grading process, namely that the reviewing managers took liberty to 'finesse' and expand some of the elements of the criteria, thus applying to the Applicant amended and sometimes distorted criteria.

The Tribunal agrees with the general principle that managers implementing the mechanism of grading should limit themselves to applying the general criteria to the particular concrete cases. They have no power to amend and expand them when applying them to individual cases. However, the requirements for a certain level or position within the Respondent's hierarchy cannot —by necessity—be completely different from those required for a job of the same nature but of a higher level or grade. The difference may simply be one of degree. In applying the criteria both the grading bodies and those who review the grading may need to interpret certain elements common to two different levels in a somewhat different manner that would be more demanding when applied to the higher grade or level.

28. It appears from a careful reading of the document entitled 'Generic Functions of Project Officers (Project Economist, Financial Analyst and Technical Specialist)' that the framers were aware of the impossibility of laying down completely different criteria for jobs of the same nature, though of different levels. The opening statement of that document declares that:

> '[T]he majority of Project Officers perform these functions within their area of assigned responsibility and expertise. Positions, however, will vary in the extent to which these responsibilities are carried out.'

29. Moreover, the examples given by the applicant of such 'finessing' of the criteria in the reviewing process do not substantiate the contention that the reviewing bodies were in fact amending or expanding the requirements. They were rather applying them within the reasonable limits of interpretation and with a view to establishing a higher level of fulfillment of certain elements of the criteria for a higher level position. . . .

35. In the judgement of all grading and reviewing individuals and committees the Applicant did not meet the criteria required for grading her position at level 24. There being no proven abuse of discretion on the part of the Respondent its decision to grade the Applicant's

position at level 23 should stand. (*Sebastian (No. 2)*, Decision No. 57 [1988], paras. 22, 24, 27–9, 35)

ii. 35. Even if the Tribunal were to conclude that there had been an abuse of discretion or a violation of the Applicant's procedural rights in the classification decision, the Tribunal should not substitute its judgment for that of the Respondent's management by directing that the Applicant's position be graded at level 17. At most, the case might be remanded for classification according to the new criteria to be promulgated. . . .

47. The decision of the Vice President, PA, must therefore be considered in order to determine whether it was an abuse of discretion. In the judgment of the Tribunal, it was not. There appears to be no question that the criteria for the level 16 position of Administrative Secretary II were properly adopted and promulgated; they were properly applied to the Applicant, who had been doing comparable work in the G level before the regrading, and whose work after October 1, 1985 matched that described in the Administrative Secretary II criteria. The Job Grading Appeals Board concluded that the Applicant's position 'matches the criteria for Administrative Secretary II,' and that it was 'unable to recommend a change in the grade 16 assigned to the Appellant's position.' It was not an abuse of discretion for the Vice President, PA, to reach the same conclusion, and—apart from the confusion created by the overlapping Office Manager classification, withdrawn earlier—the Applicant has not suggested otherwise. (*Apkarian*, Decision No. 58 [1988], paras. 35, 47)

[For similar statements see:

Benner, Decision No. 59 [1988], para. 37
Dosik, Decision No. 60 [1988], para. 37
Hovsepian, Decision No. 61 [1988], para. 37
Hunger, Decision No. 62 [1988], para. 37
Papinchak, Decision No. 63 [1988], para. 37
Witty, Decision No. 64 [1988], para. 37.]

iii. 23. The Tribunal agrees that the Job Grading Program —involving decisions regarding criteria for evaluating staff positions, the assignment of various tasks to particular positions and the ultimate determination of grade levels—constitutes an exercise of discretionary authority by the Respondent and, as such, is not subject to review by this Tribunal, unless it is contended that there has been an abuse of discretion, by reason of the action taken in a concrete case 'being arbitrary, discriminatory, improperly motivated or carried out in violation of a fair and reasonable procedure' (*Saberi*, Decision No. 5 [1982], para. 24). No such abuse of discretion has been shown. (*Gavidia*, Decision No. 66 [1988], para. 23)

iv. 34. In previous cases arising out of the Job Grading Program the Tribunal has determined that this Program —involving decisions regarding criteria for evaluating staff positions, the assignment of various tasks to particular positions, and the ultimate determination of grade levels—constitutes an exercise of discretionary authority by the Respondent, and that 'it is not for this Tribunal to substitute its own judgment for that of the competent organs of the Bank' (*Pinto*, Decision No. 56 [1988], para. 35). Consequently, the Program as such is subject to review by this Tribunal only if it is shown that there has been an abuse of discretion, by reason of the action taken in a concrete case 'being arbitrary, discriminatory, improperly motivated or carried out in violation of a fair and reasonable procedure' (*Pinto*, Decision No. 56 [1988], para. 36). (*Alan Berg*, Decision No. 73 [1988], para. 34)

v. 15. The decision not to select the Applicant was taken in the exercise of a discretionary power. As the Tribunal has held in several of its earlier decisions, when the Respondent exercises its discretion 'it is not for this Tribunal to substitute its own judgment for that of the competent organs of the Bank.' (*de Merode*, Decision No. 1 [1981], para. 45; *Pinto*, Decision No. 56 [1988], para. 35). The Tribunal will not interfere with the exercise of such discretion 'unless the decision constitutes an abuse of discretion, being arbitrary, discriminatory, improperly motivated or carried out in violation of a fair and reasonable procedure.' (*Saberi*, Decision No. 5 [1982], para. 24; *Suntharalingam*, Decision No. 6 [1982], para. 27; *Thompson*, Decision No. 30 [1986], para. 24; *Pinto*, Decision No. 56 [1988], para. 36). (*Bertrand*, Decision No. 81 [1989], para. 15)

vi. 57. The Tribunal cannot accept this view of the matter since the Applicant was never promoted to a level 25 position and was a level 24 officer at the time the offers were made. The proposed formal increase in the Applicant's grade level was denied in June 1986. He was assigned to a level 25 position in order to test his suitability for promotion to that position. In the event, the Respondent's officers who were charged with the duty of deciding on the Applicant's fitness for promotion, noted that: 'The Applicant would need to work on the areas of leadership and management if he were to be a successful SCPO candidate'. The Applicant was never graded at level 25, notwithstanding the recommendations and favorable reports made on his work. The Tribunal will not interfere with the decision not to promote him in the absence of evidence of abuse of discretion. No abuse of discretion has been shown in this case. (*Apergis*, Decision No. 83 [1989], para. 57)

vii. 21. The question is whether the Applicant's non-selection was unlawful, as he claims. The Tribunal is satisfied that on the contrary it was lawful. The decision not to select the Applicant was taken in the exercise of a discretionary power. As the Tribunal has held in several of its earlier decisions, when the Respondent exercises its discretion, 'it is not for this Tribunal to substitute its own judgment for that of the competent organs of the Bank.' (*de Merode*, Decision No. 1 [1981], para. 45; *Pinto*, Decision No. 56 [1988], para. 35). The Tribunal will not interfere with the exercise of such discretion 'unless the decision constitutes an abuse of discretion, being arbitrary, discriminatory, improperly motivated or carried out in violation of a fair and reasonable procedure.' (*Saberi*, Decision No. 5 [1982], para. 24; *Suntharalingam*, Decision No. 6 [1982], para. 27; *Thompson*, Decision No. 30 [1986], para. 24; *Pinto*, Decision No. 56 [1988], para. 36). In the case there is no evidence of the operation of any of these vitiating factors.

22. The Bank had properly exercised its managerial discretion which it had not abused. The Bank acted reasonably in concluding that the Applicant did not have sufficient skills, qualifications and experience; his skills and experience were mainly those of a project economist controlling the operation of specific projects, while the Reorganization placed greater emphasis on sectoral functions and planning ability. The Applicant himself admitted that neither his education nor his experience provided him with the sector and projected policy skills which were the criteria for selection. (*Klempin*, Decision No. 88 [1990], paras. 21, 22)

viii. 40. Even assuming that the Bank could properly promote a better qualified staff member from a level 25 position in preference to the Applicant, certain questions remain with regard to the Bank's actions in this case. One is whether the Bank in fact did properly act within its discretionary authority in making particular choices among the candidates for level 26 positions in the Reorganization. As the Tribunal has frequently stated, decisions such as these are within the Bank's discretion and may not be nullified, 'unless the decision constitutes an abuse of discretion, being arbitrary, discriminatory, improperly motivated or carried out in violation of a fair and reasonable procedure': *Saberi*, Decision No. 5 [1982], para. 24. (*Fernandes*, Decision No. 90 [1990], para. 40)

ix. 23. The Applicant questions the motivation of the Respondent in offering him the position of PTCO, contending that it 'reflected the Respondent's hope of avoiding its obligation to offer the Applicant separation under the terms of the Enhanced Separation Package, as a result of constraints on available resources for such purpose' . . .

25. Even if it were true that the Bank was in difficulty in dealing with all the Enhanced Separation payments within the limits of its budget, the Tribunal cannot see that fact as by itself supporting the allegation that, if otherwise correct, an act of the Bank was improperly motivated. Nor is there, in itself, any evident impropriety in the Bank tailoring a position to meet the circumstances of an officer of experience and quality whose services the Bank understandably wished to retain. . . .

28. The Applicant also argues that the PTCO position was substantively wrongly graded at level 25 and that this was because it was tailored for him, that he had been at level 25 and that, therefore, the level at which the position was graded was predetermined by his level, not by the nature of the position.

29. That the PTCO position was tailored for the Applicant is admitted by the Bank. But the fact does not by itself mean that the position was wrongly graded. The grading of positions is a matter of Bank management in which the Bank exercises a discretion. The Tribunal will review such matters only for the purpose of ensuring that the Administration has behaved in a procedurally correct way and that it has not reached a substantive conclusion that is not reasonably sustainable. It is not the task of the Tribunal to substitute its own assessment for that of the Bank. (*Lindsay*, Decision No. 92 [1990], paras. 23, 25, 28, 29)

x. 41. The Tribunal must now address the issue which seems to be the gravamen of the application, namely the exercise of the Bank's managerial discretion not to reassign her. The Applicant concedes, as indeed she could not dispute, that the Respondent owed no duty to reassign her. She says:

Applicant has never asserted that the Bank had 'an absolute duty' to reassign her but under the circumstances of her case, a reassignment would have been the only fair and reasonable measure.

If the Applicant has, *ex concessis*, no legal right to reassignment, then whether she should be reassigned or her employment terminated would be purely a matter for managerial discretion which, if exercised either way, would be valid, unless it was discriminatory, arbitrary or improperly motivated. . . .

44. In various parts of her application, the Applicant sought to get round the Tribunal's oft reiterated statement of principle by claims that the Bank exercise of discretion was vitiated on the ground that it was arbitrary, discriminatory, improperly motivated or carried out in violation of fair and reasonable procedure. These claims are not borne out by the record. The Tribunal considers that the various assessments of the Applicant's performance by her superior officers of all grades, Division Chiefs, Directors and supervisors, were all made in the course of their duties and were fair and reasonable. Accordingly, the Respondent's decision to terminate the Applicant's appointment constitutes a valid exercise of managerial discretion. (*Georgiev*, Decision No. 96 [1990], paras. 41, 44)

xi. 54. However, the Applicant did present a timely request for administrative review of his 1986/87 PPR. This complaint is devoid of merit. The 1986/87 PPR embodied the collective judgments of the Applicant's managers and independent persons within his department. During the administrative review he had ample opportunity to make his own views known. His managers took pains to look into his complaints and see that he had been fairly evaluated. The Tribunal is of the opinion that these factors are sufficient to dispel doubt regarding the report, and that the Bank's officers did not abuse their administrative discretion in assessing the Applicant's performance. Therefore, there is no basis for designating an 'External Financial Expert' to assess the work produced by the Applicant from July 1985–

June 1987. So this claim is dismissed. (*Kassab*, Decision No. 97 [1990], para. 54)

xii. 30. As the Tribunal has often stated, a decision by the Bank to select a staff member for a particular position rests within the Bank's discretion, and may be overturned by the Tribunal only when it concludes that this discretion has been abused. 'The Administration's appraisal in that respect is final, unless the decision constitutes an abuse of discretion, being arbitrary, discriminatory, improperly motivated or carried out in violation of a fair and reasonable procedure,' *Suntharalingam*, Decision No. 5 [1981], para. 24. The Tribunal will not set aside a decision of the Bank unless it was 'reached in an arbitrary manner, involving, for example, unfairness, failure to allow the Applicant to state his case, or other departures from established procedures, bias, prejudice, the taking into consideration of irrelevant factors or manifest unreasonableness,' *de Raet*, Decision No. 85 [1989], para. 67. This standard of scrutiny has been applied by the Tribunal in cases arising from the 1987 Reorganization, in which staff members have been displaced from their previous positions on the ground of redundancy as a result of the redefinition of job duties or the reduction in the number of departmental positions . . .

37. It is not for the Tribunal, in assessing the validity of the selection or non-selection of a member, to undertake its own examination of that staff member's record, or a criterion-by-criterion assessment of his or her qualifications. That is for the Bank to do in the first instance, subject to review by the Tribunal only for abuse of discretion. But the Tribunal is charged with determining whether the Bank's decision was the product of bias, prejudice, arbitrariness, manifest unreasonableness, or unfair or improper procedure. Thus, if the Bank's conclusion regarding the Applicant's qualifications for selection as audit analyst altogether lacks support in factual evidence or reasonable inference, that conclusion must be found to be an abuse of discretion.

The Tribunal will now consider whether such is the case here. . . .

55. The negative views of the Applicant's qualifications held by the most influential participant in the selection process were altogether without support in the Applicant's prior annual evaluation reports, and also fundamentally and clearly failed to reflect the positive views of the three senior auditors who were consulted by the Acting Director and who were fully familiar with the Applicant's work. The Bank's decision that the Applicant was unfit for a level 20 audit analyst position is found to be lacking in any evidentiary support and is therefore an abuse of discretion. . . .

59. The Respondent claims that the Selection Committee's decisions not to select the Applicant for a level 19 position, or for further training, were justified by the Applicant's written statement shortly before the selection process that he wished to be selected for a position outside IAD, or indeed that he preferred to leave the Bank altogether with the special financial benefits contained in the Enhanced Separation Package (Package B). There is considerable factual dispute about the Applicant's stated preferences in this regard. Suffice it to say that the formal minutes of the Selection Committee state that the Applicant's 'request not to be selected into IAD was taken into account. However, he did not meet the selection criteria.' It therefore appears that the principal basis, if not the exclusive basis, for the Committee's decision not to select the Applicant was his lack of qualifications rather than his preferences regarding assignment. It is that decision that the Tribunal concludes to have been an abuse of discretion. . . .

61. Because the Tribunal has concluded that the non-selection of the Applicant for the level 20 position of audit analyst in IAD constituted an abuse of discretion, and because the record indicates that three audit analyst positions were left vacant at the conclusion of the Reorganization, the appropriate remedy is to order the Respondent to reinstate the Applicant in the position. Such an order would help to place the Applicant in the

position he would be in, had the Respondent not violated his contract of employment. (*Jassal*, Decision No. 100 [1991], paras. 30, 37, 55, 59, 61)

For similar statements see *Fabara-Núñez*, Decision No. 101 [1991], paras. 31, 38, 44, 45, 50.]

xiii. 29. The discretion exercised by the Respondent as to whether the Applicant met the requirements of the position must, therefore, be scrutinized by the Tribunal in order to ensure that it is not vitiated by an abuse of discretion, being arbitrary, discriminatory, improperly motivated or carried out in violation of a fair and reasonable procedure. (*Saberi*, Decision No. 5 [1981], para. 24, *Suntharalingam*, Decision No. 6 [1981] para. 24, *de Raet*, Decision No. 85 [1989], para. 67) . . .

39. The Tribunal concludes that there was no abuse of discretion in making this evaluation. (*Mathew*, Decision No. 103 [1991], paras. 29, 39)

2. Error of law

[See also Sect. 16, 'Classification', 3.i; Sect. 32, 'Miscellaneous', 2.i.]

i. 21. Staff Principle 6.2 (*b*) directs the Respondent to 'institute and maintain programs of systematic job evaluation, the purpose of which is to grade jobs according to their purpose, function, and level of responsibility so as to provide a sound and equitable basis for the remuneration of staff members'. The Applicant contends that the generic evaluation criteria leaves wide room for discretion and judgment, and hence for abuse by managers. In particular, she contends that the inclusion of terms and expressions like 'regular', and 'technical authority', 'sensitive' and 'general guidance' etc. introduces such vague criteria for evaluating jobs that the standard of Staff Principle 6.2 (*b*) is not satisfied.

22. The Tribunal does not agree with the Applicant's criticism of the generic criteria for grade 24. The

discretion given to the grading individuals and committees under the mechanism established and applied by the Respondent does not differ in nature or scope from the discretion possessed by management in other areas relating to the conditions of employment. In all cases of discretion, unless otherwise proven, it is assumed that the administrative authority will exercise its discretion in an objective and non-discriminatory manner. The very fact of allowing the grading and reviewing bodies a wide range of discretion does not by itself invalidate the scheme. It is the exercise of discretion by individuals and committees in particular cases that may be challenged and criticized. Such an exercise can be invalidated only if it is shown that there has been an abuse of discretion, the action taken in a concrete case 'being arbitrary, discriminatory, improperly motivated or carried out in violation of a fair and reasonable procedure' (*Saberi*, Decision No. 5 [1982], para. 24). . . .

25. The Tribunal observes that in the particular case of the Applicant no such withholding of assignment took place. The Applicant admits that since 1978 she was continuously assigned the leadership function of 'complex, new type projects in sectors or operations that were never before tried in the Bank'.

26. The Tribunal, therefore, concludes that the generic evaluation criteria for PRJ—C (grade 24) did not fall short of meeting the standard required by Staff Principle 6.2 (*b*).

27. The Tribunal turns next to the Applicant's second criticism of the grading process, namely, that the reviewing managers took liberty to 'finesse' and expand some of the elements of the criteria, thus applying to the Applicant amended and sometimes distorted criteria. The Tribunal agrees with the general principle that managers implementing the mechanism of grading should limit themselves to applying the general criteria to the particular concrete cases. They have no power to amend and expand them when applying them to individual cases. However, the requirements for a certain level or position within the Respondent's hierarchy cannot—by

necessity—be completely different from those required for a job of the same nature but of a higher level or grade. The difference may simply be one of degree. In applying the criteria both the grading bodies and those who review the grading may need to interpret certain elements common to two different levels in a somewhat different manner that would be more demanding when applied to the higher grade or level.

28. It appears from a careful reading of the document entitled 'Generic Functions of Project Officers (Project Economist, Financial Analyst and Technical Specialist)' that the framers were aware of the impossibility of laying down completely different criteria for jobs of the same nature, though of different levels. The opening statement of that document declares that:

> '[T]he majority of Project Officers perform these functions within their area of assigned responsibility and expertise. Positions, however, will vary in the extent to which these responsibilities are carried out.'

29. Moreover, the examples given by the Applicant of such 'finessing' of the criteria in the reviewing process do not substantiate the contention that the reviewing bodies were in fact amending or expanding the requirements. They were rather applying them within the reasonable limits of interpretation and with a view to establishing a higher level of fulfillment of certain elements of the criteria for a higher level position. (*Sebastian (No. 2)*, Decision No. 57 [1988], paras. 21–2, 25–9)

ii. 42. This is enough to dispose of the substance of the case. The Applicant should have been medically examined and she was not. It is unnecessary, therefore, to consider her other contentions. (*Arellano*, Decision No. 98 [1990], para. 42)

3. Erroneous conclusion

[See Sect. 1, 'Jurisdiction', 1 (*b*) v; Sect. 14, 'Performance', 1.ii; Sect. 28, 'Reorganization', 2.x.]

4. Considerations of irrelevant facts

[See Sect. 1, 'Jurisdiction', 1 (*b*) v.]

5. Omission of relevant facts

[See Sect. 28, 'Reorganization', 2.ix.]

13. PROCEDURAL IRREGULARITY

1. General

[See also Sect. 12, 'Substantive Irregularity', 1.ii and xii; Sect. 16, 'Classification', 13.iii; Sect. 28, 'Reorganization', 2.i and xi; Sect. 29, 'Remedies', 4.i; Sect. 30, 'Procedure before Tribunal', 3 (*a*) vi.]

i. 39. Decisions made by the Bank regarding the criteria for evaluating staff positions, the assignment of various tasks to particular positions, and the ultimate determination of grade levels for such positions, are properly regarded as within the discretion of the Bank. The Tribunal does, however, have the power and responsibility to determine whether the Respondent's decision 'constitutes an abuse of discretion, being arbitrary, discriminatory, improperly motivated or carried out in violation of a fair and reasonable procedure.' *Saberi*, Decision No. 5 [1982], para. 24. (*Apkarian*, Decision No. 58 [1988], para. 39)

[See Decisions Nos. 59–64 for similar statements.]

ii. 45. The Tribunal notes that from the time the Applicant expressed her dissatisfaction with the grading of her position by the JEU, the Respondent took a series of measures aimed at confirming and consolidating the decision to grade the Applicant's position at level 17. Many of these measures fell short of meeting the requirements of due process and a fair and reasonable procedure. . . .

52. In the light of the above the Tribunal concludes

that the Respondent's decision to grade the Applicant's position at level 17 and to reject the recommendation of the JGAB was taken as a result of a series of measures carried out in violation of fair and reasonable procedures. As a result of these measures the Applicant was deprived of her right effectively to participate in the grading exercise and to be notified in good time of the measures, communications and decisions taken affecting different aspects of her employment with the Respondent. Consequently, in these circumstances the decision should be quashed and remanded to the Respondent, and compensation should be granted to the Applicant for the tangible and intangible injury suffered by the Applicant as a result of the irregular procedure followed in determining the grade of her position. (*Rae*, Decision No. 74 [1988], paras. 45, 52)

iii. 20. The Applicant contended that Staff Rule 5.09, Section 8, sets out a detailed procedure for the grading of new positions and asserted that, in the case of the PTCO position, there is no evidence that this procedure was followed. The Applicant did not develop this argument in full detail but instead included in his application three interrogatories and two requests for documents in which he sought information and documents closely reflecting the procedural requirements set out in Staff Rule 5.09, para. 8.03. . . .

22. In these circumstances, the Tribunal finds it impossible to conclude either that the procedures laid down in Staff Rule 5.09, Section 8, were not applicable to the PTCO position or that the conduct of the Respondent satisfied those procedures. The consequences of this procedural irregularity will be considered later in this judgment . . .

24. The evidence adduced by the Applicant in support of this contention is no more than circumstantial and consists principally of the fact that the post was newly created, that the job description was precisely tailored to suit his qualifications and that, after he declined it, the post was not offered to anyone else. However, apart from

the procedural irregularity that the Tribunal already found (question (I) above), the only real evidence on the point is the statement in a memorandum from Mr. Dyck to the Applicant: 'of course . . . the Region was also cognizant of Senior Management's desire to place as many qualified staff as possible at their level before the end of Round 2'. This observation must be read in its context, as following a sentence describing the objective justification for the post to the Applicant: ' . . . the Region offered him this position by virtue of his past experience and expertise as a Project Specialist (and his knowledge of technical assistance) including but not limited to the human resources section.'

25. Even if it were true that the Bank was in difficulty in dealing with all the Enhanced Separation payments within the limits of its budget, the Tribunal cannot see that fact as by itself supporting the allegation that, if otherwise correct, an act of the Bank was improperly motivated. Nor is there, in itself, any evident impropriety in the Bank tailoring a position to meet the circumstances of an officer of experience and quality whose services the Bank understandably wished to retain.

26. The Applicant has also sought to support his general contention by claiming that when he left the PTCO position it was not again advertised and no attempt was made to fill it. The Respondent has explained that the functions of the position were then redistributed over a number of other posts.

27. The Applicant then suggest that this development confirms the arbitrariness of the establishment and grading of the post, a situation which he feared might have led, if he had remained in the post, to the Bank deciding that the post had no real role to perform and that its incumbent should be declared redundant. The Respondent has replied that there is nothing to support this speculation. The Tribunal agrees. (*Lindsay*, Decision No. 92 [1990], paras. 20, 22, 24–7)

v. 38. It is not for the Tribunal, in assessing the validity of the selection or non-selection of a staff member, to undertake its own examination of that staff member's record, or a criterion-by-criterion assessment of his or her qualifications. That is for the Bank to do in the first instance, subject to review by the Tribunal only for abuse of discretion. But the Tribunal is charged with determining whether the Bank's decision was the product of bias, prejudice, arbitrariness, manifest unreasonableness, or unfair or improper procedure. Thus, if the Bank's conclusion regarding the Applicant's qualifications for selection as audit analyst altogether lacks support in factual evidence or reasonable inference, or was the product of an improper procedure, that conclusion must be found to be an abuse of discretion. The Tribunal will now consider whether such is the case here. . . .

48. The Tribunal also finds that the selection process was likely tainted by a serious procedural irregularity. The Respondent asserts in its answer that the Acting Director and the other members of the Selection Committee had before them the Applicant's career file and that the Acting Director supplemented this with highly critical comments that had been previously related to him by the Applicant's supervisor in EDP; these critical comments were later (on November 5, 1987) put into writing by that supervisor. The Tribunal gives no weight to this memorandum. First, it must be noted that the November 5, 1987 memorandum was prepared at the explicit request of the Acting Director, who was the subject of an investigation by an impartial panel appointed slightly more than one week before, in light of charges of mismanagement that had been leveled by staff members against him; its preparation under these circumstances and long after the selection decisions were made in July 1987 cast grave doubt upon the credibility of its contents. Moreover, the negative comments set forth in the November 1987 memorandum and assertedly communicated orally as well to the Selection Committee some months before are flatly contradictory to the very positive evaluations contemporaneously made by that same supervisor in several previous annual

evaluation reports. [*Fabara-Núñez*, Decision No. 101 [1991], paras. 38, 48)

2. Warnings

[See Sect. 6, 'Administrative Review', 1.iii; Sect. 14, 'Performance', 1.iv.]

3. Statement of reasons

[See also Sect. 13, 'Procedural Irregularity', 5.iv; Sect. 28, 'Reorganization', 2.iv.]

i. 43. Nonetheless, in all the circumstances of the Reorganization the Bank's notification can only be read as informing the Applicant that others in the pool of eligible staff members had been regarded as better qualified for selection to level 26 positions in the managerial-selection round. This seems to the Tribunal to constitute a sufficient initial statement of reasons for the non-selection of a staff member within a comprehensive reorganization process. Such selection process necessarily involved the subjective assessment on the part of management of a variety of skills, aptitudes and the like possessed by thousands of staff members vying for positions in the reorganized Bank. Given the nature of the process, the statement given by the Bank to the Applicant may be regarded as an adequate statement of reasons as required under Principle 7.1 (*b*). (*Fernandes*, Decision No. 90 [1990], para. 43)

4. Classification

[See also Sect. 16, 'Classification', 14.i.]

i. 35. In the present case the Applicant has contended that improper procedures were followed by the Respondent concerning his grading at the time when he was transferred to the Agriculture and Rural Development Department in 1975. According to documents in the

Respondent's files, which were not made available to the Applicant, the position then assigned to him, as Senior Nutrition Advisor, had a grade level (grade N) lower than that of his previous assignment as Deputy Director (grade O). According to the same documents, the Applicant was nevertheless allowed to retain his former grade O but on a personal basis. . . .

40. The consequences of that improper procedure have materialized at the present time as a result of the application to the staff member of the Job Grading exercise. The Applicant rightly contends that if he had been made aware of his true situation in 1975 he might have been able to dispute the decision taken and to take remedial action, either to obtain another suitable assignment within the Bank or to seek a position outside it. While at that time he had prospects of outside employment, it is now too late for him to be considered for an outside position by reason of his age. (*Alan Berg*, Decision No. 73 [1988], para. 35, 40)

5. Notice

[See also Sect. 7, 'Appeals Committee', 1.ii; Sect. 14, 'Performance', 1.ii and iv; Sect. 18, 'Benefits', 3.i; Sect. 27, 'Termination', 1 (*a*) ii; Sect. 28, 'Reorganization', 2.iv and vii, 3.viii; Sect. 29, 'Remedies', 8.ii.]

i. 60. The Applicant appears to consider that a significant distinction is to be drawn between the suspension of 'terms of the redundancy notice' and the suspension of the notice itself. The Tribunal is unable to identify any relevant distinction. If the terms of a notice are suspended without any qualification or limitation, there is nothing in the notice that remains unsuspended. The notice therefore becomes legally inoperative. . . .

63. There is another aspect of the redundancy procedure that occasions concern, namely, that it appears that it can take place without the staff member whose position is being redesigned, and whose qualifications for the new position are being examined, being informed of

what is happening. This happened in the present case. During much of the period when the Applicant was discussing with his manager his APR for 1985–86, in the apparent belief that this was the only process going on at that time that might affect his position in the Bank, the redundancy process was concurrently taking place, unknown to the Applicant. In it the Applicant's post was being redesigned and determinations were being made by the Bank that the Applicant was not qualified to perform the duties of his position. . . .

66. The fact that the terms of the notice of redundancy were withdrawn by the Bank shortly afterwards makes it unnecessary for the Tribunal to say more about that process in the present case. But Principle 2.1 of Staff Employment ('The Organizations shall at all times act with fairness and impartiality and shall follow a proper process in their relations with staff members') should be borne in mind; and clarification now of the mode of operation of the redundancy provisions may assist in avoiding difficulties in the future. (*de Raet*, Decision No. 85 [1989], paras. 60, 63, 66)

ii. 41. What, then, is the date of notification of the decision the administrative review of which the Applicant requested? The announcement of the salary increases in the 'For Your Information' bulletin on June 11, 1986 and May 8, 1987, respectively, can be disregarded in this respect since these announcements were of a general character and did not allow the individual staff member to know the amount of the merit increases awarded personally to him. On the other hand, the Applicant must have become aware of the size of his individual merit increases at the latest when he received his pay check, i.e., on July 31 for 1986 and on June 30 for 1987. The Applicant accepts this view in respect of the 1987 increase, since both in his memorandum of April 5, 1988 and his appeal to the Appeals Committee of June 8, 1988 he writes: 'Through my payroll statement of end June 1987, I learned that I had been awarded a low merit increase for 1987'. As for the 1986 increase, the Applicant states in the same documents that he learned of its below level size only during his meeting of early July 1987 with his personnel officer.

42. Although the Applicant thus concedes that '(he) was advised factually of (his) 1986 and 1987 merit increases in early July 1987', he does not, however, accept that early July 1987 should be taken as the *dies a quo* for the purposes of ascertaining whether Rule 9.01, para. 2.01, has been complied with. He was not in a position, he maintains, to respond meaningfully to the assertions of malperformance and to challenge the low merit increases awarded to him until he received the explicit performance review by his Division Manager, i.e., until January 28, 1988. Accordingly, he says, this has to be regarded as the decision contested in the present procedure. His request for administrative review of April 25, 1988, he concludes, therefore, complied with the requirements of Staff Rule 9.01, para. 2.01.

43. The Tribunal does not share the Applicant's view on this issue. Not only did the Applicant, according to his own admission, know that the size of his 1986 and 1987 merit increases were below normal level by early July 1987 at the latest, but by then he also had knowledge of the reasons for this low level. It appears clearly from the Applicant's memorandum to Personnel Files of April 5, 1988 and from his appeal to the Appeals Committee of July 8, 1988 that he was aware for some time before July 1987, or alternatively that he became aware at the latest during his discussions with his superiors in June– July 1987, of the negative views of his Division Manager on his performance, and that he ascribed these views to the 'untenable relationship', the 'bad chemistry', which had evolved between his Division Manager and himself. He explicitly states, for example, that in early July 1987 his personnel officer explained to him that his low 1987 increase 'implied a low performance as sessment by (his) supervisor'. He admits also that he had previously discussed with his Division Manager the latter's assessment. The situation was such, he explains, that as early as in July 1987 one of his supervisors advised him

to seek reassignment in the Bank. To all this the performance review of January 28, 1988 did not add much that the Applicant was not already aware of from his June–July 1987 discussions with his supervisors. In effect, the performance review did not go much further than ascribing the low merit increases awarded to the Applicant in 1986 and 1987 to his poor performance. 'I told him the reasons for this action in June last year', the Division Manager added.

44. In the light of the preceding, the Tribunal determines that end June-beginning July 1987 is the latest date conceivably to be taken as the *dies a quo* for the purpose of compliance with Rule 9.01, para. 2.01. It remains, therefore, to be seen whether the administrative review has been requested within the time limits prescribed by this Rule.

45. Even assuming that the Applicant's discussions with his supervisors in 1987 are to be regarded as complying with the provisions of paragraph 2.02 defining 'step 1' of the administrative review procedure, the fact of the matter is that the formal written request for administrative review was filed only on April 25, 1988, i.e., 9 months after the *dies a quo* defined in the most liberal way. Rule 9.01, para. 2.01, it may be recalled, provides for a maximum of 132 days, i.e. less than 5 months from the date of decision the administrative review of which the Applicant requests. (*de Jong*, Decision No. 89 [1990], paras. 41–3, 44–5)

iii. 38. In deciding to acquire U.S. citizenship on June 1, 1984 the Applicant should and could have investigated the legal and financial consequences of her decision due to the absence of any provision allowing restoration of financial benefits in case of subsequent renunciation of that citizenship. On her appointment to the Bank the Applicant was informed of the conditions of eligibility for Home Leave, Education and Repatriation Benefits, by a letter dated March 7, 1974. In that letter the Applicant was informed of the Personnel Manual Circular No. 820–2–74 dated February 20, 1974 concerning elimination of discrimination in access to staff benefits which stated that:

> All expatriate staff appointed by the Bank Group on or after January 1, 1974 will be eligible for expatriate benefits . . . under the following terms and conditions provided that if stationed at headquarters, the staff members who join the Bank Group in permanent-resident status and who change to G-4 Status on or before confirmation of appointment and thereafter maintain such status shall also be eligible for expatriate benefits.

The information in the letter should have alerted the Applicant to the fact that eligibility required maintaining the status of a non-citizen of the duty station country. (*Wahie*, Decision No. 93 [1990], para. 38)

iv. 43. The Applicant's complaints refer separately to the procedures followed in Rounds 1 and 2 of the Reorganization. As to Round 1, the Applicant contends that the Bank did not comply with assurances to the effect that support staff, prior to stating their preferences, should be informed of where their most recent colleagues would be working. In particular, he complains that the selection of Section Chief was not communicated to the Staff of S-3 before all the staff had submitted their Round 1 statements of preferences for available positions and that this denied him the opportunity to make an informed choice. This grievance relates to the Applicant's dissatisfaction with the selection of his immediate supervisor —the new Section Chief—and his preference for the former incumbent. But the Tribunal does not find this allegation to be relevant, because no harm was caused to the Applicant by the fact that he learned only on July 28 of the name of the new Section Chief. As the sequence of actions shows, the Applicant had prior cognizance of the name of his new Section Chief and had time to consider that fact before deciding on August 3 to reject the position offered to him. Moreover, the fact that he signed a preference form before learning of the new supervisor had no damaging effect, since he retained the possibility of changing his mind and refusing the offer, as he in fact did. (*Pavesich*, Decision No. 94 [1990], para. 43)

6. Due process/right of defence

[See also Sect. 6, 'Administrative Review', 1.i; Sect. 8, 'Sources of Law', 1 (*b*) i; Sect. 16, 'Classification', 14.i; Sect. 28, 'Reorganization', 1.i; Sect. 29, 'Remedies', 8.ii.]

i. 37. The Applicant contends that he learned of the arrangement made in 1975 only as a result of the Bank-wide job grading program in 1985, and there is no direct evidence to contradict this assertion. He was then informed that, as part of this program, his personal grade was being abolished and he would be entitled to retain the salary corresponding to his personal grade level only for a two year grandfathering period. After September 30, 1987 his compensation would be based on a lower salary range.

38. The Respondent has observed that in 1975 there was no formal procedure for notifying staff members that the grade they held was personal. The Tribunal considers, nevertheless, that the Bank has an obligation to inform the staff member of a change in his employment status, especially when constituting a demotion to a lower level position. Such a communication must also indicate the reasons for that demotion. This obligation is demanded by elementary considerations of due process. Its existence is independent of the adoption of the Principles of Staff Employment.

39. Consequently, the Tribunal finds that in not advising the Applicant, at the time of transfer, that his new work assignment had a lower grade level, and that he retained his former grade only on a personal basis, the Bank did not follow a proper procedure. This is recognized by the Vice President, PA, in his letter of May 11, 1987 which is the decision contested by the Applicant. In that letter the Vice President, PA admits that 'there had not been sufficient clarity with respect to your downgrading at the time of your transfer in 1975. This is not only regrettable but unacceptable. . . . at the time the system did not work in your case'.

40. The consequences of that improper procedure

have materialized at the present time as a result of the application to the staff member of the Job Grading exercise. The Applicant rightly contends that if he had been made aware of his true situation in 1975 he might have been able to dispute the decision taken and to take remedial action, either to obtain another suitable assignment within the Bank or to seek a position outside it. While at that time he had prospects of outside employment, it is now too late for him to be considered for an outside position by reason of his age.

41. For these reasons, the Tribunal concludes that the treatment of the Applicant fell short of the required standards and this has effectively caused him harm. . . . (*Alan Berg*, Decision No. 73 [1988], paras. 37–41)

ii. 46. At the stage of administrative review corrections had been made to the Applicant's submission without the prior involvement or knowledge of the Applicant, thereby unduly depriving the Applicant of an opportunity to comment on the intended revision. On December 31, 1985 the Applicant submitted a memorandum to the JEU enumerating the areas she felt needed to be re-evaluated or more fully described. The Applicant's Department made the following remarks on the certificate sheet:

> 'We have certified much of the additional information provided; however, we have excised certain statements which would ascribe to the job greater responsibilities or skills requirements than management intends. The revised statement is attached, together with a copy of the incumbent's draft, with. . . . materials marked in yellow.'

(*Rae*, Decision No. 74 [1988], para. 46)

iii. 19. The Tribunal does not believe that the reopening by the JGAB was in excess of its powers or that it deprived the Applicant of due process. It was reasonable for the Vice President, PA, to request a reopening and an opportunity to respond to the Applicant's earlier comments. Staff Rule 9.04 announces rules for appeals to the Job Grading Appeals Board. Paragraph 2 (*a*) of that Rule provides: 'The Secretary [to the Board] shall be responsible for transmitting copies of documents related to an appeal to the Appellant and the Respondent (the parties) and to members of the Board designated by the Chairman to act as the panel for an appeal (the Panel) and shall keep a record of documents so transmitted.' Paragraph 12 provides: 'In the event that the Panel accepts jurisdiction to entertain the appeal, the Secretary shall . . . ensure that the parties have received copies of all documents and evidence considered by the Panel to be of possible relevance to the appeal. . . .' Apparently by oversight, the Secretary neglected to send to the Respondent the Applicant's comments upon the answer. This obviously disadvantaged the Respondent, which learned of the untransmitted comments only upon examination of the initial report of the JGAB. (*Spier*, Decision No. 77 [1989], para. 19)

iv. 55. The Applicant's main contention is that he was denied the right to be heard because he was not given an opportunity to answer a memorandum from the Assistant Director, EAP, dated December 10, 1986, which allegedly was the basis for declaring him redundant. The Applicant complains that he had access to it only during the procedure before the Appeals Committee. On this issue, the Appeals Committee found that 'the Applicant was not given an appropriate opportunity to respond to statements or comments made by [the Assistant Director's] report.' This report ends by stating that the Applicant should be informed 'of the outcome of the present review' but not of its contents.

56. The Tribunal has in a previous case expressed 'its grave concern over certain procedural irregularities and other practices that did not conform with the requirements of due process of law. In no case, however, has it found them serious enough to warrant a finding that the substantive decisions based upon them were null and void.' (*Gyamfi*, Decision No. 28 [1986], para. 47). The exception at the time was *Gyamfi*, where the situation was found to be different. The criterion adopted in that case to find fault with the procedures followed was

the consideration that the 'failure to inform the Applicant seriously impaired his ability to defend himself.' (Ibid. para. 43). (*Kassab*, Decision No. 97 [1990], paras. 55, 56)

14. PERFORMANCE

1. Evaluation

[See also Sect. 8, 'Sources of Law', 1 (*e*) ii; Sect. 11, 'Prejudice/ Discrimination', 2.v; Sect. 12, 'Substantive Irregularity', 1.x and xi; Sect. 13, 'Procedural Irregularity', 1.iv, 5.i; Sect. 16 'Classification', 3.i, 8.i; Sect. 20, 'Fixed-Term Contracts', 1.i, 2.i; Sect. 27, 'Termination', 1 (*a*) ii; Sect. 28, 'Reorganization', 2.v and ix.]

i. 32. Moreover, the disagreement between the Applicant and her previous Division Chief related mainly to the evaluation of the Applicant's performance and her work attitudes. The grading committees did not concern themselves with the actual performance of the Applicant. They concerned themselves exclusively with finding out whether the assignments and tasks carried out by the Applicant in her position met the criteria for grading her position as 24 or 23. (*Sebastian (No. 2)*, Decision No. 57 [1988], para. 32)

ii. 61. The Tribunal accepts that there was a sufficient degree of doubt regarding the 1986 assessment to warrant modifying the performance rating for that year. The Tribunal notes that the rating was founded on an assessment by Mr. Mossop based on contact with the Applicant going no further back than January 1, 1986 and extending no later than April 1, 1986. It was clearly affected by Mr. Karp's 'critical review' (to use Mr. Mossop's language) of February 20, 1986.

62. But the fact that the Bank may have recognized that the 1986 assessment should be changed does not mean that such doubt as there may be about the 1985

assessment is sufficient to justify its invalidation. For one thing, the period of strained relations between the Applicant and Mr. Karp was not so extended between April and June 1985 (the date of the 1985 assessment) as it obviously became by February 1986 (the date of Mr. Karp's interim review for use in the 1986 assessment).

63. For another, in contrast with the 1986 assessment which was reviewed, and changed, only by Mr. Cosgrove, the 1985 assessment was reviewed by Mr. Williams (in July 1985 and May 1986) and by Mr. Cosgrove (in October 1986). Mr. Cosgrove delegated the review to Carol Word who, amongst other things, interviewed Messrs. Williams, Dyck, Karp, Manickavasagam, Mossop and Rosenfeld, identified the fact that the decision to rate the Applicant at level 2+ was taken jointly by Messrs. Kaji, Ritchie and Dyck, with input from Mr. Karp, and noted that the decision had taken into account the fact that the Applicant had been assigned to an extremely difficult client area, ERS.

64. The Tribunal considers that these factors, especially the identification of the participants in the joint decision to rate the Applicant at level 2+ in 1985, are sufficient to reduce the element of doubt in respect of that assessment effectively to the point of disappearance. There does not seem to be doubt of a sufficient degree to warrant giving the applicant the benefit of it. Nor does the Tribunal perceive any such discrepancy between the facts stated in the relevant documents and the conclusions reached by the Bank as to establish that those conclusions so lacked justification that they were unreasonable and therefore invalid. (*Buyten*, Decision No. 72 [1988], paras. 61–4]

iii. 69. The procedure to be followed in the preparation of APRs is set out in Staff Rule 5.03, Section 2.02. In summary, this requires a meeting between the manager and the staff member at which they are to review the staff member's performance plan. The staff member is to be shown the manager's written review and may respond to it. (*de Raet*, Decision No. 85 [1989], para. 69)

iv. 32. The record shows that the Applicant received written warnings from her supervisors who were anything but satisfied, both with her technical competence and with her brusque personality. In March 1988 her Division Chief felt obliged to subject her to a three-month evaluation period. The Applicant was not only informed of this, but well knew what was required of her. At the end of the evaluation period, she again failed to measure up. It was found that her performance in the evaluation period fell short of the requirements of the Division and that her work relationships had deteriorated. This conclusion was brought to her notice. It is clear, therefore, that the procedure prescribed by Staff Rule 7.01 was followed.

33. The Applicant also contends that it was unreasonable to give her only three months to improve her work quality. The Tribunal notes that, although the relevant Staff Rule prescribes a maximum testing period of six months, no minimum period is laid down. Therefore, what length of time, say between one week and six months, is appropriate in any given case is a matter for the judgment of the Respondent. In this case the two deficiencies of the Applicant which troubled the Bank and which were brought to her notice were first, the unsatisfactory quality of her work and output, and second, the deficiencies in her character which jeopardized harmonious working relationships. The Applicant was not given a heavier workload during her testing period. Indeed, her workload was reduced. She was in the same familiar environment and should have had no problem of adjustment. Moreover, the Respondent could reasonably have concluded that a three-month period was adequate time for the Applicant to show improvement in her interpersonal relationships with her peers and superiors. Therefore, the Tribunal holds that the Respondent was not manifestly unreasonable in deciding that three months was an adequate period in which to demonstrate improvement or for a fair evaluation of her performance. . . .

39. The Applicant also argues that the termination of

service which the Respondent imposed on her was wholly out of proportion to whatever lapses may have been found in her work. She therefore stigmatizes it as 'not fair and reasonable.' But the Tribunal's view is that the Applicant does not and cannot contend with any plausibility that termination of the employment of an employee whose performance was adjudged unsatisfactory and who failed to avail herself of an opportunity to improve, must be unreasonable. Nonetheless, the Applicant asserts that she worked satisfactorily in different units of the Bank for almost three and a half years, and her so-called unsatisfactory performance of barely seven months at EM4IE should not have attracted the sanction of termination of service. As to this the 'Tribunal agrees that the penalty should bear a reasonable relation to the 'offence'. In *Gregorio*, Decisions No. 14 [1983], para. 47, this Tribunal held that:

> The Tribunal has the authority to determine whether a sanction imposed by the Bank upon a staff member is significantly disproportionate to the staff members offence, for if the Bank were so to act, its action would properly be deemed arbitrary or discriminatory.

40. It is admitted by the Respondent that the Applicant's performance in AGREP was consistently good. That may well have been the reason why, when that unit was disbanded in the Reorganization she was selected in Round 1 of the selection process. But soon after her appointment to her new unit, significant deterioration was noticed in her work. Practically all her supervisors were anything but satisfied with her performance with regard both to her technical competence and working relationships. She received warnings which she failed to heed. The Respondent then decided to invoke the procedure which put her on formal notice that her removal from the unit and consequent termination were distinctly probable. The conclusion of her Division Chief after the evaluation was:

> that Ms. Georgiev's performance in the evaluation period has fallen far short of the requirements of the division and of the stated performance improvement objectives.

On these facts, it would hardly make sense to say because she worked satisfactorily in another unit for some length of time in the past, she should be spared the sanction which her present continuing and unremedied default deserves. The Tribunal concludes that the sanction of termination of service was not significantly disproportionate to her offence and rejects the Applicant's contention on this score. (*Georgiev*, Decision No. 96 [1990], para. 32–3, 39–40)

v. 32. Although the Applicant challenges the Respondent's evaluation of his performance as being discriminatory and motivated by a general hostile attitude on the part of the VPCOF towards the Applicant, the Tribunal does not find in the record any evidence that substantiates that contention.

33. As to the Applicant's contention that he was evaluated on the basis of work assignments of a purely administrative nature which did not represent his performance on the more technical aspects of his responsibilities as a Cofinancing Advisor, the Tribunal notes that as a result of the Reorganization the nature and the priorities of work within the Cofinancing Department changed, and the Applicant, as the Appeals Committee noticed in its conclusions, 'found himself performing tasks that he either did not like (administrative tasks) or was not well suited to perform'. . . .

38. On the basis of the above negative evaluation the Applicant's supervisor expressed his inability to recommend that the Applicant be offered a position as a permanent staff member of the Cofinancing Department.

39. The Tribunal concludes that there was no abuse of discretion in making this evaluation.

40. The Tribunal does not find merit in the Applicant's complaint that he was negatively evaluated by a Vice President who had no first-hand contact or knowledge of the Applicant's performance. Vice Presidents and heads of departments commonly base their evaluations of their staff members on a review of the

evaluations made by more immediate supervisors. (*Mathew*, Decision No. 103 [1991], paras. 32–3, 38–40)

15. TERMS AND CONDITIONS OF EMPLOYMENT

[See also Sect. 8, 'Sources of Law', 2 (*a*) i, (*b*) i, ii, (*c*) i–v.]

1. Acquired rights/fundamental conditions

[See also Sect. 16, 'Classification', 1.ii; Sect. 25, 'Salary', 3 (*a*) i; Sect. 28, 'Reorganization', 2.ix.]

i. 37. The Tribunal does not deem it necessary to pronounce in the present case on the question whether . . . the Respondent has the power to deprive a staff member of a grade previously held by him. In particular, with respect to the Job Grading exercise, there can be no certainty that in all cases an exact correspondence exists between the former grades and the present ones, . . . [T]he Applicant herself has not invoked the existence of a right indefinitely to maintain her former grade. Her contentions and arguments have been essentially concerned with . . . her entitlement to continued salary increases. . . .

39. The Applicant's principal contention is that her salary review increases after the effective date of her job regrading should not be limited by the two-year grandfathering provision in Staff Rule 5.06, para. 3.01. . . . In her reply, the Applicant invokes . . . para. 5 (1) f of the Principles of Staff Employment, . . . [T]he Applicant contends . . . that she should be 'grandfathered' in her previous salary level. She also contends that by freezing her salary the Bank would deny her a 'fundamental

element in Applicant's conditions of employment which the Bank does not have the right to change unilaterally,' namely, the right as embodied in de Merode (Decision No. 1 [1981], para. 112) to benefit from 'periodic adjustments reflecting changes in the cost of living and other factors.'

40. In *de Merode* (Decision No. 1 (1981), paras. 111 and 112) the Tribunal found 'that a consistent practice of periodic adjustment has been established, and that the Bank makes these adjustments out of the conviction that it is legally obliged to do so'. The Tribunal concluded:

> '... in consequence ... the Bank is obliged to carry out periodic reviews of salaries, taking into account various relevant factors ... the established practice, and statements confirming that practice, have created a legal obligation to make periodic adjustments reflecting changes in the cost of living and other factors. In the opinion of the Tribunal such an obligation is a fundamental element in the Applicant's condition of employment with the Bank does not have the right to change unilaterally.'

The Tribunal concludes that the freezing of the Applicant's salary, from September 30, 1987, would deprive her, without justifiable cause, of the right to benefit from periodic adjustments reflecting changes in the cost of living and other factors, which the Tribunal has found to be a fundamental element in the Applicant's conditions of employment which the Bank does not have the right to change unilaterally. This is not to suggest that a staff member may under no circumstances have his or her grade reduced or salary frozen, for example, when this is done for cause as for disciplinary action. In the present case, however, the downgrading of the Applicant and her position was done not because of her misconduct but because of the organizational needs of the Bank; in such circumstance, the staff member is reasonably entitled to more equitable treatment, as appears to be contemplated by Staff Principle 5 (1) f. (*Pinto*, Decision No. 56 [1988], paras. 37, 39–40)

ii. 26. In *de Merode* (paras. 111 and 112) the Tribunal found 'that a consistent practice of periodic adjustment has been established, and that the Bank makes these adjustments out of the conviction that it is legally obliged to do so'. The Tribunal concluded:

> '. . . in consequence . . . the Bank is obliged to carry out periodic reviews of salaries, taking into account various relevant factors . . . the established practice, and statements confirming that practice, have created a legal obligation to make periodic adjustments reflecting changes in the cost of living and other factors. In the opinion of the Tribunal such an obligation is a fundamental element in the Applicant's conditions of employment which the Bank does not have the right to change unilaterally.'

The Tribunal concludes that the freezing of the Applicant's salary, from September 30, 1987, would deprive her, without justifiable cause, of the right to benefit from periodic adjustments reflecting changes in the cost of living and other factors, which the Tribunal has found to be a fundamental element in the Applicant's conditions of employment which the IFC does not have the right to change unilaterally. This is not to suggest that a staff member may under no circumstances have his or her grade reduced or salary frozen, for example, when this is done for cause as for disciplinary action. In the present case, however, the downgrading of the Applicant and her position was done not because of her misconduct but because of the organizational needs of the IFC; in such circumstance, the staff member is reasonably entitled to more equitable treatment, as appears to be contemplated by Staff Principle 5 (1) f. (*Gavidia*, Decision No. 66 [1988], para. 26)

iii. 29. The Applicant's main contention is that his salary review increases after the effective date of the job regrading should not be limited by the two-year grandfathering requirement. The paragraph of Staff Rule 5.06 which provides for this reads:

> A staff member whose position is graded at a lower level as a result of a formal job evaluation assumes the lower grade upon

the effective date of the evaluation. However, for a period of 24 months thereafter, he will be eligible for increases as if the salary range formerly applicable to the position, adjusted for any increases in the salary structure, had remained in effect. . . . If after 24 months the staff member has not been selected for a position at his previous or a higher level, future increases in his salary will be administered within the range of his new grade. If at this time the staff member's salary exceeds the maximum of the salary range of the position occupied, the salary will remain unchanged until the maximum of the range exceeds that amount.

In his reply, the Applicant invokes, in support of his claim, para. 5 (1) f of the Principles of Staff Employment, which states that the Respondent shall:

establish procedures and conditions under which staff members may be assigned to positions graded at various levels, while providing reasonable measures to alleviate adverse effects on staff members assigned to positions graded or regraded at a lower level.

The Applicant contends, on the basis of the above Principle, that he should be grandfathered in his previous salary level. He also contends that by freezing his salary the Bank would deny him a 'fundamental element in Applicant's conditions of employment which the Bank does not have the right to change unilaterally,' namely, the right as embodied in *de Merode* (Decision No. 1 [1981], para. 112) to benefit from 'periodic adjustments reflecting changes in the cost of living and other factors.'

30. In *de Merode* (Decision No. 1 [1981], paras. 111 and 112) the Tribunal found 'that a consistent practice of periodic adjustment has been established, and that the Bank makes these adjustments out of the conviction that it is legally obliged to do so'. The Tribunal concluded:

[I]n consequence . . . the Bank is obliged to carry out periodic reviews of salaries, taking into account various relevant factors. . . . [T]he established practice, and statements confirming that practice, have created a legal obligation to make periodic adjustments reflecting changes in the cost of living and other factors. In the opinion of the Tribunal such an obligation is a fundamental element in the Applicant's conditions of employment which the Bank does not have the right to change unilaterally.

In *Pinto* (Decision No. 56 [1988], para. 40), where the same contention was raised as has been raised in this case, the Tribunal held:

> The Tribunal concludes that the freezing of the Applicant's salary, from September 30, 1987, would deprive her, without justifiable cause, of the right to benefit from periodic adjustments reflecting changes in the cost of living and other factors, which the Tribunal has found to be a fundamental element in the Applicant's conditions of employment which the Bank does not have the right to change unilaterally. This is not to suggest that a staff member may under no circumstances have his or her grade reduced or salary frozen, for example, when this is done for cause as for disciplinary action. In the present case, however, the downgrading of the Applicant and her position was done not because of her misconduct but because of the organizational needs of the Bank; in such circumstance, the staff member is reasonably entitled to more equitable treatment, as appears to be contemplated by Staff Principle 5 (1) f.

The Tribunal will apply the same ruling in this case and decides that the Applicant should, as from September 30, 1987, receive the periodic salary review increases approved by the Respondent for staff members in grade 16, the grade in which he was before his position was regraded. (*Chakra*, Decision No. 70 [1988], paras. 29–30)

[For a similar statement see *Cardenas*, Decision No. 71 [1988], paras. 30–1].

iv. 31. The record of this case does not substantiate the contention by the Applicants that the Respondents had in fact unilaterally amended the rule requiring a comprehensive review every three years. The postponement in 1987, and again in 1988, does not amount to an amendment of this rule. What is under consideration is not an attempt by the Respondents unilaterally to change a rule affecting the conditions of employment, but rather a departure from strict adherence to such rule. . . .

33. It may be added that in *von Stauffenberg*, where the Bank had maintained that the three year requirement 'was changed by the Executive Directors to a period of four years until the second comprehensive review', the Tribunal was of the view that

> This minor change in periodicity related to a non-essential element in the conditions of employment and the principle of periodic comprehensive review was not affected. (Decision No. 38 [1987], para. 84)

The Tribunal, in this case, does not find the postponement of the comprehensive review for two years to be, in itself, a violation of an essential element of the conditions of employment of the Applicants. (*Hammond et al.*, Decision No. 86 [1989], paras. 31, 33)

v. 26. The Applicant contends that his non-selection constitutes a violation, or improper unilateral amendment, of an 'essential element' of his conditions of employment. He invokes the Tribunal's decisions in *de Merode*, Decision No. 1 [1981], and *Harrison*, Decision No. 53 [1987], which held that certain elements of a staff member's employment conditions—in those cases, periodic adjustment in salary and access to the Tribunal—are so fundamental as not to permit of unilateral change by the Bank. He asserts that a number of bank documents and policies, in particular the *Principles of Staff Employment* and Staff Rule 5.09, create for staff members a right to selection for positions at their grade level that they are qualified to perform in preference to a promoted lower-level staff member. He then goes on to claim that this right is of 50 fundamental a character, comparable to the rights considered in *de Merode* and *Harrison*, that it too should be held by the Tribunal to be an essential element of employment for all staff members.

27. Upon an examination of the documents and policies invoked by the Applicant, the Tribunal concludes

that they do not warrant the inference of any such right. It is therefore not necessary to consider whether any such right, if found, should properly be regarded as an 'essential element' of employment. (*Fernandes*, Decision No. 90 [1990], paras. 26–7)

vi. 31. The essence of the first contention is that paragraph 5.03 of Staff Rule 5.09 should be invalidated because it undermines an essential element of staff member conditions of employment in that it permits 'individual staff members identified by the VPP as ready for promotion to be selected.' The Applicant contends that the Articles of Agreement, the Principles of Staff Employment and the Staff Rules promulgated thereunder, and the past practice of the Bank, all create an obligation on the part of the Bank to secure to each staff member continued employment at his grade level, unless there is some fault on the part of the staff member which renders him unfit for continued service.

32. In *Fernandes*, Decision No. 90 [1990], the Applicant invoked Principle 2.1 (*d*) of the Principles of Staff Employment providing that the Bank shall 'provide staff members security in their employment consistent with the terms of their appointment, their satisfactory performance and conduct, and the efficient administration of the Bank,' and Principle 6.1 providing that 'the basic objectives of the [Bank's] compensation policy shall be to . . . enable the [Bank] to recruit staff of the highest caliber appropriate to job requirements,' which the Applicant also invokes in this case. The Tribunal there concluded:

> . . . these two principles do not justify inferring a staff right to priority of assignment over a lower graded staff member, when in the course of a comprehensive reorganization the Bank, within the range of its allowable discretion, determines that the promotable employee is in fact more qualified to perform the job. (para. 28)

33. In application of the decision in *Fernandes* the Tribunal concludes that by eventually selecting a lower

grade staff member to occupy positions at the level of the Applicant's previous position, but after first considering the Applicant for those positions, the Respondent had acted within the requirements of all pertinent Principles and Staff Rules. Para. 1.06 (6) of Staff Rule 5.09 cannot properly be invoked to question the validity of the Applicant's non-selection. Para. 1.06 provides that in the selection process, candidates occupying positions graded at a level higher than that of the position to be filled are to be 'considered' first; it does not provide that such candidates are also to be 'offered' the positions in preference to lower graded promotable staff members. It, therefore, becomes unnecessary to determine whether any such right should properly be regarded as an 'essential element' of the conditions of employment, as claimed by the Applicant.

34. The Tribunal, therefore, concludes that the selection of a lower grade staff member to occupy a position graded at level 26 in preference to the Applicant, and the non-selection of the Applicant to a level 26 position, do not violate his conditions of employment. (*Klaus Berg (No. 2)*, Decision No. 99 [1990], paras. 31–4)

2. Security of employment

[See Sect. 28, 'Reorganization', 1.ii.]

16. CLASSIFICATION

1. Salary

[See also Sect. 28, 'Reorganization', 2.iv, v, and ix, 3.v.]

i. 39. The Applicant's principal contention is that her salary review increases after the effective date of her job regrading should not be limited by the two-year grandfathering provision in Staff Rule 5.06, para. 3.01. That section provides:

'A staff member whose position is graded at a lower level as a result of a formal job evaluation assumes the lower grade upon the effective date of the evaluation. However, for a period of 24 months thereafter, he will be eligible for increases as if the salary range formerly applicable to the position, adjusted for any increases in the salary structure, had remained in effect. . . . If after 24 months the staff member has not been selected for a position at his previous or a higher level, future increases in his salary will be administered within the range of his new grade. If at this time the staff member's salary exceeds the maximum of the salary range of the position occupied, the salary will remain unchanged until the maximum of the range exceeds that amount.'

In her reply, the Applicant invokes, in support of her claim, Para. 5 (1) f of the Principles of Staff Employment, which states that the Respondent shall:

'establish procedures and conditions under which staff members may be assigned to positions graded at various levels, while providing reasonable measures to alleviate adverse effects on staff members assigned to positions graded or regraded at a lower level.'

The Applicant contends, in the basis of the above Principle, that she should be 'grandfathered' in her previous salary level. She also contends that by freezing her salary the Bank would deny her a 'fundamental element in Applicant's conditions of employment which the Bank does not have the right to change unilaterally,' namely, the right as embodied in *de Merode* (Decision No. 1 [1981], para. 112) to benefit from 'periodic adjustments reflecting changes in the cost of living and other factors.'

40. In *de Merode* (Decision No. 1 [1981], paras. 111 and 112) the Tribunal found 'that a consistent practice of periodic adjustment has been established, and that the Bank makes these adjustments out of the conviction that it is legally obliged to do so'. The Tribunal concluded:

'. . . in consequence . . . the Bank is obliged to carry out periodic reviews of salaries, taking into account various relevant factors . . . the established practice, and statements confirming that practice, have created a legal obligation to make periodic adjustments reflecting changes in the cost of living and other factors. In the opinion of the Tribunal such an obligation is a fundamental element in the Applicant's conditions of employment which the Bank does not have the right to change unilaterally.'

The Tribunal concludes that the freezing of the Applicant's salary, from September 30, 1987, would deprive her, without justifiable cause, of the right to benefit from periodic adjustments reflecting changes in the cost of living and other factors, which the Tribunal has found to be a fundamental element in the Applicant's conditions of employment which the Bank does not have the right to change unilaterally. This is not to suggest that a staff member may under no circumstances have his or her grade reduced or salary frozen, for example, when this is done for cause as for disciplinary action. In the present case, however, the downgrading of the Applicant and her position was done not because of her misconduct but because of the organizational needs of the Bank; in such circumstance, the staff member is reasonably entitled to more equitable treatment, as appears to be contemplated by Staff Principle 5 (1) f.

Decision:
For the above reasons the Tribunal unanimously decides that the decision of the Vice President, PA, of September 18, 1986 is rescinded so far as it does not provide for the payment to the Applicant, as from September 30, 1987 of the periodic salary review increases approved by the Respondent for staff members in grade 16. (*Pinto*, Decision No. 56 [1988], paras. 39, 40, Decision)

ii. 23. The Tribunal agrees that the Job Grading Program —involving decisions regarding criteria for evaluating staff positions, the assignment of various tasks to particular positions and the ultimate determination of grade levels—constitutes an exercise of discretionary authority by the Respondent and, as such, is not subject to review by this Tribunal, unless it is contended that there has been an abuse of discretion, by reason of the action taken in a concrete case 'being arbitrary, discriminatory, improperly motivated or carried out in violation of a fair and reasonable procedure' (*Saberi*, Decision No. 5 [1982], para. 24). No such abuse of discretion has been shown.

24. The Tribunal does not deem it necessary to pronounce in the present case on the question whether and, if so, under what conditions, the Respondent has the power to deprive a staff member of a grade previously held by him. In particular, with respect to the Job Grading exercise, there can be no certainty that in all cases an exact correspondence exists between the former grades and the present ones, so as consider a grade under the previous system the indisputable source of a right to maintain the grade previously held or to be assigned a new grade of a similar value. Moreover, the Applicant herself has not invoked the existence of a right indefinitely to maintain her former grade. Her contentions and arguments have been essentially concerned with the grading of her position but, as the Tribunal has decided in *von Stauffenberg* (Decision No. 38 [1987], para. 43), it is within its judicial mission to address the legal questions really in issue in the submissions formulated in an application.

25. In a case similar to this one, namely, *Pinto* (Decision No. 56 [1988]), the Applicant's principal contention was that her salary review increases after the effective date of her job regrading should not be limited by the two-year grandfathering provision in Staff Rule 5. 06, para. 3.01. That section provides:

'A staff member whose position is graded at a lower level as a result of a formal job evaluation assumes the lower grade upon the effective date of the evaluation. However, for a period of 24 months thereafter, he will be eligible for increases as if the salary range formerly applicable to the position, adjusted for any increases in the salary structure, had remained in effect . . . If after 24 months the staff member has not been selected for a position at his previous or a higher level, future increases in his salary will be administered within the range of his new grade. If at this time the staff member's salary exceeds the maximum of the salary range of the position occupied, the salary will remain unchanged until the maximum of the range exceeds that amount.'

In her reply, the Applicant in *Pinto* invoked, in support of her claim, Para. 5 (1) f of the Principles of Staff Employment, which states that the Respondent shall:

'establish procedures and conditions under which staff members may be assigned to positions graded at various levels, while providing reasonable measures to alleviate adverse effects on staff members assigned to positions graded or regraded at a lower level.'

The Applicant in *Pinto* contended, on the basis of the above Principle, that she should be indefinitely 'grandfathered' in her previous salary level. She also contended that by freezing her salary the Bank would deny her a 'fundamental element in Applicant's conditions of employment which the Bank does not have the right to change unilaterally,' namely, the right, as embodied in *de Merode* (para. 112) to benefit from 'periodic adjustments reflecting changes in the cost of living and other factors.'

26. In *de Merode* (paras. 111 and 112) the Tribunal found 'that a consistent practice of periodic adjustment has been established, and that the Bank makes these adjustments out of the conviction that it is legally obliged to do so'. The Tribunal concluded:

'. . . in consequence . . . the Bank is obliged to carry out periodic reviews of salaries, taking into account various relevant factors . . . the established practice, and statements confirming that practice, have created a legal obligation to make periodic adjustments reflecting changes in the cost of living and other factors. In the opinion of the Tribunal such an obligation is a fundamental element in the Applicant's conditions of employment which the Bank does not have the right to change unilaterally.'

The Tribunal concludes that the freezing of the Applicant's salary, from September 30, 1987, would deprive her, without justifiable cause, of the right to benefit from periodic adjustments reflecting changes in the cost of living and other factors, which the Tribunal has found to be a fundamental element in the Applicant's conditions of employment which the IFC does not have the right to change unilaterally. This is not to suggest that a staff member may under no circumstances have his or her grade reduced or salary frozen, for example, when this is done for cause as for disciplinary action. In the present case, however, the downgrading of the Applicant and her position was done not because of her misconduct but because of the organizational needs of the IFC; in such circumstance, the staff member is reasonably entitled to more equitable treatment, as appears to be contemplated by Staff Principle 5 (1) f. (*Gavidia*, Decision No. 66 [1988], paras. 23–6)

iii. 49. It does not follow, however, that staff members suffering interim economic or other injury by virtue of the Respondent's ultimately corrected mistakes must be altogether without recourse. That is especially true in a case such as this, where at the time of the Applicant's formal grading, the Office Manager classification was still in effect after a period of some months; where that mistaken classification was not withdrawn until several months thereafter; and where a principal inducement for such withdrawal was the administrative review proceedings instituted by the Applicant and several similarly situated co-workers (whose applications are also presently before the Tribunal). Until the formal withdrawal of the Office Manager classification, and the exhaustion of administrative review, the Applicant harbored a reasonable belief that she satisfied the criteria of that level 17 position. No immediate impact on the Applicant's pay, however, would flow even had her belief been vindicated; her salary as Administrative Secretary in October 1985 was in the midst of the grade 17 salary range, so that a grade of 17 would not have brought any salary increase. (*Apkarian*, Decision No. 58 [1988], para. 49)

[For identical statements see:

Benner, Decision No. 59 [1988], para. 37
Dosik, Decision No. 60 [1988], para. 37
Hovsepian, Decision No. 61 [1988], para. 37
Hunger, Decision No. 62 [1988], para. 37
Papinchak, Decision No. 63 [1988], para. 37
Witty, Decision No. 64 [1988], para. 37.]

2. Arbitrariness

[See also Sect. 9, 'Discretionary Power', 1.i, 2.i; Sect. 11, 'Prejudice/Discrimination', 2.i; Sect. 12, 'Substantive Irregularity', 1.ii and ix.]

i. 38. As to the effects of the program upon the Applicant, she complains of arbitrariness and discrimination. However, the grading of the staff position occupied by her was not addressed to her personally nor did it take into account her performance. A considerable number of the staff have been similarly affected by the downgrading of their positions and the same treatment has been accorded to them all. The Applicant has also complained of defective placement efforts in her respect, but the record shows that the Respondent complied with the requirements demanded by para. 3.01 of Staff Rule 5.06. (*Pinto*, Decision No. 56 [1988], para. 38)

ii. 38. The Applicant contends that the Respondent's grading of her position as Administrative Secretary at level 16, rather than as Office Manager at level 17, constitutes willful and arbitrary action in violation of her contract of employment. As the Tribunal has frequently stated, a staff member's terms of employment include pertinent staff rules promulgated by management of the Bank. Among those staff rules are those governing the standards and procedures of the Job Grading Program instituted by the Respondent in 1982.

39. Decisions made by the Bank regarding the criteria for evaluating staff positions, the assignment of various tasks to particular positions, and the ultimate

determination of grade levels for such positions, are properly regarded as within the discretion of the Bank. The Tribunal does, however, have the power and responsibility to determine whether the Respondent's decision 'constitutes an abuse of discretion, being arbitrary, discriminatory, improperly motivated or carried out in violation of a fair and reasonable procedure.' *Saberi*, Decision No. 5 [1982], para. 24. (*Apkarian*, Decision No. 58 [1988], paras. 38, 39)

[For identical statements see:

Benner, Decision No. 59 [1988], para. 37
Dosik, Decision No. 60 [1988], para. 37
Hovsepian, Decision No. 61 [1988], para. 37
Hunger, Decision No. 62 [1988], para. 37
Papinchak, Decision No. 63 [1988], para. 37
Witty, Decision No. 64 [1988], para. 37.]

iii. 26. The Applicant has also sought to support his general contention by claiming that when he left the PTCO position it was not again advertised and no attempt was made to fill it. The Respondent has explained that the functions of the position were then redistributed over a number of other posts.

27. The Applicant then suggests that this development confirms the arbitrariness of the establishment and grading of the post, a situation which he feared might have led, if he had remained in the post, to the Bank deciding that the post had no real role to perform and that its incumbent should be declared redundant. The Respondent has replied that there is nothing to support this speculation. The Tribunal agrees. . . .

30. The Applicant argues that the Respondent's decision to grade the PTCO position at this level did not reflect the position's 'purpose, function and level of responsibility so as to provide a sound and equitable basis for the remuneration of staff members'. He dismisses as 'a meaningless post hoc exercise' the filing by the Respondent of a statement by the Senior Job Evaluation Officer, PERPD, that 'the job could be considered

as equivalent to the grading criteria for technical specialists as level 25'. The Applicant does not, however, grapple with the substance of that evaluation. The Job Evaluation Officer's statement concludes with the words: 'I have indicated the key phrases in the job description which support this match'. On comparing the job description (on the basis of which the Applicant accepted the post) with the portion of the Career Progression Summary for Technical Specialists that relates to 'Principal (Technical) Specialist: Grade 25', the Tribunal can find no real discrepancy between the two, certainly none to suggest that the Evaluation Officer's assessment was manifestly unreasonable. For example, it may be observed that the indications in the Career Progression Summary that the specialist at Grade 25 would serve as lead authority to other staff and would lead major sector or appraisal missions is matched in the position description by the statement that the PTCO may, under the overall direction of the TCU chief, have a lead role and responsibility for one or more countries and would take the principal lead in identifying and resolving broad policy and institutional problems affecting the implementation of the TCU strategy. Similarly, there are elements in the 'Qualification/Requirements' paragraph of the Career Progression Summary at Grade 25 which correspond to some of the items in the 'Skills/Abilities' section of the Selection Criteria that appear in the PTCO position description.

31. The Tribunal is, therefore, unable to conclude that the level accorded to the PTCO position departed from previously established standards for grading positions at level 25 so as to be manifestly unreasonable. (*Lindsay*, Decision No. 92 [1990], paras. 26–7, 30–1)

3. Discrimination

[See also Sect. 9, 'Discretionary Power', 1.ii; Sect. 12, 'Substantive Irregularity', 1.i.]

i. 22. The Tribunal does not agree with the Applicant's criticism of the generic criteria for grade 25. The discretion given to the grading individuals and committees under the mechanism established and applied by the Respondent does not differ in nature or scope from the discretion possessed by management in other areas relating to the conditions of employment. In all cases of discretion, unless otherwise proven, it is assumed that the administrative authority will exercise its discretion in an objective and non-discriminatory manner. The very fact of allowing the grading and reviewing bodies a wide range of discretion does not by itself invalidate the scheme. It is the exercise of discretion by individuals and committees in particular cases that may be challenged and criticized. Such an exercise can be invalidated only if it is shown that there has been an abuse of discretion, the action taken in a concrete case 'being arbitrary, discriminatory, improperly motivated or carried out in violation of a fair and reasonable procedure' (*Saberi*, Decision No. 5 [1982], para. 24). . . .

30. The Applicant finally alleges discrimination in the process of grading her position. She alleges discrimination based on sex, and lack of fairness in evaluating her performance, on the part of her first Division Chief where evaluation of her performance and the tasks she was carrying out constituted the point of departure for subsequent evaluations by the various grading and grading reviewing bodies.

31. In grading the position of the Applicant and subsequently in reviewing that grading, the Respondent did not confine itself to the assessment of the Division Chief whose attitude and evaluation of the Applicant's performance were the subject of the Applicant's complaint. In the course of the administrative review the Matching Committee conferred with the Applicant herself as well as with her present and former supervisors.

32. Moreover, the disagreement between the Applicant and her previous Division Chief related mainly to the evaluation of the Applicant's performance and her work attitudes. The grading committees did not concern themselves with the actual performance of the Applicant. They concerned themselves exclusively with finding out whether

the assignment and tasks carried out by the Applicant in her position met the criteria for grading her position as 24 or 23.

33. In the judgment of the grading and reviewing committees, as well as in the judgment of the JGAB, the Applicant did not meet all the components of the criteria for a grade 24. The record does not substantiate the Applicant's contention that in grading her position as a 23 grade position anything other than the officially established criteria had been taken into account.

34. Discrimination against the Applicant cannot be proven by the mere presentation of general statistics purporting to show that as a class the women employees of the Bank are not treated as well as male employees. The issue before the Tribunal is whether the Applicant in this case has been subjected to discrimination or arbitrary and unfair treatment, a contention that the Applicant could not substantiate.

35. In the judgment of all the grading and reviewing individuals and committees the Applicant did not meet the criteria required for grading her position at level 24. There being no proven abuse of discretion on the part of the Respondent its decision to grade the Applicant's position at level 23 should stand. (*Sebastian (No. 2)*, Decision No. 57 [1988], paras. 22, 30–5)

4. Transfer

[See Sect. 16, 'Classification', 2.i.]

5. Improper motive

[See Sect. 16, 'Classification', 2.iii, 3.i.]

6. Abuse of discretion

[See Sect. 16, 'Classification', 2.iii, 3.i.]

7. Administrative review

i. 46. The Applicant contends that at the time her position was graded, the level 17 Office Manager description was in effect, and that the subsequent withdrawal (and later the cancellation) of that classification cannot retroactively deprive her of the grade to which she had become entitled. The Tribunal notes, however, that the decision being challenged here, as properly stated in the application, is the October 17, 1986 decision of the Vice President, PA, to confirm the assignment of the Applicant's position to grade level 16. By that time, the Respondent had taken action to rectify the error manifested in the overlapping position descriptions for Administrative Secretary II and Office Manager: it had removed the latter position from the secretarial stream. The Applicant's classification effective October 1, 1985, whether or not consistent with the revised grading criteria promulgated some months earlier, was subject to challenge by the Applicant and reconsideration by the Respondent in the course of the administrative review proceedings contemplated by Staff Rule 9.04. At each state of administrative review, recommendations were made to successively higher levels of supervision, culminating with the Vice President, PA, who had effective decision making authority. . . .

50. The Tribunal concludes that it is appropriate to direct the Respondent to recompense the Applicant for the intangible injury suffered by her. Such an award was made by the Tribunal under comparable circumstances in *Durrant-Bell* (Decision No. 24 [1985], para. 36). The Applicant seeks two months' compensation—one month for an alleged inability to use funds which would have been obtained had she been promptly graded at level 17, and one month for 'time spent pursuing a remedy frivolously denied.' There has been no proof that the Respondent's grading decision resulted in the Applicant's loss of any funds, or that the Respondent's adherence to its position through administrative review has been frivolous. Nonetheless, the Tribunal decides that the Respondent shall pay the Applicant an amount equivalent to one

month of her net base salary, in compensation for the intangible injury suffered. (*Apkarian*, Decision 58 [1988], paras. 46, 50)

[For identical statements see:

Benner, Decision No. 59 [1988], para. 37
Dosik, Decision No. 60 [1988], para. 37
Hovsepian, Decision No. 61 [1988], para. 37
Hunger, Decision No. 62 [1988], para. 37
Papinchak, Decision No. 63 [1988], para. 37
Witty, Decision No. 64 [1988], para. 37.]

8. Qualifications

[See also Sect. 12, 'Substantive Irregularity', 1.ix and xii.]

i. 28. The Applicant also argues that the PTCO position was substantively wrongly graded at level 25 and that this was because it was tailored for him, that he had been at level 25 and that, therefore, the level at which the position was graded was predetermined by his level, not by the nature of the position.

29. That the PTCO position was tailored for the Applicant is admitted by the Bank. But his fact does not by itself mean that the position was wrongly graded. The grading of positions is a matter of Bank management in which the Bank exercises a discretion. The Tribunal will review such matters only for the purpose of ensuring that the Administration has behaved in a procedurally correct way and that it has not reached a substantive conclusion that is not reasonably sustainable. It is not the task of the Tribunal to substitute its own assessment for that of the Bank.

30. The Applicant argues that the Respondent's decision to grade the PTCO position at this level did not reflect the position's 'purpose, function and level of responsibility so as to provide a sound and equitable basis for the remuneration of staff members'. He dismisses as 'a meaningless post hoc exercise' the filing by the Respondent of a statement by the Senior Job Evaluation Officer,

PERPD, that 'the job could be considered as equivalent to the grading criteria for technical specialists at level 25'. The Applicant does not, however, grapple with the substance of that evaluation. The Job Evaluation Officer's statement concludes with the words: 'I have indicated the key phrases in the job description which support this match'. On comparing the job description (on the basis of which the Applicant accepted the post) with the portion of the Career Progression Summary for Technical Specialists that relates to 'Principal (Technical) Specialist: Grade 25', the Tribunal can find no real discrepancy between the two, certainly none to suggest that the Evaluation Officer's assessment was manifestly unreasonable. For example, it may be observed that the indications in the Career Progression Summary that the specialist at Grade 25 would serve as lead authority to other staff and would lead major sector or appraisal missions is matched in the position description by the statement that the PTCO may, under the overall direction of the TCU chief, have a lead role and responsibility for one or more countries and would take the principal lead in identifying and resolving broad policy and institutional problems affecting the implementation of the TCU strategy. Similarly, there are elements in the 'Qualification/Requirements' paragraph of the Career Progression Summary at Grade 25 which correspond to some of the items in the 'Skills/Abilities' section of the Selection Criteria that appear in the PTCO position description.

31. The Tribunal is, therefore, unable to conclude that the level accorded to the PTCO position departed from previously established standards for grading positions at level 25 so as to be manifestly unreasonable. . . .

34. The Tribunal has determined in paragraph 22 above that the Respondent did not follow the procedure prescribed in Staff Rule 5.09, Section 8, for the grading of the new position, but has rejected the other grounds of the Applicant's complaint. The first determination does not necessarily lead to a finding that the decision reached by the Respondent after failing to follow the prescribed procedure is a nullity. As the Tribunal

recalled in its decision in *Broemser* (Decision No. 27 [1985], para. 40):

> There have been a number of cases in which the Tribunal, though finding that there has been a procedural irregularity in the Bank's treatment of a staff member, has concluded that the rescission of the decision contested or specific performance of the obligation invoked was not a remedy appropriate to the injury done . . . Instead, the Tribunal has ordered the payment to the staff member of compensation for the intangible injury thus suffered.

35. In the present case, the Tribunal can find no basis on which to say that the Applicant was unjustly or harshly treated. The Tribunal notes that the Applicant was, in fact, originally offered in Round 1 the position of Chief of the Technical Cooperation Unit, a post immediately above that of PTCO, and declined it; that the Applicant had presumably understood the position description for PTCO before he accepted that position; and that, when the Applicant resigned the position after less than a week, he cited family reasons for wishing to leave the Bank, in addition to his feeling that the job did not meet his interests or professional skills. (*Lindsay*, Decision No. 92 [1990], paras. 28–31, 34–5)

9. Internal appeals procedure

[See Sect. 1, 'Jurisdiction', 1 (*b*) i; Sect. 16, 'Classification', 10.ii, 13.iv.]

10. Staff rules

i. 51. While this application was pending before the Tribunal, the Applicant informed the Tribunal that the Report of the JGAB in her case, along with the decision of the Vice President, PA were sent without her consent to her Division Chief. She contends that this was an illegal act, was intended to intimidate her, and was inconsistent with the rules of confidentiality set forth in Staff Rule 9.04 governing Job Grading Appeals. The Tribunal rejects these contentions. It was surely appropriate for the Applicant's Division Chief to be made aware of the management's decision, and supporting reasons, regarding the important matter of the grading of positions within his division. Moreover, the job grading decision in the Applicant's case related only to the general content of her position, is no way related to her competence or to any other factors that would bear adversely upon her, such that confidentiality might be appropriate. Finally, the Tribunal is convinced that the disclosure challenged by the Applicant is in fact consistent with Staff Rule 9.04, and with Personnel Manual Statement No. 4.015 which deals more generally with confidentiality of a staff member's personnel records. (*Apkarian*, Decision No. 58 [1988], para. 51)

[For identical statements see:

Benner, Decision No. 59 [1988], para. 37
Dosik, Decision No. 60 [1988], para. 37
Hovsepian, Decision No. 61 [1988], para. 37
Hunger, Decision No. 62 [1988], para. 37
Papinchak, Decision No. 63 [1988], para. 37
Witty, Decision No. 64 [1988], para. 37.]

ii. 21. Staff Rule 9.04, para. 4, provides: 'At any stage of the proceedings, the Panel may . . . (*d*) suspend, terminate or otherwise dispose of the appeal as it considers appropriate in the circumstances; . . . (*f*) on its own initiative or, on the request of a party, call upon any person to file within a specified time limit any document related to the appeal.' These provisions appear to contemplate flexibility and discretion on the part of the JGAB in conducting the appeal, as is consistent with its function in rendering informed recommendations to the Vice President, PA. It is true that Staff Rule 9.04 contains an express provision dealing with reopening, and that this provision, in para. 19, expressly authorizes reopening of proceedings 'prior to submitting a Report . . . in exceptional circumstances.' But the Tribunal does not read this paragraph to negate the inherent power of the JGAB to reopen a proceeding in order to correct a potentially serious miscarriage of justice, in this case the receipt by the JGAB of comments from the Applicant in what was, albeit inadvertently, essentially an *ex parte* manner. (*Spier*, Decision No. 77 [1989], para. 21)

11. Violation of staff principles

i. 21. Staff Principle 6.2 (*b*) directs the Respondent to 'institute and maintain programs of systematic job evaluation, the purpose of which is to grade jobs according to their purpose, function, and level of responsibility so as to provide a sound and equitable basis for the remuneration of staff members'. The Applicant contends that the generic evaluation criteria for PRJ—C (grade 24) do not meet the standard of objectivity and fairness required by Staff Principle 6.2 (*b*). According to her each element of the criteria leaves wide room for discretion and judgment, and hence for abuse by managers. In particular, she contends that the inclusion of terms and expressions like 'regular', 'technical authority', 'sensitive' and 'general guidance' etc. introduces such vague criteria for evaluating jobs that the standard of Staff Principle 6.2 (*b*) is not satisfied. (*Sebastian (No. 2)*, Decision No. 57 [1988], para. 21)

12. Procedural irregularity

[See Sect. 16, 'Classification', 2.iii.]

13. Grading exercise

[See also Sect. 28, 'Reorganization', 3.i; Sect. 29, 'Remedies', 1.ii.]

i. 27. The Applicant is requesting the rescission of the decision not to accord her a grade 23, when her position was graded at level 22. She is requesting that the Respondent maintain her, for purposes of compensation administration at grade 23, contending that she has a right to be 'grandfathered' indefinitely.

28. The Tribunal notes that there was no reduction of the Applicant's salary at the time her position was graded but that her salary would have been frozen when it had reached or exceeded the ceiling of the salary of the new grade accorded to her position as a result of the grading exercise. Thus, the decision complained of had no immediate effect on her salary and could not have had any effect until at least two years had elapsed. (*Kaplan*, Decision No. 65 [1988], paras. 27–8)

ii. 28. Having occupied, prior to the Job Grading Exercise, a level 3 position (equivalent to present grade 18), and seeing her position allocated to grade 19 in that exercise, the Applicant sought administrative review and a grade 21 or 22. Administrative review resulted in the conduct of a job audit by the Job Evaluation Unit at the request of the Vice President and Controller and his subsequent decision, with proffered reasons, on February 26, 1987 to grade the Applicant's position at level 20. The Applicant has not at this time sought review by the Tribunal of that decision by the VPCTR. Rather, she contests the refusal of the Chief, JEU, on March 10, 1987 in effect to provide her with another administrative review and the documents she claims are necessary to determine whether the job audit was conducted properly. The Applicant seeks to have those decisions of the Chief, JEU, rescinded and a determination by the Tribunal that she shall be allowed ninety days from the release of the requested findings in order to appeal the decision of February 26, 1987 of the VPCTR to place her job at level 20. Shortly after the Applicant filed her application to the Tribunal the Chief, JEU, offered her access to the documents relating to the job audit, but she has since declined to examine those documents, seeking the Tribunal's determination that she should have been given access initially as a matter of right.

29. The issues for determination by the Tribunal are:

(i) Was the JEU right to refuse the administrative review of the decision to place the Applicant's job at level 20?

(ii) Should the Tribunal order release of the audit findings?

(iii) Should the Tribunal reserve the Applicant's right to appeal to the Tribunal the decision of the VPCTR to confirm the grade of her position at level 20 until 90 days after the release of the job audit findings?

30. On the first issue the Applicant argues that the JEU was wrong to refuse on March 10 administrative review of the February 26 decision. She is mistaken. The administrative review provided for by Staff Rule 9.04 is a step in the process leading to an appeal to the JGAB. There was in fact such a review. The Staff Rule does not, however, give the Applicant the right to request a further administrative review of a job audit undertaken subsequent to, and in implementation of, a recommendation of the JGAB made as the outcome of an appeal. (*Breton*, Decision No. 69 [1988], paras. 28–30)

iii. 48. Staff Rule 9.04 dealing with Job Grading Appeals does not stipulate for any such right of the Vice President, PA, to refer back to the JGAB or to the Chief of its panel to reconsider the decision taken. The Vice President may be free to seek whatever advice he deems useful or helpful for taking his decision as to whether he should go along with the recommendation of the JGAB. He should not, however, without advising the Applicant, involve the JGAB, which is intrusted with a quasi-judicial mission of deciding on appeals seeking review of the grading decision. Moreover, the Vice President's letter of December 5, 1986 was sent even before the decision of the JGAB itself was communicated to the Applicant. In these circumstances the Tribunal finds the action of the Vice President, in referring back the decision of the JGAB for reconsideration of its substance to be in violation of Principle 2.1 of Staff Employment which states that:

'The Organizations shall at all times act with fairness and impartiality and shall follow a proper process in their relations with staff members.' . . .

51. The Tribunal finds nothing wrong or arbitrary in the criterion of career level stream itself. The flaw in this case results from the fact that the mechanism was applied to the Applicant retroactively. It was in fact applied before being finalized by the Respondent.

52. In the light of the above the Tribunal concludes that the Respondent's decision to grade the Applicant's position at level 17 and to reject the recommendation of the JGAB was taken as a result of a series of measures carried out in violation of fair and reasonable procedures. As a result of these measures the Applicant was deprived of her right effectively to participate in the grading exercise and to be notified in good time of the measures, communications and decisions taken affecting different aspects of her employment with the Respondent. Consequently, in these circumstances the decision should be quashed and remanded to the Respondent, and compensation should be granted to the Applicant for the tangible and intangible injury suffered by the Applicant as a result of the irregular procedure followed in determining the grade of her position. (*Rae*, Decision No. 74 [1988], paras. 48, 51–2)

iv. 24. The Tribunal does not intend to suggest that the proper recourse for the Vice President, PA, in dealing with JGAB recommendations with which he does not agree, is to request or induce the Board to reopen its proceedings. It is the function of the JGAB to investigate, report and recommend, and it is the function of the Vice President, PA, to make effective job grading decisions, subject to the possibility of judicial review by the Tribunal. Under the circumstances of this case, however, the conduct of the JGAB and of the Vice President, PA, was reasonable, within their powers, and caused no injury to the Applicant and was therefore not a violation of the Applicant's contract of employment or terms of appointment. (*Spier*, Decision No. 77 [1989], para. 24)

14. Downgrading

[See also Sect. 13, 'Procedural Irregularity', 4.i; Sect. 16, 'Classification', 1.ii, Sect. 28, 'Reorganization', 1.i, 3.iv.]

i. 34. In previous cases arising out of the Job Grading Program the Tribunal has determined that this Program —involving decisions regarding criteria for evaluating staff positions, the assignment of various tasks to particular positions, and the ultimate determination of grade levels—constitutes an exercise of discretionary authority by the Respondent, and that 'it is not for this Tribunal to substitute its own judgment for that of the competent organs of the Bank' (*Pinto*, Decision No. 56 [1988], para. 35). Consequently, the Program as such is subject to review by this Tribunal only if it is shown that there has been an abuse of discretion, by reason of the action taken in a concrete case 'being arbitrary, discriminatory, improperly motivated or carried out in violation of a fair and reasonable procedure' (*Pinto*, Decision No. 56 [1988], para. 36)....

39. Consequently, the Tribunal finds that in not advising the Applicant, at the time of transfer, that his new work assignment had a lower grade level, and that he retained his former grade only on a personal basis, the Bank did not follow a proper procedure. This is recognized by the Vice President, PA, in his letter of May 11, 1987 which is the decision contested by the Applicant. In that letter the Vice President, PA, admits that 'there had not been sufficient clarity with respect to your downgrading at the time of your transfer in 1975. This is not only regrettable but unacceptable . . . at the time the system did not work in your case'.

40. The consequences of that improper procedure have materialized at the present time as a result of the application to the staff member of the Job Grading exercise. The Applicant rightly contends that if he had been made aware of his true situation in 1975 he might have been able to dispute the decision taken and to take remedial action, either to obtain another suitable assignment within the Bank or to seek a position outside it. While at that

time he had prospects of outside employment, it is now too late for him to be considered for an outside position by reason of his age.

41. For these reasons, the Tribunal concludes that the treatment of the Applicant fell short of the required standards and this has effectively caused him harm. However, the decision adopted by the Respondent in 1985 assigning grade 26 to the position occupied by the Applicant is not disputed. Moreover, the Tribunal considers the suppression of personal grades to be one of the legitimate purposes of the Job Grading exercise. Consequently, rescission of that 1985 decision is not a remedy appropriate to the intangible injury done. In these circumstances the Tribunal will order the payment to the Applicant of compensation which it equitably assesses at two months net base salary. (*Alan Berg*, Decision No. 73 [1988], paras. 34, 39–41)

ii. 42. It is pertinent to note that at the time of the reorganization and the offer to her of a position graded at her then-current 15 level, the Applicant's principal grievance was directed at her downgrading from level G to level 15, a grading decision that was made some two years before and that the Applicant admittedly failed to challenge in a timely way. The core of her case before the Tribunal, in substance, is that her work in TAP and her skills used there warranted a grade higher than level 15—so that the offer of a grade-15 position in September 1987 was effectively a demotion. The Tribunal cannot countenance at this time what is in effect an untimely challenge to the Applicant's grading decision of years before. Her application must be dismissed. (*Montesa*, Decision No. 82 [1989], para. 42)

15. Hay formulae

[See also Sect. 29, 'Remedies', 8.i.]

i. 25. As was stated in *Einthoven*, so long as 'policy formulation is not arbitrary, discriminatory, improperly motivated or reached without fair procedure, there is no violation of the contract of employment or of the terms of appointment of the staff member.' (Decision No. 23 [1985], para. 43). The Tribunal will review the application of a policy to an Applicant in an individual case in order to ascertain whether there has been an abuse of discretion.

26. The Applicant challenges the Respondent's policy of not assigning a higher grade to a position in which bilingual skills are required but rather recognizing the value of such skills by placing the incumbent of the position at the time of recruitment at a higher point in the salary scale of the grade. Not to take into account bilingual skills in the evaluation of a position, where such skills are a requirement for that position, is an abuse of discretion. No reason has been given by the Respondent to explain why a required language skill is not properly to be treated as a 'know-how' component deserving of points under the Hay job-grading formula, and no such reason is self-evident to the Tribunal. The Tribunal, therefore, concludes that the grading of the Applicant's position at level 15 was arbitrary.

27. It is not certain, however, that even had the Bank awarded Hay points to the Applicant's position for the required bilingual skills, this would have resulted in an increase in the grade level of that position. Therefore, the Tribunal quashes the decision to assign to the Applicant's position to level 15 and remands the case to the Respondent so that a new decision on the grade of the Applicant's position may be taken. (*Chakra*, Decision No. 70 [1988], paras. 25–7)

[For a similar statement see *Cardenas*, Decision No. 71 [1988], paras. 26–8.]

16. Grandfathering

[See also Sect. 15, 'Terms and Conditions of Employment', 1.iii; Sect. 16, 'Classification', 1.i; Sect. 25, 'Salary', 2.i.]

i. 29. On October 31, 1987 the Applicant left the service of the Bank, and in connection with her departure she received the Enhanced Separation Package (Package B) of severance pay and benefits. The Applicant's departure took place one month after the expiration of the two-year grandfathering period. During that month no salary review took place, and consequently the Applicant did not incur any financial loss as a result of the expiration of the limited grandfathering period. On March 18, 1988 the Respondent informed the Tribunal of the Applicant's separation from service, and of its contention that, as a result of these developments, the Applicant was not entitled to any further compensation. Although the Applicant was duly notified, she did not respond to that contention.

30. In light of the above the application has become moot. (*Kaplan*, Decision No. 65 [1988], paras. 29, 30)

ii. 37. Although the case was listed as ready for hearing on July 22, 1987, the Respondent on March 18, 1988 informed the Tribunal that the Applicant had left the service of the Bank on November 30, 1987, having received the Enhanced Separation Package (Package B) of severance pay and benefits. It follows that, apart from the relevance of any possible increase in the salaries of staff that might have become effective during the two-month period September 30–November 30, 1987, none of the remedies sought by the Applicant remains relevant. As to that two-month period following September 30, 1987, no salary review took place and consequently the Applicant did not incur any financial loss as a result of the expiration of the limited grandfathering period.

38. A copy of the Respondent's letter of March 18, 1988 was sent to counsel for the Respondent who, being unable to make contact with the Applicant, in a letter dated March 25, 1988, contended, by reference to the Rules of the Tribunal, that the letter should not be made part of the record. The Tribunal rejects this contention, bearing in mind particularly that under Article XIII of the Statute of the Tribunal it is the facts as known to the Tribunal at the date of the judgment that are material

to its decision. Since the Tribunal is now aware of the fact that the Applicant has left the Bank's service, there is no point in giving effect to a purely formal objection to the admissibility of the Respondent's letter of March 18, 1988. The Tribunal has therefore made both the letters of March 18 and 25, 1988 part of the record.

39. In light of the above, the application has become moot. (*Tucker*, Decision No. 68 [1988], paras. 37–9.)

iii. 30. In *de Merode* (Decision No. 1 [1981], paras. 111 and 112) the Tribunal found 'that a consistent practice of periodic adjustment has been established, and that the Bank makes these adjustments out of the conviction that it is legally obliged to do so'. The Tribunal concluded:

> [I]n consequence . . . the Bank is obliged to carry out periodic reviews of salaries, taking into account various relevant factors. . . . [T]he established practice, and statements confirming that practice, have created a legal obligation to make periodic adjustments reflecting changes in the cost of living and other factors. In the opinion of the Tribunal such an obligation is a fundamental element in the Applicant's conditions of employment which the Bank does not have the right to change unilaterally.

In *Pinto* (Decision No. 56 [1988], para. 40), where the same contention was raised as has been raised in this case, the Tribunal held:

> The Tribunal concludes that the freezing of the Applicant's salary, from September 30, 1987, would deprive her, without justifiable cause, of the right to benefit from periodic adjustments reflecting changes in the cost of living and other factors, which the Tribunal has found to be a fundamental element in the Applicant's conditions of employment which the Bank does not have the right to change unilaterally. This is not to suggest that a staff member may under no circumstances have his or her grade reduced or salary frozen, for example, when this is done for cause as for disciplinary action. In the present case, however, the downgrading of the Applicant and her position was done not because of her misconduct but because of the organizational needs of the Bank; in such circumstance, the staff member is reasonably entitled to more

equitable treatment, as appears to be contemplated by Staff Principle 5 (1) f.

The Tribunal will apply the same ruling in this case and decides that the Applicant should, as from September 30, 1987, receive the periodic salary review increases approved by the Respondent for staff members in grade 16, the grade in which he was before his position was regraded. (*Chakra*, Decision No. 70 [1988], para. 30)

[For similar statements see:

Cardenas, Decision No. 71 [1988], para. 31
Alan Berg, Decision No. 73 [1988], para. 43.]

17. Job description

[See also Sect. 16, 'Classification', 8.i; Sect. 28, 'Reorganization', 1.iii, 3.ix.]

i. 20. The Applicant contended that Staff Rule 5.09, Section 8, sets out a detailed procedure for the grading of new positions and asserted that, in the case of the PTCO position, there is no evidence that this procedure was followed. The Applicant did not develop this argument in full detail but instead included in his application three interrogatories and two requests for documents in which he sought information and documents closely reflecting the procedural requirements set out in Staff Rule 5.09, para. 8.03. . . .

24. The evidence adduced by the Applicant in support of this contention is no more than circumstantial and consists principally of the fact that the post was newly created, that the job description was precisely tailored to suit his qualifications and that, after he declined it, the post was not offered to any one else. However, apart from the procedural irregularity that the Tribunal already found (question (I) above), the only real evidence on the point is the statement in a memorandum from Mr. Dyck to the Applicant: 'of course . . . the Region was also cognizant of Senior Management's desire to place as

many qualified staff as possible at their level before the end of Round 2'. This observation must be read in its context, as following a sentence describing the objective justification for offering the post to the Applicant: '. . . the Region offered him this position by virtue of his past experience and expertise as a Project Specialist (and his knowledge of technical assistance) including but not limited to the human resources section.'

25. Even if it were true that the Bank was in difficulty in dealing with all the Enhanced Separation payments within the limits of its budget, the Tribunal cannot see that fact as by itself supporting the allegation that, if otherwise correct, an act of the Bank was improperly motivated. Nor is there, in itself, any evident impropriety in the Bank tailoring a position to meet the circumstances of an officer of experience and quality whose services the Bank understandably wished to retain. . . .

30. The Applicant argues that the Respondent's decision to grade the PTCO position at this level did not reflect the position's 'purpose, function and level of responsibility so as to provide a sound and equitable basis for the remuneration of staff members'. He dismisses as 'a meaningless post hoc exercise' the filing by the Respondent of a statement by the Senior Job Evaluation Officer, PERPD, that 'the job could be considered as equivalent to the grading criteria for technical specialists as level 25'. The Applicant does not, however, grapple with the substance of that evaluation. The Job Evaluation Officer's statement concludes with the words: 'I have indicated the key phrases in the job description which support this match'. On comparing the job description (on the basis of which the Applicant accepted the post) with the portion of the Career Progression Summary for Technical Specialists that relates to 'Principal (Technical) Specialist: Grade 25', the Tribunal can find no real discrepancy between the two, certainly none to suggest that the Evaluation Officer's assessment was manifestly unreasonable. For example, it may be observed that the indications in the Career Progression Summary that the specialist at Grade 25 would serve as lead authority to

other staff and would lead major sector or appraisal missions is matched in the position description by the statement that the PTCO may, under the overall direction of the TCU chief, have a lead role and responsibility for one or more countries and would take the principal lead in identifying and resolving broad policy and institutional problems affecting the implementation of the TCU strategy. Similarly, there are elements in the 'Qualification/Requirements' paragraph of the Career Progression Summary at Grade 25 which correspond to some of the items in the 'Skills/Abilities' section of the Selection Criteria that appear in the PTCO position description.

31. The Tribunal is, therefore, unable to conclude that the level accorded to the PTCO position departed from previously established standards for grading positions at level 25 so as to be manifestly unreasonable. (*Lindsay*, Decision No. 92 [1990], paras. 20, 24, 25, 30, 31)

ii. 33. It is alleged by the Respondent that the Bank when it declined to appoint the Applicant to an audit analyst position, concluded that the Applicant's previous position in the IAD had been significantly redefined in the Reorganization, so as to be more demanding, and that the Applicant lacked the qualifications for the position as redefined. The Applicant contends, however, that the post-Reorganization audit analyst position at level 20 was in fact not materially different from his pre-Reorganization position and that he was fully qualified for selection.

34. The Respondent, on several occasions in its pleadings, insists that 'the responsibilities of Applicant's position were changed as a result of the reorganization,' that 'Applicant was found to be unqualified for the new position,' that 'the skills requirements of [the audit analyst position] were altered, and generally new priorities were adopted,' and that 'changes were made and the requirements for positions were enlarged.' Yet the Respondent fails altogether to go beyond these general assertions to state with any particularity the respects in which the audit analyst position was changed in the

course of the Reorganization. It was surely contemplated that in the Reorganization certain positions would be changed in their job content such that, for example, new technical skills (such as in macroeconomics or computers) would henceforth be required. The Bank might well, in such circumstances, reasonably conclude that the present occupant of that position lacked the requisite skills for the position as redefined, and indeed that such skills could not be acquired after a reasonable period of training. Non-selection by virtue of redundancy might then be appropriate even though that position would remain vacant for lack of any other qualified staff member. But the Respondent has failed to provide any specific information that would warrant a conclusion that the audit analyst position was redefined in so substantial a manner. (*Jassal*, Decision No. 100 [1991], paras. 33, 34)

[For a similar statement see *Fabara-Núñez*, Decision No. 101 [1991], paras. 34, 35.]

17. RECRUITMENT

1. Permanent employment/re-employment

[See also Sect. 22, 'Transfer and Reassignment', 1.iii; Sect. 28, 'Reorganization', 2.iv; Sect. 29, 'Remedies', 1.vi, 2.v.]

i. 43. The Applicant seeks rescission of the original decision of the Bank not to employ her in a permanent position. Such rescission is unnecessary because she has already been given a permanent position. (*Arellano*, Decision No. 98 [1990], para. 43)

2. Temporary Assignment Program

[See also Sect. 8, 'Sources of Law', 3 (*a*) i; Sect. 28, 'Reorganization', 3.iv.]

i. 39. Equally unconvincing is the contention that para. 7.06 requires, before the Applicant would lose her claim to the Enhanced Separation Package, an offer of a position at a level comparable to the level of positions to which she was currently being temporarily assigned in the TAP program. The Applicant contends (although the Respondent takes issue) that almost all of her service in TAP was in level-16 positions and that therefore the Bank's offer of a Staff Assistant position at level 15 did not comport with para. 7.06. The Tribunal gives the pertinent language its obvious meaning: that 'a position of [the Applicant's] current . . . grade level' means a level-15 position. The principal document establishing the terms of the TAP program —Pers./11/81, dated June 30, 1981—reinforces this conclusion in its provision to the effect that 'When staff members join the Temporary Assignment Program, they will retain their salary and level.' Level 15 is indisputably the grade level given to the Applicant's position in TAP (as it was the grade of her previous position), and this is evidenced by the unambiguous reference to Level 15 in all of the Applicant's pertinent personnel documents.

40. Even apart from its clear language, para 7.06 should be read as the Respondent contends lest the current grade level of a staff member working in TAP constantly vacillate, depending upon the temporary work assignment at any given time. It is not likely that the separation rights of staff members were intended to be left in such an unsettled state, one which could just as easily redound to the serious detriment of a staff member (if temporarily working in a lower graded position) as to his or her benefit.

41. Although the Applicant relies upon some colorably supportive language in a document dated February 10, 1986, from the Assistant Director, PMD, to another supervisor in the department, that is too slender a reed upon which to rest the Applicant's claim. First, it is not explained how this memorandum could supersede the clear language of Pers./11/81. Nor is there any evidence that the memorandum or the personnel manual circular was applied with respect to any other staff member so as

to vary the grade level of TAP positions form time to time. Finally, the memorandum of the Assistant Director, PMD, continued as follows: 'In future the following provisions apply: a staff member who joins TAP will carry the grade of their [*sic*] previous regular assignment on a personal basis for up to two years and will be given assignments appropriate to their grade to the extent possible.' In other words, staff members in TAP were to have their grade level fixed, with temporary assignments to be made consistently therewith—not, as the Applicant contends, the other way around, with the grade level being temporarily determined by work assignments. (*Montesa*, Decision No. 82 [1989], paras. 39–41)

3. Classification

[See Sect. 16, 'Classification', 15.i.]

18. BENEFITS

1. Severance pay

[See also Sect. 4, 'Release Agreements', 2.iii; Sect. 16, 'Classification', 16.ii; Sect. 28, 'Reorganization', 3.i, ii, and vi, 5.i; Sect. 32, 'Miscellaneous', 5.i, 6.i.]

i. 51. Despite not being required by Rule 7.01, the Bank subsequently decided to offer six months compensation to staff in the Applicant's situation. Those were the conditions offered to the Applicant by close of business on September 30 and he accepted the offer, signing the Separation Agreement in October 1987. There was no duress in the mutual separation agreement, because the situation in which the Applicant found himself was of his own choosing. (*Pavesich*, Decision No. 94 [1990], para. 51)

2. External training

[See Sect. 22, 'Transfer and Reassignment', 1.iii.]

3. Expatriate

[See also Sect. 7, 'Appeals Committee', 1.ii; Sect. 8, 'Sources of Law', 2 (*c*) iv.]

i. 38. In deciding to acquire U.S. citizenship on June 1, 1984 the Applicant should and could have investigated the legal and financial consequences of her decision due to the absence of any provision allowing restoration of financial benefits in case of subsequent renunciation of that citizenship. On her appointment to the Bank the Applicant was informed of the conditions of eligibility for Home Leave, Education and Repatriation Benefits, by a letter dated March 7, 1974. In that letter the Applicant was informed of the Personnel Manual Circular No. 820–2–74 dated February 20, 1974 concerning elimination of discrimination in access to staff benefits which stated that:

> All expatriate staff appointed by the Bank Group on or after January 1, 1974 will be eligible for expatriate benefits . . . under the following terms and conditions provided that if stationed at headquarters, the staff members who join the Bank Group in permanent-resident status and who change to G-4 Status on or before confirmation of appointment and thereafter maintain such status shall also be eligible for expatriate benefits.

The information in the letter should have alerted the Applicant to the fact that eligibility required maintaining the status of a non-citizen of the duty station country.

39. In reaching this conclusion the Tribunal has borne in mind its understanding of the rationale behind the whole system of expatriate benefits and the proper approach to citizenship as a reflection of allegiance to and connection with a particular State. To provide for the reacquisition of certain economic benefits when a staff member renounces his or her nationality might encourage a casual approach to the responsibilities and implications of citizenship. The Applicant does not conceal

the real purpose of her decisions first to acquire U.S. citizenship and then to consider renouncing it. In her application before the Tribunal she 'affirms that she took U.S. citizenship because of rumors that the Bank was planning a reduction in force and if deprived of a job she felt that she would stand a better chance of finding another one in the U.S. market if she had U.S. citizenship'. She equally admits that her desire to renounce U.S. citizenship stems, partly at least, from her realization that her decision to take U.S. citizenship had cost her eligibility for expatriate benefits.

40. The Tribunal does not accept the Applicant's contention that by denying her re-eligibility for expatriate benefits if she renounces her U.S. citizenship the Respondent would be interfering with the right of staff members freely to acquire and reassume their citizenship. The Applicant remains free to renounce her previously acquired U.S. citizenship and to revert to the G-4 visa status, but she cannot use that freedom as the basis for requiring the Respondent to grant her certain benefits. The Respondent's regulation of eligibility for expatriate benefits is a proper exercise of its power to regulate the rights and obligations of staff members.

41. The Tribunal concludes that, by denying the Applicant's request to regain expatriate benefits on her renunciation of U.S. citizenship, the Respondent has not violated any element of the Applicant's rights under her contract of employment or terms of appointment. (*Wahie*, Decision No. 93 [1990], paras. 38–41)

4. Home country travel

[See also Sect. 18, 'Benefits', 3.i.]

i. 33. The controlling rules are Staff Rule 6.13 on eligibility for home country travel and Staff Rule 6.41 on Education Benefits. Para. 2.01 of both rules reads:

> A staff member appointed on or before January 28 1985, whose service has been continuous since that date, is eligible for [home country/education benefits] in respect of that period of service

during which he is not a citizen of the duty station country. However, eligibility will cease when the staff member becomes a citizen of the duty station country, or becomes a permanent resident of the duty station country on the basis of a petition or an application filed after January 29, 1986.

(*Wahie*, Decision No. 93 [1990], para. 33)

5. Education benefits

[See Sect. 18, 'Benefits', 4.i.]

19. STAFF ASSOCIATION

[See also Sect. 25, 'Salary', 3 (*a*) i.]

i. 29. The Kafka System as adopted by the Executive Directors of the Respondents on May 24, 1979 stipulated that staff compensation should be reviewed in accordance with the following principles.

(i) there should be a comprehensive review of staff compensation every third year and in the intervening years pay should, in normal circumstances, be adjusted in the light of movements in the pay levels of comparator organizations in the chosen markets;

(ii) in abnormal situations pay adjustments in the intervening years should also take account of pay movements in real terms among comparator organizations in other countries and, in the case of the U.S. market, should not be subject to sharp deviations from market forces as a result of changing U.S. Government practices towards the pay of its civil service; and

(iii) there should be full Staff Association participation in the review process . . .

38. The Applicants also maintain that the postponement of the comprehensive review for two consecutive years deprived them of the right to participate, through consultation of the Staff Association with the management, in the process of periodic salary adjustments.

39. In their meeting of May 24, 1979 in which the Executive Directors approved the management's Staff Compensation Review, the Executive Directors decided that:

> [T]here should be full Staff Association participation in the review process.

The record shows that the Staff Association was consulted by management before the salary adjustment recommendations were put forward. On December 21, 1987, the Staff Association was informed of the management's decision to conduct an intervening year survey as a basis for the 1988 Compensation Review. On March 31, 1988 the Staff Association was provided with the Preliminary Hay Survey Data, and a meeting was scheduled for April 1, 1988 to discuss the further consultation process. On April 7, 1988 the management solicited the Staff Association's views on certain aspects of the 1988 structure adjustment and salary increase. In that letter of April 7 the management went on to state that:

> It is understood that this step does not complete the consultation process and that the Staff Association will have the usual opportunity to present their views for inclusion in the Board Paper and to make an oral presentation to the Executive Directors. . . .

Again on April 4, 1988 the Staff Association was informed of a meeting with the Board Committee on Staff Compensation issues, to take place on April 25, and the Staff Association was offered the opportunity to present their views on the 1988 compensation review. The Tribunal, therefore, cannot share the Applicants' view that their right to consult with the management in the review process was impaired by the Respondents' postponement of the Comprehensive Review. (*Hammond et al.*, Decision No. 86 [1989], paras. 29, 38–9)

20. FIXED-TERM CONTRACTS

1. Expectancy

[See also Sect. 14, 'Performance', 1.v.]

i. 26. The record shows that the Respondent did promise to convert the Applicant's appointment into a permanent one but that the fulfillment of that promise was conditional upon the Applicant's satisfactory performance.

27. By a letter dated December 22, 1986, the Applicant's supervisor informed the Personnel Management Department (PMD) of the Applicant's selection as a Cofinancing officer. He stated that:

> It was agreed at the time of the Applicant's transfer that his performance would be reviewed at the end of the calendar year against the objectives which have been set for him here and at which time his fixed-term appointment should be changed to permanent.

These comments were endorsed by the Vice President Cofinancing, (VPCOF) on May 14, 1987. The Applicant himself does not contest the Respondent's contention as to the requirement of satisfactory performance. (*Mathew*, Decision No. 103 [1991], paras. 26–7]

2. Conversion

i. 26. The record shows that the Respondent did promise to convert the Applicant's appointment into a permanent one but that the fulfillment of that promise was conditional upon the Applicant's satisfactory performance. . . .

28. In the case of *Mr. X*, Decision No. 16 [1984], this Tribunal decided that:

> The fixed-term staff member thus had no absolute right to a regular appointment but was necessarily exposed to the exercise of the Bank's discretion as to whether he met the requirements of the position . . .

29. The discretion exercised by the Respondent as to whether the Applicant met the requirements of the position must therefore, be scrutinized by the Tribunal in order to ensure that it is not vitiated by an abuse of discretion, being arbitrary, discriminatory, improperly motivated or carried out in violation of a fair and reasonable procedure. (*Saberi*, Decision No. 5 [1981], para. 24, *de Raet*, Decision No. 85 [1989], para. 67.) . . .

39. The Tribunal concludes that there was no abuse of discretion in making this evaluation. . . .

41. The Applicant also contends that the Respondent did little or nothing to assist him in finding another position in the Bank. Without pronouncing on the question whether the Respondent has such a duty vis-a-vis a fixed-term employee, the Tribunal finds that several attempts were made by the PMD to assist the Applicant to find a position outside the Cofinancing Department, both before and after the January 1989 decision not to renew or convert his appointment. The fact that those efforts were not successful does not constitute any breach or non-observance of the Applicant's contract of employment or terms of appointment. (*Mathew*, Decision No. 103 [1991], paras. 26, 28–9, 39, 41)

3. Renewal

[See Sect. 20, 'Fixed-Term Contracts', 2.i.]

21. PROBATION

[See Sect. 28, 'Reorganization', 3.iii; Sect. 29, 'Remedies', 10.iv.]

22. TRANSFER AND REASSIGNMENT

1. General

[See also Sect. 11, 'Prejudice/Discrimination', 2.i; Sect. 12, 'Substantive Irregularity', 1.x; Sect. 13, 'Procedural Irregularity', 6.i; Sect. 16, 'Classification', 2.i; Sect. 20, 'Fixed-Term Contracts', 1.i; Sect. 28, 'Reorganization', 1.i.]

i. 38. As to the effect of the [job grading] program upon the Applicant, she complains of arbitrariness and discrimination. However, the grading of the staff position occupied by her now was not addressed to her personally nor did it take into account her performance. A considerable number of the staff have been similarly affected . . . and the same treatment has been accorded to them all. The Applicant has also complained of defective placement efforts . . . but the record shows that the Respondent complied with requirements demanded by para. 3. 01 of Staff Rule 5.06. (*Pinto*, Decision No. 56 [1988], para. 38)

ii. 38. The Respondent has observed that in 1975 there was no formal procedure for notifying staff members that the grade they held was personal. The Tribunal considers, nevertheless, that the Bank has an obligation to inform the staff member of a change in his employment status, especially when constituting a demotion to a lower level position. Such a communication must also indicate the reasons for that demotion. This obligation is demanded by elementary considerations of due process. Its existence is independent of the adoption of the Principles of Staff Employment.

39. Consequently, the Tribunal finds that in not advising the Applicant, at the time of transfer, that his new work assignment had a lower grade level, and that he retained his former grade only on a personal basis, the

Bank did not follow a proper procedure. This is recognized by the Vice President, PA, in his letter of May 11, 1987 which is the decision contested by the Applicant. In that letter the Vice President, PA, admits that 'there had not been sufficient clarity with respect to your downgrading at the time of your transfer in 1975. This is not only regrettable but unacceptable . . . at the time the system did not work in your case'. (*Alan Berg*, Decision No. 73 [1988], paras. 38–9)

iii. 38. In support of her contentions the Applicant invokes Principle 5 (*d*) of the Principles of Staff Employment, which provides that the Respondent shall 'establish programs and arrangements for staff training and development for the purpose of updating and improving staff skills to meet the needs of the Organization'. The Applicant further invokes in support of her claims Personnel Manual Statement (PMS) 4.03, Section 1 which reads as follows:

> The World Bank's long-term effectiveness in providing assistance to its member countries is largely dependent upon the professional excellence of its staff.
>
> Professional excellence, however, cannot be assumed to be self-sustaining in a context where standards of performance, the state of knowledge and the range of Bank Group activities are steadily evolving. It must be systematically maintained and renewed through suitable training programs.

These statements merely describe the Bank's policy to encourage and support staff members to develop further their own education and skills through a partially subsidized program. But neither Principle 5 (*d*) nor PMS 4. 03 creates for the Respondent the legal obligations claimed by the Applicant (see *de Merode*, Decision No. 1 [1981], para. 22).

39. The Applicant asserts that an implied obligation on the part of the Respondent results from the fact that she had assumed, on her part, the obligation to stay with the Bank for a specified period of time. This argument refers to the fact that the Bank, in subsidizing full-time external training, requires from the staff member the under-

taking to remain in the service of the Bank for at least three years upon completion of the full-time study program. If the beneficiary leaves the Bank within three years for any reason, he is required to repay the Bank a prorated portion of the costs it incurred. Such a commitment was obtained from the Applicant, although she continued working in the Bank on a part time basis. However, this 'bonding', as it is called, does not signify the existence of a corresponding, mutual obligation on the part of the Bank to retain for a period of time the services of the beneficiary of a full time external program. There is no indication that the Bank has given up its power of declaring a position redundant. This is confirmed by the letter of September 23, 1985 approving the Applicant's study program, where reference is made to the possibility of a termination grant and of resettlement upon termination. In any event, the 'mutuality' sought by the Applicant in her bilateral contract was already amply provided when the Bank paid a substantial portion of her educational expenses.

40. The Applicant further contends that by inducing her to enter on a prolonged training program, partially paid for by the Respondent and supervised by its Training Division, the Bank assumed an implied obligation, resulting from the reasonable expectations of the parties, to the effect that she would be entitled to return to full time work to use and demonstrate her newly acquired skills. However, the record of the case shows that there was no exact correspondence between the expectations of the parties. While the Applicant intended to pursue a Master's degree in the School of Advanced International Studies at Johns Hopkins University, so as to qualify for a post as Project Economist/Operations Officer, her supervisors insisted that the acceptance of her educational program did not imply any commitment or encouragement for promotion or reassignment, and made clear that she would be returning to work at her previous level as Operations Assistant.

41. As a matter of fact, when the Applicant returned to full-time work at the Bank, in June 1986, she occupied

her former position as Operations Assistant and in that position she was not able to use or demonstrate her newly acquired skills. She had only a mere expectation of upward mobility if there was an opening for a promotion to a higher position, such as that of sector economist. . . .

46. On the other hand, the Tribunal notes that the commitment assumed by the Respondent in its letter of November 14, 1988, to the effect that the Applicant 'may apply for suitable openings through the Bank's VIS system and will be given consideration similar to staff on active duty', is in force and will continue to be in force until September 30, 1990. While deliberating on the case, the Tribunal was informed by the Respondent that the Senior Operations Advisor, Latin America and the Caribbean Regional Office, had selected the Applicant for a position as Operations Assistant, Level 20. The Respondent further advised the Tribunal that before the Applicant's reemployment can be finalized the question of appropriate restitution for the benefits received under Package B will need to be settled. The Respondent pointed out that this is its first occasion to determine the extent of the restitution appropriate in a case where an offer of a position is made to a former staff member who had previously accepted a separation package, adding that, while the conclusion will be tailored to the particular circumstances, guidelines have not yet been adopted. The Tribunal takes notice of this development which ensures that the time and effort spent by the Applicant on an education selected by the Staff Training Division with a Bank career in mind, and the money invested by the Respondent in subsidizing that education, would not be completely lost. (*Sukkar*, Decision No. 84 [1989], paras. 38, 39, 40, 41, 46)

2. Alternative post

[See Sect. 20, 'Fixed-Term Contracts', 1.i, 2.i.]

23. PROMOTION AND DEMOTION

1. Promotion

[See also Sect. 15, 'Terms and Conditions of Employment', 1.vi; Sect. 22, 'Transfer and Reassignment', 1.iii; Sect. 23, 'Promotion and Demotion', 1.i; Sect. 28, 'Reorganization', 2.iv, 3.v.]

i. 56. The relief requested by the Applicant appears to imply that the job offers made would, if accepted by him, have meant his demotion to a level 24 position, while he occupied a level 25 position.

57. The Tribunal cannot accept this view of the matter since the Applicant was never promoted to a level 25 position and was a level 24 officer at the time the offers were made. The proposed formal increase in the Applicant's grade level was denied in June 1986. He was assigned to a level 25 position in order to test his suitability for promotion to that position. In the event, the Respondent's officers who were charged with the duty of deciding on the Applicant's fitness for promotion, noted that: 'The Applicant would need to work on the areas of leadership and management if he were to be a successful SCPO candidate'. The Applicant was never graded at level 25, notwithstanding the recommendations and favorable reports made on his work. The Tribunal will not interfere with the decision not to promote him in the absence of evidence of abuse of discretion. No abuse of discretion has been shown in this case. (*Apergis*, Decision No. 83 [1989], paras. 56, 57)

2. Demotion

[See Sect. 13, 'Procedural Irregularity', 6.i; Sect. 16, 'Classification', 1.ii, 14.ii; Sect. 22, 'Transfer and Reassignment', 1.i; Sect. 28, 'Reorganization', 2.ix, 3.iv; Sect. 29, 'Remedies', 1.vii.]

24. DISCIPLINARY MEASURES

[See Sect. 11, 'Prejudice/Discrimination', 2.ii; Sect. 15, 'Terms and Conditions of Employment', 1.ii; Sect. 16, 'Classification', 1.i and ii.]

25. SALARY

[See Sect. 14, 'Performance', 1.ii; Sect. 28, 'Reorganization', 3.iv]

1. Reduction

[See also Sect. 16, 'Classification', 13.i, 16.ii; Sect. 28, 'Reorganization', 3.ii.]

2. Review

[See also Sect. 11, 'Prejudice/Discrimination', 2.ii; Sect. 13, 'Procedural Irregularity', 5.ii; Sect. 15, 'Terms and Conditions of Employment', 1.iii; Sect. 16, 'Classification', 1.i and ii, 13.i, 16.i–iii; Sect. 28, 'Reorganization', 3.i and ii; Sect. 29, 'Remedies', 1.i, 2.ii, 8.i.]

i. 29. The Applicant's main contention is that his salary review increases after the effective date of the job re-grading should not be limited by the two-year grand-fathering requirement. The paragraph of Staff Rule 5.06 which provides for this reads:

> A staff member whose position is graded at a lower level as a result of a formal job evaluation assumes the lower grade upon the effective date of the evaluation. However, for a period of 24 months thereafter, he will be eligible for increases as if the salary range formerly applicable to the position, adjusted for any increases in the salary structure, had remained in effect. . . . If after 24 months the staff member has not been selected for a

position at his previous or a higher level, future increases in his salary will be administered within the range of his new grade. If at this time the staff member's salary exceeds the maximum of the salary range of the position occupied, the salary will remain unchanged until the maximum of the range exceeds that amount.

In his reply the Applicant invokes, in support of his claim, para. 5 (1) f of the Principles of Staff Employment, which states that the Respondent shall

establish procedures and conditions under which staff members may be assigned to positions graded at various levels, while providing reasonable measures to alleviate adverse effects on staff members assigned to positions graded or regraded at a lower level.

The Applicant contends, on the basis of the above Principle, that he should be grandfathered in his previous salary level. He also contends that by freezing his salary the Bank would deny him a 'fundamental element in Applicant's conditions of employment which the Bank does not have the right to change unilaterally,' namely, the right as embodied in *de Merode* (Decision No. 1 [1981], para. 112) to benefit from 'periodic adjustments reflecting changes in the cost of living and other factors.'

30. In *de Merode* (Decision No. 1 [1981], paras. 111 and 112) the Tribunal found 'that a consistent practice of periodic adjustment has been established, and that the Bank makes these adjustments out of the conviction that it is legally obliged to do so'. The Tribunal concluded:

[I]n consequence . . . the Bank is obliged to carry out periodic reviews of salaries, taking into account various relevant factors. . . . [T]he established practice, and statements confirming that practice, have created a legal obligation to make periodic adjustments reflecting changes in the cost of living and other factors. In the opinion of the Tribunal such an obligation is a fundamental element in the Applicant's conditions of employment which the Bank does not have the right to change unilaterally.

In *Pinto* (Decision No. 56 [1988], para. 40), where the same contention was raised as has been raised in this case, the Tribunal held:

> The Tribunal concludes that the freezing of the Applicant's salary, from September 30, 1987, would deprive her, without justifiable cause, of the right to benefit from periodic adjustments reflecting changes in the cost of living and other factors, which the Tribunal has found to be a fundamental element in the Applicant's conditions of employment which the Bank does not have the right to change unilaterally. This is not to suggest that a staff member may under no circumstances have his or her grade reduced or salary frozen, for example, when this is done for cause as for disciplinary action. In the present case, however, the downgrading of the Applicant and her position was done not because of her misconduct but because of the organizational needs of the Bank; in such circumstance, the staff member is reasonably entitled to more equitable treatment, as appears to be contemplated by Staff Principle 5 (1) f.

The Tribunal will apply the same ruling in this case and decides that the Applicant should, as from September 30, 1987, receive the periodic salary review increases approved by the Respondent for staff members in grade 16, the grade in which he was before his position was regraded. (*Chakra*, Decision No. 70 [1988], paras. 29–30)

[For similar statements see *Cardenas*, Decision No. 71 [1988], paras. 30–1.]

ii. 43. In *de Merode* (Decision No. 1 [1981], paras. 111 and 112) the Tribunal found 'that the Bank makes these adjustments out of the conviction that it is legally obliged to do so'. The Tribunal concluded:

> [I]n consequence . . . the Bank is obliged to carry out periodic reviews of salaries, taking into account various relevant factors. . . . [T]he established practice, and statements confirming that practice, have created a legal obligation to make periodic adjustments reflecting changes in the cost of living and other factors. In the opinion of the Tribunal such an obligation is a fundamental element in the Applicant's conditions of employment which the Bank does not have the right to change unilaterally.

In *Pinto* (Decision No. 56 [1988], para. 40), the Tribunal held:

The Tribunal concludes that the freezing of the Applicant's salary, from September 30, 1987, would deprive her, without justifiable cause, of the right to benefit from periodic adjustments reflecting changes in the cost of living and other factors, which the Tribunal has found to be a fundamental element in the Applicant's conditions of employment which the Bank does not have the right to change unilaterally. This is not to suggest that a staff member may under no circumstances have his or her grade reduced or salary frozen, for example, when this is done for cause as for disciplinary action. In the present case, however, the downgrading of the Applicant and her position was done not because of her misconduct but because of the organizational needs of the Bank; in such circumstances, the staff member is reasonably entitled to more equitable treatment, as appears to be contemplated by Staff Principle 5 (1) f.

The Tribunal will apply the same ruling in this case and decides that the Applicant should as from September 30, 1987 receive the periodic salary review increases approved by the Respondent for staff members in grade 27, the grade which he held before his position was regraded.

Decision:
For the above reasons the Tribunal unanimously decides that:

1. the Respondent shall pay the Applicant a sum equivalent to two months net base salary;
2. the decision of the Vice President, PA, of May 11, 1987 is rescinded so far as it does not provide for the payment to the Applicant, as from September 30, 1987, of the periodic salary review increases approved by the Respondent for staff members in grade 27;
3. the Respondent shall pay the Applicant costs in the amount of $1,000; and
4. all other pleas in the application are dismissed. (*Alan Berg*, Decision No. 73 [1988], para. 43, Decision)

3. Periodic adjustments

[See Sect. 28, 'Reorganization', 2.ix.]

(a) Comprehensive review

[See also Sect. 8, 'Sources of Law', 2 *(b)* i; Sect. 9, 'Discretionary Power', 1.iii.]

i. 27. The Respondents, on the other hand, view their postponement of the comprehensive review for two consecutive years, and their reliance, instead, on intervening years review, to be a valid exercise of their discretion in implementing the rule of periodicity of salary adjustment, prescribed by the Kafka System, and sanctioned by the Tribunal in a consistent line of decisions.

28. In order to dispose of the applications, the Tribunal will have to answer several interrelated questions concerning the proper application of the Kafka System: particularly, whether by postponing the Comprehensive Review the Respondents meant to amend that system, and whether such postponement constituted a reasonable exercise of the discretionary powers of the Respondents.

29. The Kafka System as adopted by the Executive Directors of the Respondents on May 24, 1979 stipulated that staff compensation should be reviewed in accordance with the following principles:

(i) there should be a comprehensive review of staff compensation every third year and in the intervening years pay should, in normal circumstances, be adjusted in the light of movements in the pay levels of comparator organizations in the chosen markets;

(ii) in abnormal situations pay adjustments in the intervening years should also take account of pay movements in real terms among comparator organizations in other countries and, in the case of the U.S. market, should not be subject to sharp deviations from market forces as a result of changing U.S. Government practices towards the pay of its civil service; and

(iii) there should be full Staff Association participation in the review process.

30. There is no disagreement between the Applicants and the Respondents as to the legal nature of the principles governing staff compensation laid down by the Kafka System. This legal nature was affirmed by the Tribunal which concluded in *von Stauffenberg* that:

> There can, therefore, be no doubt that a violation of the rules laid down in 1979 would amount to non-observance of the conditions of employment of the Applicant under Article II of the Statute of the Tribunal. (Decision No. 38 [1987], para. 7)

The Tribunal therefore does not need further to examine this issue in the present case.

31. The record of this case does not substantiate the contention by the Applicants that the Respondents had in fact unilaterally amended the rule requiring a comprehensive review every three years. The postponement in 1987, and again in 1988, does not amount to an amendment of this rule. What is under consideration is not an attempt by the Respondents unilaterally to change a rule affecting the conditions of employment, but rather a departure from strict adherence to such rule.

32. The real disagreement between the Applicants and the Respondents lies in the way each of them reads the requirements of the Kafka System relating to a comprehensive review to be carried out every three years. Whereas the Applicants read the requirement in a literal and strict manner, the Respondents, on the other hand, refer to the recognition in the Kafka Committee report of 1979 that comprehensive reviews be held every three years 'unless, after the first review, the Board decided that a longer period between reviews would be justified though the period should never exceed five years.' Although the President of the Bank did not make a similar qualifying statement in recommending to the Executive Directors that comprehensive reviews be held every third year, there is no reason to suppose that he meant to reject the flexibility proposed by the Kafka Committee.

33. It may be added that in *von Stauffenberg*, where the Bank had maintained that the three year requirement 'was changed by the Executive Directors to a period of four

years until the second comprehensive review', the Tribunal was of the view that

> This minor change in periodicity related to a non-essential element in the conditions of employment and the principle of periodic comprehensive review was not affected. (Decision No. 38 [1987], para. 84)

The Tribunal, in this case, does not find the postponement of the comprehensive review for two years to be, in itself, a violation of an essential element of the conditions of employment of the Applicants.

34. The Tribunal finds, however, that the discretion enjoyed by the Respondents in implementing the principle of periodicity of salary adjustments is not without limitations. Under the Kafka System, the Respondents are undoubtedly required, as a general rule, to carry out comprehensive reviews every three years. If for valid reasons and in good faith they decide to postpone the conducting of such comprehensive review, the postponement should meet two conditions:

(i) It should rest on a reasonable basis justifying the departure from the strict observance of the three year rule.
(ii) It should not lead to exceeding the five year limit prescribed by the Kafka Committee in 1979.

35. In 1984 a Joint Bank/Fund Committee was constituted 'to consider whether changes in such aspects of the compensation system are desirable and to recommend the changes that appear appropriate in order that they may be taken into account to the maximum extent possible in the 1985 compensation review.' However, it became clear that the joint committee needed much more time to accomplish its mission than was initially anticipated by the Respondents. The Respondents' decision to postpone carrying out a comprehensive review in 1987 and again in 1988 was in fact caused by the delay in the work of the joint committee and not by a deliberate decision to depart from the norm stipulated by the Kafka System. In the minutes of the Executive Directors meeting on November 20, 1986 'many directors expressed their

concern for, and disappointment at that delay and urged the committee to complete its work as expeditiously as possible, while a few stressed that the quality of the final outcome was a greater importance than speed.' In a memorandum to the Executive Directors, dated April 29, 1988, the President of the Respondents explained the reasons for the second postponement of the due comprehensive review as follows:

> The planning and commissioning of a major survey for 1988 would have had to begin in 1987. However, since it was earlier expected that the report of the Joint Bank/Fund Committee of Executive Directors on Staff Compensation (JCC) would be available in time for the 1988 salary review, it was not considered appropriate to conduct a major survey based on the 'Kafka I' comparators. Moreover, such a survey would have conflicted with the major survey which Hay Associates were already carrying out for the JCC. In December 1987, the Board Committee on Staff Compensation Issues agreed, therefore, with management's recommendations that an 'intervening year' survey be conducted this year . . .

36. In both 1987 and 1988 the Executive Directors of the Respondents found that the circumstances justified recourse to intervening year reviews rather than engaging in the process of a comprehensive review when the Joint Committee was fully absorbed in its mission and the consultants were busy preparing the survey for the Joint Committee.

37. The Tribunal finds the explanation given by the Respondents for their decisions to postpone the comprehensive review for two consecutive years to be reasonable enough to bring those decisions within the margin of discretion left to them.

38. The Applicants also maintain that the postponement of the comprehensive review for two consecutive years deprived them of the right to participate, through consultation of the Staff Association with the management, in the process of periodic salary adjustments.

39. In their meeting of May 24, 1979 in which the Executive Directors approved the management's Staff Compensation Review, the Executive Directors decided that:

> [T]here should be full Staff Association participation in the review process.

The record shows that the Staff Association was consulted by management before the salary adjustment recommendations were put forward. On December 21, 1987, the Staff Association was informed of the management's decision to conduct an intervening year survey as a basis for the 1988 Compensation Review. On March 31, 1988 the Staff Association was provided with the Preliminary Hay Survey Data, and a meeting was scheduled for April 1, 1988 to discuss the further consultation process. On April 7, 1988 the management solicited the Staff Association's views on certain aspects of the 1988 structure adjustment and salary increase. In that letter of April 7 the management went on to state that:

> It is understood that this step does not complete the consultation process and that the Staff Association will have the usual opportunity to present their views for inclusion in the Board Paper and to make an oral presentation to the Executive Directors . . .

Again on April 4, 1988 the Staff Association was informed of a meeting with the Board Committee on Staff Compensation issues, to take place on April 25, and the Staff Association was offered the opportunity to present their views on the 1988 compensation review. The Tribunal, therefore, cannot share the Applicants' view that their right to consult with the management in the review process was impaired by the Respondents' postponement of the Comprehensive Review. (*Hammond et al.*, Decision No. 86 [1989], paras. 27–39)

(*b*) *Intervening years review*
[See Sect. 25, 'Salary', 3 (*a*) i.]

(*c*) *Kafka System*
[See Sect. 25, 'Salary', 3 (*a*) i.]

4. Classification

[See also Sect. 9, 'Discretionary Power', 1.i and ii; Sect. 15, 'Terms and Conditions of Employment', 1.i.]

i. 37. The Tribunal does not deem it necessary to pronounce in the present case on the question whether . . . the Respondent has the power to deprive a staff member of a grade previously held by him. In particular, with respect to the Job Grading exercise, there can be no certainty that in all cases an exact correspondence exists between the former grades and the present ones, . . . [T]he Applicant herself has not invoked the existence of a right indefinitely to maintain her former grade. Her contentions and arguments have been essentially concerned with . . . her entitlement to continued salary increases. (*Pinto*, Decision No. 56 [1988], para. 37)

ii. 23. Nor does the Tribunal agree with the Applicant's contention that the grading mechanism does not meet the requirements of Staff Principle 6.2 (*b*) because it leaves a certain degree of discretion in applying the requirements of that Staff Principle. All that Staff Principle 6.2 (*b*) requires is the establishment and maintenance of programs of systematic job evaluation, and that such programs should provide a sound and equitable basis for remuneration of staff members. . . . (*Sebastian (No. 2)*, Decision No. 57 [1988], para. 23)

iii. 41. Prior to and during the Bank's review of its job grading system, the Applicant served as Administrative Secretary . . . a position given grade G. Acting pursuant to the revised mid-1985 grading criteria, the Respondent informed the Applicant . . . that . . . her position would be assigned to grade 16, the approximate equivalent of grade G under the old system. Grade level 16 carried a salary range with a maximum of $27,870 (the Applicant's salary at that time). . . .

49. It does not follow, however, that the staff members suffering interim economic or other injury by virtue of the Respondent's ultimately corrected mistakes must be altogether without recourse. That is especially true . . . where at the time of the Applicant's formal grading, the Office Manager classification was still in effect after a period of some months; . . . and where a principal

inducement for . . . withdrawal was the administrative review proceedings instituted by the Applicant and several . . . co-workers. . . . Until the formal withdrawal of the Office Manager classification, and the exhaustion of administrative review, the Applicant harbored a reasonable belief that she satisfied the criteria of that level 17 position . . . [H]er salary as Administrative Secretary . . . was in the midst of the grade 17 salary range, so that a grade of 17 would not have brought any salary increase. (*Apkarian*, Decision No. 58 [1988], para. 41, 49]

[For identical statements see:

Benner, Decision No. 59 [1988], paras. 41, 9
Dosik, Decision No. 60 [1988], paras. 41, 9
Hovsepian, Decision No. 61 [1988], paras. 41, 9
Hunger, Decision No. 62 [1988], paras. 41, 9
Papinchak, Decision No. 63 [1988], paras. 41, 9
Witty, Decision No. 64 [1988], paras. 41, 9.]

26. TAXATION

1. Tax law: Retroactivity

[See also Sect. 1, 'Jurisdiction', 1 (*b*) iii; Sect. 8, 'Sources of Law', 2 (*c*) i.]

i. 36. Although, as the Tribunal will note shortly, its own jurisdiction is not limited to review of affirmative administrative decisions but can encompass as well certain omissions or failures to act, the reference in Staff Rule 9. 01 to review of an 'administrative decision' can obviously give rise to uncertainties on the part of staff members. In the circumstances of this case in particular, it is difficult to say what kind of specific relief or decision the Applicant could have expected from the Pension Information Assistant, in view of the fact that the revised U.S. tax law was indisputably applicable to her late-1966 commuted pension payments; she was indeed informed by him that there was nothing that the Bank could do for her. If, as the Respondent sometimes argues in this case, this did not amount to an 'administrative decision' that this Tribunal can review, it is understandable that there could be uncertainty on the part of the Applicant as to whether the Bank's internal administrative review provisions in Staff Rule 9.01 were applicable and as to whom the Applicant should turn to for recourse. She was therefore not unreasonable when she moved promptly to seek the advice of the Staff Association and then of the Ombudsman. The Applicant might well have moved equally promptly to file an appeal with the Appeals Committee had she not been accurately advised by the Ombudsman that she need not do so because of a pending appeal that the Bank had agreed to apply to her should the outcome favor the Staff member. It is noteworthy, in any event, that when the Applicant did take her case to the Appeals Committee, the Bank challenged the Committee's jurisdiction for lack of an 'administrative decision' from which administrative review and ultimately appeal could be taken. . . .

40. The Tribunal concludes that the Applicant has adequately framed her claim as one for the 'non-observance of [her] contract of employment or terms of appointment.' Her claim is that the Respondent undertook to provide accurate tax advice to its retiring staff members, that she reasonably relied on this undertaking, and that the Respondent neglected to inform her in a timely manner of the retroactive change in the U.S. tax law so that she could accordingly conform her decisions regarding the commutation of her pension payments. These claims fall within the jurisdiction of the Tribunal to decide on the merits. . . .

43. Even so, the advice given by the Pension Information Assistant when the Applicant met with him on August 8, 1986 was also sound. The Applicant sought assurance that any commuted pension payments received by her after October 31, 1986 would be free of tax (to the extent they did not exceed her own contributions), and in providing

that assurance the Pension Information Assistant acted reasonably. Such was the then current U.S. law, and it would have been unreasonable for him to anticipate at that time that any pertinent change in the tax law would be made retroactive, effective July 2, 1986.

44. But the record before the Tribunal demonstrates that the retroactivity feature that was incorporated in the Conference bill and report could reasonably have come to the attention of the Bank on September 23, 1986, and that its passage by both Houses of Congress had taken place by September 27. The Respondent had more than one month in which to become appraised of the retroactivity provision, to identify that this change was of pertinence to Bank staff members, and to contact the ten to fifteen staff members whose pension payment would fall within the statutory retroactivity period. Having known of the Applicant's meeting of August 8 and of her intention to retire on October 31 with commuted pension payments, the Respondent should reasonably have been expected to alert the Applicant during the month of October 1986 to the important change in her tax liabilities.

45. It is true, as the Respondent contends, that the tax reform act was not formally signed into law until October 22, only a week before the Applicant's retirement. But the passage by both Houses of Congress of compromise legislation a month before surely afforded a firm expectation of the imminent change in the statute. It is also true that all staff members could have had recourse to their own individual tax attorneys or advisers during the period of uncertainty in the legislative revision process, and that this was particularly true given the expressions of doubt and unpredictability on the part of the lecturers at the April 1986 seminar. But the Bank did hold out the Pension Information Assistants as providers of pertinent information in the period after the seminar, and it appears that at the meeting between the Applicant and the Pension Information Assistant on August 8, 1986, the advice that she was given—unequivocal as it was—provided her with no intimation that she needed any further advice to keep abreast of legislative developments.

46. For these reasons, and on the particular facts of this case, the Tribunal concludes that the failure to inform the Applicant of the adverse tax consequences of her pension payments until December 1986 (and possibly, as the Applicant claims, even later, in February 1987) was a violation of the Respondent's duty to act reasonably in all the circumstances. (*Robinson*, Decision No. 78 [1989], paras. 36, 40, 43–6)

27. TERMINATION

1. Unsatisfactory performance

(*a*) *General*

[See also Sect. 10, '*Détournement de Pouvoir*', 1.i; Sect. 14, 'Performance', 1.iv; Sect. 20, 'Fixed-Term Contracts', 2.i; Sect. 27, 'Termination', 1 (*b*) ii; Sect. 28, 'Reorganization', 1.iii, 2.x; Sect. 30, 'Procedure before Tribunal', 3 (*a*) i.]

i. 39. The analogy, however, is not convincing. Once the Applicant's position as Division Chief was eliminated, he had no comparable claim upon other vacancies at the same grade level—any more so than other qualified staff members, each of whom was vying for the vacancy. The Bank, by thus making a comparative judgment about the abilities of the various canditates for the vacancy, cannot be said to be acting in a manner comparable to terminating the service of an incumbent staff member. In the process of selecting for vacancies, it is reasonable for the Bank to employ the criterion of comparative skills and abilities, unlike the case of a termination where a more 'absolute' standard—such as 'cause' for dismissal—is customary and correct. This seems equally to be the case whether the contenders for the vacancy are at the same grade level or whether they include highly qualified 'promotables'. (*Fernandes*, Decision No. 90 [1990], para. 39)

ii. 31. First the Applicant contends that the termination action was 'seriously flawed since it was carried out in violation of a fair and reasonable procedure.' The procedure by which the employment of a member of the staff may be terminated for unsatisfactory performance is spelled out in the Staff Rules. The relevant provision in this case is Staff Rule 7.01, para. 11.02, which provides in pertinent part that:

> When a staff member is not performing satisfactorily, the manager will inform him so as to provide the staff member an opportunity to improve. If after a reasonable period of time, which shall not exceed six months . . . the staff member's performance remains unsatisfactory, the manager shall request his department director . . . to remove the staff member from the position. . . .

32. The record shows that the Applicant received written warnings from her supervisors who were anything but satisfied, both with her technical competence and with her brusque personality. In March 1988 her Division Chief felt obliged to subject her to a three-month evaluation period. The Applicant was not only informed of this, but well knew what was required of her. At the end of the evaluation period, she again failed to measure up. It was found that her performance in the evaluation period fell short of the requirements of the Division and that her work relationships had deteriorated. This conclusion was brought to her notice. It is clear, therefore, that the procedure prescribed by Staff Rule 7.01 was followed.

33. The Applicant also contends that it was unreasonable to give her only three months to improve her work quality. The Tribunal notes that, although the relevant Staff Rule prescribes a maximum testing period of six months, no minimum period is laid down. Therefore, what length of time, say between one week and six months, is appropriate in any given case is a matter for the judgment of the Respondent. In this case the two deficiencies of the Applicant which troubled the Bank and which were brought to her notice were first, the unsatisfactory quality of her work and output, and second, the deficiencies in her character which jeopardized harmonious working relationships. The Applicant was not given a heavier workload during her

testing period. Indeed, her workload was reduced. She was in the same familiar environment and should have had no problem of adjustment. Moreover, the Respondent could reasonably have concluded that a three-month period was adequate time for the Applicant to show improvement in her interpersonal relationships with her peers and superiors. Therefore, the Tribunal holds that the Respondent was not manifestly unreasonable in deciding that three months was an adequate period in which to demonstrate improvement or for a fair evaluation of her performance. . . .

36. Unless it can be said that the Personnel Department was not under a duty to ensure that only competent persons are recruited into its service, no valid objection can be taken to the position of the Personnel Department on this matter. In *Mr. X*, Decision No. 16 [1984], where an oral offer of a position was withdrawn after the Personnel Department expressed concern that the Applicant's file had not been reviewed before the offer was made, the Tribunal observed:

> For the Personnel Department to remind the relevant Department that before formalizing an oral offer of employment, it should take into account the entire record of employment within the Bank of prospective candidates constitutes a proper administrative action. (para. 42)

By the same token the personnel officer's advice to the Manager to refrain from considering, so to speak, a tainted candidate unless she was superior to taintless ones, was a proper administrative action. . . .

38. Accordingly, the question that falls for decision here is whether management acted unfairly or unreasonably in deciding that the Applicant's work should be evaluated during the three-month period. It is clear from the record that the quality of her work was thought to be unsatisfactory by a number of her supervisors. More important still, her ability to work harmoniously with her peers or superiors was, to put it mildly, debatable. This was because she took a rather generous view of her own ability and thus disabled herself from appreciating the

need for improvement. In those circumstances it was the plain duty of management to appraise her not only of its dissatisfaction with her performance, but to proceed to an evaluation of her work within the true intendment of Staff Rule 7.01, para. 11.02. The Tribunal is unable to accept that there is anything unfair or unreasonable about the Respondent's decision.

39. The Applicant also argues that the termination of service which the Respondent imposed on her was wholly out of proportion to whatever lapses may have been found in her work. She therefore stigmatizes it as 'not fair and reasonable.' But the Tribunal's view is that the Applicant does not and cannot contend with any plausibility that termination of the employment of an employee whose performance was adjudged unsatisfactory and who failed to avail herself of an opportunity to improve, must be unreasonable. Nonetheless, the Applicant asserts that she worked satisfactorily in different units of the Bank for almost three and a half years, and her so called unsatisfactory performance of barely seven months at EM4IE should not have attracted the sanction of termination of service. As to this the Tribunal agrees that the penalty should bear a reasonable relation to the 'offence'. In *Gregorio*, Decision No. 14 [1983], para. 47, this Tribunal held that:

> The Tribunal has the authority to determine whether a sanction imposed by the Bank upon a staff member is significantly disproportionate to the staff member's offence, for if the Bank were so to act, its action would properly be deemed arbitrary or discriminatory. (*Georgiev*, Decision No. 96 [1990], paras. 31, 32, 33, 36, 38, 39)

iii. 31. In earlier cases arising from the Reorganization, the Tribunal has been confronted with claims that an applicant was improperly denied selection to a position that the Bank in fact gave to another staff member. This is the first case before the Tribunal in which an applicant claims to be qualified to serve in a post-Reorganization position that was left vacant. In such a case, a finding of redundancy must turn upon a conclusion that the content

> redundancy must turn upon a conclusion that the content of the position was so defined as to render its previous occupant no longer qualified to discharge its responsibilities. Unsatisfactory performance by a staff member in his or her position prior to the Reorganization cannot alone furnish a basis for terminating service with the Bank on the ground of redundancy. To do so would be an improper use of the Reorganization procedures in order to avoid the protections otherwise afforded by the Bank's governing documents—Staff Rule 7.01 in particular—for termination of employment, and would therefore constitute *dé*tournement de pouvoir, subject to reversal by the Tribunal. (*Jassal*, Decision No. 100 [1991], para. 31)

[For a similar statement see *Fabara-Núñez*, Decision No. 101 [1991], para. 32.]

(*b*) *Alternative employment*

[See also Sect. 12, 'Substantive Irregularity', 1.x; Sect. 27, 'Termination', 1 (*a*) ii, Sect. 28, 'Reorganization', 2.vii.]

i. 47. The Applicant deliberately decided to reject his former position in order, in his own words, 'to look for something better in Round 2', believing that 'Round 2 offers the opportunity to market my organizing, analytical and report-writing, as well as my technical and training skills'. However, the record shows that the Applicant did not pursue the search for alternative positions with the required dedication and urgency. He sent off applications for other positions only after the end of August despite having decided to market his technical skills on August 3. For various reasons, some of them legitimate, he was absent from the Bank in the final crucial days in the Round 2 exercise, at the end of September. Taking into account all the circumstances, the Tribunal concludes that the lack of response or interest in selecting the Applicant cannot be attributed to a defective assistance by the Personnel services, nor to the absence of a correct telephone connection. As the Appeals Committee found, this latter fact alone 'should not have prevented the

Appellant from looking for other jobs'. (*Pavesich*, Decision No. 94 [1990], para. 47)

ii. 41. The Tribunal must now address the issue which seems to be the gravamen of the application, namely the exercise of the Bank's managerial discretion not to reassign her. She says:

> Applicant has never asserted that the Bank had 'an absolute duty' to reassign her but under the circumstances of her case, a reassignment would have been the only fair and reasonable measure.

If the Applicant has, *ex concessis*, no legal right to reassignment, then whether she should be reassigned or her employment terminated would be purely a matter for managerial discretion which, if exercised either way, would be valid, unless it was discriminatory, arbitrary or improperly motivated. . . .

44. In various parts of her application, the Applicant sought to get round the Tribunal's oft reiterated statement of principle by claims that the Bank's exercise of discretion was vitiated on the ground that it was arbitrary, discriminatory, improperly motivated or carried out in violation of fair and reasonable procedure. These claims are not borne out by the record. The Tribunal considers that the various assessments of the Applicant's performance by her superior officers of all grades, Division Chiefs, Directors and supervisors, were all made in the course of their duties and were fair and reasonable. Accordingly, the Respondent's decision to terminate the Applicant's appointment constitutes a valid exercise of managerial discretion. (*Georgiev*, Decision No. 96 [1990], paras. 41, 44)

(*c*) *Retirement*

[See Sect. 26, 'Taxation', 1.i.]

28. REORGANIZATION

1. Redundancy/redundancy notice

[See also Sect. 12, 'Substantive Irregularity', 1.xii; Sect. 13, 'Procedural Irregularity', 6.i; Sect. 16, 'Classification', 14.i, 17.ii; Sect. 22, 'Transfer and Reassignment', 1.i; Sect. 32, 'Miscellaneous', 6.iii.]

i. 37. The Applicant contends that he learned of the arrangement made in 1975 only as a result of the Bank-wide job grading program in 1985, and there is no direct evidence to contradict this assertion. He was then informed that, as part of this program, his personal grade was being abolished and he would be entitled to retain the salary corresponding to his personal grade level only for a two year grandfathering period. After September 30, 1987 his compensation would be based on a lower salary range.

38. The Respondent has observed that in 1975 there was no formal procedure for notifying staff members that the grade they held was personal. The Tribunal considers, nevertheless, that the Bank has an obligation to inform the staff member of a change in his employment status, especially when constituting a demotion to a lower level position. Such a communication must also indicate the reasons for that demotion. This obligation is demanded by elementary considerations of due process. Its existence is independent of the adoption of the Principles of Staff Employment.

39. Consequently, the Tribunal finds that in not advising the Applicant, at the time of transfer, that his new work assignment had a lower grade level, and that he retained his former grade only on a personal basis, the Bank did not follow a proper procedure. This is recognized by the Vice President, PA, in his letter of May 11, 1987 which is the decision contested by the Applicant. In that letter the Vice President, PA, admits that 'there had not been sufficient clarity with respect to your

downgrading at the time of your transfer in 1975. This is not only regrettable but unacceptable . . . at the time the system did not work in your case'. (*Alan Berg*, Decision No. 73 [1988], paras. 37–9)

ii. 25. The Principles of Staff Employment do not require the Bank to guarantee security of employment where separation is on the grounds of redundancy. Principle 2.1 (*d*) of Staff Employment cannot be construed as a guarantee of lifetime employment. It must be read in conjunction with Principle 7.1 (*b*) (iii) which expressly recognizes the possibility of separation on the ground of redundancy, as occurred in this case. (*Klempin*, Decision No. 88 [1990], para. 25)

iii. 30. As the Tribunal has often stated, a decision by the Bank to select a staff member for a particular position rests within the Bank's discretion, and may be overturned by the Tribunal only when it concludes that this discretion has been abused. 'The Administration's appraisal in that respect is final, unless the decision constitutes an abuse of discretion, being arbitrary, discriminatory, improperly motivated or carried out in violation of a fair and reasonable procedure,' *Suntharalingam*, Decision No. 6 [1981], para. 24. The Tribunal will not set aside a decision of the Bank unless it was 'reached in an arbitrary manner, involving, for example, unfairness, failure to allow the Applicant to state his case, or other departures from established procedures, bias, prejudice, the taking into consideration of irrelevant factors or manifest unreasonableness,' *de Raet*, Decision No. 85 [1989], para. 67. This standard of scrutiny has been applied by the Tribunal in cases arising from the 1987 Reorganization, in which staff members have been displaced from their previous positions on the ground of redundancy as a result of the redefinition of job duties or the reduction in the number of departmental positions.

31. In earlier cases arising from the Reorganization, the Tribunal has been confronted with claims that an applicant was improperly denied selection to a position

that the Bank in fact gave to another staff member. This is the first case before the Tribunal in which an applicant claims to be qualified to serve in a post-Reorganization position that was left vacant. In such a case, a finding of redundancy must turn upon a conclusion that the content of the position was so defined as to render its previous occupant no longer qualified to discharge its responsibilities. Unsatisfactory performance by a staff member in his or her position prior to the Reorganization cannot alone furnish a basis for terminating service with the Bank on the ground of redundancy. To do so would be an improper use of the Reorganization procedures in order to avoid the protection otherwise afforded by the Bank's governing documents—Staff Rule 7.01 in particular—for termination of employment, and would therefore constitute *détournement de pouvoir*, subject to reversal by the Tribunal. . . .

34. The Respondent, on several occasions in its pleadings, insists that 'the responsibilities of Applicant's position were changed as a result of the reorganization,' that 'Applicant was found to be unqualified for the new position,' that 'the skills requirements of [the audit analyst position] were altered, and generally new priorities were adopted,' and that 'changes were made and the requirements for positions were enlarged.' Yet the Respondent fails altogether to go beyond these general assertions to state with any particularity the respects in which the audit analyst position was changed in the course of the Reorganization. It was surely contemplated that in the Reorganization certain positions would be changed in their job content such that, for example, new technical skills (such as in macro-economics or computers) would henceforth be required. The Bank might well, in such circumstances, reasonably conclude that the present occupant of that position lacked the requisite skills for the position as redefined, and indeed that such skills could not be acquired after a reasonable period of training. Non-selection by virtue of redundancy might then be appropriate even though that position would remain vacant for lack of any other

qualified staff member. But the Respondent has failed to provide any specific information that would warrant a conclusion that the audit analyst position was redefined in so substantial a manner. (*Jassal*, Decision No. 100 [1991], paras. 30, 31, 34)

[For a similar statement see *Fabara-Núñez*, Decision No. 101 [1991], 31, 32, 35.]

2. Selection process

[See Sect. 8, 'Sources of Law', 3 (*a*) ii; Sect. 12, 'Substantive Irregularity', 1.vii and xi; Sect. 13, 'Procedural Irregularity', 1.iv; Sect. 16, 'Classification', 17.i; Sect. 29, 'Remedies', 1.iv, 6.i; Sect. 30, 'Procedure before Tribunal', 1.vi, x.]

i. 18. The Tribunal considers, as a matter of law, that it is not inappropriate for the Bank to take policy differences into account in choosing among eligible candidates in the reorganization. But this does not dispose of the issue presented in this case. In any particular case, though the management may be entitled to take a given factor into account, there must at the least be some plausible indication that there is factual support for the factor given negative weight, that such factor has not been weighed in a manner that is discriminatory when compared with its application to other staff members, and that the weight given to such factor can lead to a distortion of the process of decision, and what might otherwise have been relevant and reasonable in a limited quantity could become unreasonable and improper in a greater quantity. Similarly, the weight given by senior managers to policy differences should properly turn upon such considerations as the level and responsibilities of the staff member, the position-relationship with his or her superior, and the traditions of the discipline or of the work unit and the manner in which such differences are articulated. It might also be the case that a negative assessment of a staff member's performance might, even if relating to a minor matter, loom larger when the other staff members with whom he is competing for an assignment have especially strong credentials. Indeed, that the Bank designates certain staff members rather than another, in the course of a reorganization, need not in any way imply that the latter staff member is not qualified for the post or that he has rendered performance that is less than satisfactory; such a situation is in fact to be frequently expected in an organization with personnel standards such as those of the Bank.

19. Applying these considerations to the present case, the Tribunal notes that the Applicant was a division chief at the time of the management-selection round of the 1987 reorganization. Although this imposed upon him the duty to conform his decisions and actions to Bank policy, it is also true that staff members at this level can reasonably be expected frankly to air their differences with their superiors when preparing policy statements. Moreover, the record supports the conclusion that robust mutual criticism was quite characteristic of the working relationships within the Applicant's department, and that the Applicant appears not to have been previously admonished therefor. It is also clear that by the time of the management-selection round, a personal element had crept into the relationship between the Applicant and his director and indeed that the director was candid enough to concede that he might have been partly to blame therefor. (*Bertrand*, Decision No. 81 [1989], paras. 18, 19)

ii. 4. In its interrogatory and document request, the Applicant seeks information relating to 'positions graded at level 26 which were filled during the reorganization selection process by persons who prior to their selection held positions grade at a lower level.' Because the Tribunal considers that any such information might prove to be relevant to the Tribunal's decision on the merits of this case, it concludes that the Respondent should be directed to respond to the interrogatory posed and produce any related documents as requested. (*Fernandes*, Order [1989], para. 4)

iii. 4. In its Interrogatory No. 1, the Applicant requests that the Respondent furnish a list of 'the post-reorganization positions assigned the duties performed by Applicant prior to the reorganization.' The Bank has purported to furnish this information in the pleas and annexes in its Answer. At this time, this appears to be an adequate response to Interrogatory No. 1. The Applicant's request for this preliminary measure is therefore denied.

5. In its Interrogatory No. 2, the Applicant requests that for each position listed by the Respondent in response to Interrogatory 1, it also list the 'pre-reorganization position and grade of the staff member who was selected' for that post-reorganization position. Because the Tribunal considers that this information (but not the names of the staff members) might prove to be relevant to the Tribunal's decision on the merits of this case, it concludes that the Respondent should respond to Interrogatory No. 2.

6. In its Document Request No. 1, the Applicant requests that for each post-reorganization position listed by the Respondent in response to Interrogatory No. 1, the Respondent produce the pertinent 'statements of responsibility and selection criteria' prepared for use in the management-selection process. Because the Tribunal considers that any such documents might prove to be relevant to the Tribunal's decision on the merits of this case, it concludes that the Respondent should produce them. The Respondent in its Answer appears to assert that there are no such documents for it to produce. If the Respondent reasserts that contention in response to the Applicant's Document Request No. 1, then the Respondent should produce any pertinent job description for the specified post-reorganization positions, should identify the pertinent position grade levels, and should identify the stage of the reorganization process when these positions were filled by decision of the Bank's representatives.

7. In its Document Request No. 2, the Applicant requests that for each pre-organization position listed by the Respondent in response to Interrogatory No. 2, the

Respondent produce the 'last written job description for that position.' Because the Tribunal considers that any such documents might prove to be relevant to the Tribunal's decision on the merits of this case, it concludes that the Respondent should produce them. (*Harrison (No. 2)*, Order [1989], paras. 4–7)

iv. 28. The Applicant places great weight on several Principles contained in the *Principles of Staff Employment*. Principle 2.1 (*d*) provides, in pertinent part, that the Bank shall 'provide staff members security in their employment consistent with the terms of their appointments, their satisfactory performance and conduct, and the efficient administration of the [Bank].' Principle 6.1 provides, in pertinent part: 'The basic objectives of the [Bank's] compensation policy shall be to . . . enable the [Bank] to recruit staff of the highest caliber appropriate to job requirements.' The Tribunal concludes that these two Principles do not justify inferring a staff right to priority of assignment over a lower-graded staff member, when in the course of a comprehensive reorganization the Bank, within the range of its allowable discretion, determines that the promotable employee is in fact more qualified to perform the job.

29. Indeed, the emphasis in both of these Principles upon the 'efficient administration' of the Bank and the need to 'recruit staff members of the highest caliber' rather more clearly justified the opposite conclusion: that the Bank acts reasonably when it takes into consideration, in making staff appointments in a reorganized structure, not only the grade of the competing staff members and their minimum capacity to perform a job but also their relative qualifications when weighed one against the other. The 1987 Reorganization contemplated a redirection and restructuring of Bank operations, a reassessment of the content of jobs resulting not only in changes in job requirements but also the merging of certain jobs and the elimination of others, and the selection of staff members on a Bank-wide basis after a comprehensive and fair assessment

of their qualifications. These objectives, and the overall procedures by which the Bank sought to achieve them, have been sustained by the Tribunal in earlier cases. These objectives—and the objectives of the above-quoted Principles—would be unduly frustrated were the Bank disabled from selecting the best qualified staff members for vacancies created by the Reorganization whenever those staff members were at the time serving in lower-graded positions. This would introduce an element of rigidity inconsistent with the very objectives of a comprehensive staff reorganization.

30. The Applicant also invokes Principle 7.1 (*b*) of the *Principles of Staff Employment*. That Principle deals with separation from service that is initiated by the Bank, and provides that such separation 'shall be based on the needs for efficient administration and for upholding the standards of the [Bank]. Staff members separated at the initiative of the [Bank] have the right to be notified in writing of the decision and the reason for it, which shall be based on the following . . . :

> (iii) when the [Bank] determine(s) that a position or positions are no longer necessary, or that the responsibilities of a position have changed so that the staff member is not qualified to fill it, provided that no vacant position in the same type of appointment exists for which the [Bank] determine(s) that the staff member is eligible and has the required qualifications or for which he or she can be retrained in a reasonable period of time.

The Applicant asserts that under this principle he should not have been denied appointment to a level 26 position in which he was actually or potentially qualified to serve and which was awarded to a lower graded staff member. He also claims that the Bank failed to provide him with a specific reason for his non-selection, contrary to the terms of Principle 7.1 (*b*). . . .

34. The Applicant contends that paragraph 5.03 of Staff Rule 5.09, which contemplates the selection of promotable lower-graded staff members in preference to qualified higher-graded staff, is inconsistent with paragraph 1.06 (*c*) of the same Rule and that it must be regarded as superseded thereby. The Tribunal concludes

that there is no inconsistecy between these two paragraphs, and that the Bank in fact complied with both in its treatment of the Applicant in the 1987 Reorganization.

35. The Tribunal first notes that—when viewed in isolation—paragraph 5.03 reflects a reasonable approach to the Reorganization selection process. By providing for consideration of highly qualified lower graded employees who are 'ready for promotion' to higher graded positions in the course of the Reorganization, paragraph 5.03 can be viewed as deriving from the Bank's responsibility to attract, retain and place highly qualified staff members. This responsibility is manifested in the *Principles of Staff Employment* and other pertinent Bank documents and policies.

36. Moreover, the Tribunal concludes that the Respondent complied with paragraph 1.06 (*c*) of Staff Rule 5.09. It will be recalled that that paragraph provides that in the selection process, candidates occupying positions graded at or higher than the level of the position to be filled are to be 'considered' first; it does not provide that such candidates are also to be 'offered' these positions first, in preference to lower-graded promotable staff members. In this case, the Bank did in fact fully consider the Applicant for selection in the managerial-selection rounds, first for one of the four remaining Division Chief positions in the EMENA Region and thereafter for other level 26 positions. It is worth noting that the Appeals Committee, while commenting most favorably upon the Applicant's character and skills, concluded that 'the selection process [for level 26 positions] was carried out in a fair and unbiased manner as it relates to the Appellant' and that 'every effort was made to place him in a suitable level 26 position'.

37. The second sentence of paragraph 1.06 (*c*) quoted above gives priority in the management-selection process to 'Regular and Fixed Term staff' already mployed with the Bank, as compared with persons recruited 'externally'. It appears not at all to deal with the question of priorities as between full-time Bank staff members of different grade levels. By including

'promotable' regular staff members in considering filling level 26 vacancies, and by filling those vacancies with staff members then graded at level 25 or 26 rather than with 'external' recruits, the Bank appears to have fully satisfied its obligations under paragraph 1.06 (*c*) of Staff Rule 5.09.

38. The Applicant contends that denying him selection to a level 26 position for which he was qualified, in order to promote another staff member, is tantamount to discharging a fully qualified staff member from his current position in order to replace him with someone whom the Bank believes to be better qualified. Such a discharge would be improper because lacking any 'cause'—such as unfitness or other fault on the part of the incumbent—and so too, claims the Applicant, should be his displacement from a level 26 position through the promotion of a lower graded staff member.

39. The analogy, however, is not convincing. Once the Applicant's position as Division Chief was eliminated, he had no comparable claim upon other vacancies at the same grade level—any more so than other qualified staff members, each of whom was vying for the vacancy. The Bank, by thus making a comparative judgment about the abilities of the various candidates for the vacancy, cannot be said to be acting in a manner comparable to terminating the service of an incumbent staff member. In the process of selecting for vacancies, it is reasonable for the Bank to employ the criterion of comparative skills and abilities, unlike the case of a termination where a more 'absolute' standard—such as 'cause' for dismissal—is customary and correct. This seems equally to be the case whether the contenders for the vacancy are at the same grade level or whether they include highly qualified 'promotables'. . . .

42. Finally, the Applicant questions whether the Bank satisfied the requirements set forth in paragraph 7.1 (*b*) of the *Principles of Staff Employment* that staff members separated from the Bank have the right to be notified in writing 'of the decision and reason for it.' He claims that, when the Bank wrote to him to inform him

of his non-selection in the managerial-selection round, it did not provide any reasons therefor but simply stated that he had 'not been selected for a position at your grade at this stage in the selection process.' There is something to be said for the Applicant's claim that the Bank's language is more a statement of its decision than it is the provision of a reason for that decision.

43. Nonetheless, in all the circumstances of the Reorganization the Bank's notification can only be read as informing the Applicant that others in the pool of eligible staff members had been regarded as better qualified for selection to level 26 positions in the managerial-selection round. This seems to the Tribunal to constitute a sufficient initial statement of reasons for the non-selection of a staff member within a comprehensive reorganization process. Such selection process necessarily involved the subjective assessment on the part of management of a variety of skills, aptitudes and the like possessed by thousands of staff members vying for positions in the reorganized Bank. Given the nature of the process, the statement given by the Bank to the Applicant may be regarded as an adequate statement of reasons as required under Principle 7.1 (*b*). (*Fernandes*, Decision No. 90 [1990], paras. 28–30, 34–9, 42–3)

v. 26. It is noteworthy that the Appeals Committee also concluded that the Applicant was a 'manager' under the pertinent Staff Rule. It stated: 'Simply put, the Bank accepted that the Appellant met the definition of a manager, and managers who were not selected had the right to select Package B without having to go through the Bank-wide staff selection process . . . The Committee agrees with the Bank that the Appellant meets the definition of a 'manager' . . .' The Respondent has failed to explain why it is taking a position that is contrary to its position taken at those earlier times in the course of the termination of the Applicant's service.

27. It appears that the Respondent simply overlooked the Applicant at the time of the management-selection round. Less apparent is the Bank's reason for having

done so. Its oversight may very well have been the result of the fact that the management-selection round took place in very early June 1987, while the grade level of the Applicant's position was not upgraded from 24 to 25 through administrative review until some seven weeks later. In its pleadings before the Tribunal, the Respondent attempts to attribute the Applicant's non-selection to ambiguities in the pertinent Staff Rule, which the Bank promptly acted to rectify as soon as they were called to its attention. The Tribunal does not believe that the Staff Rule was unclear; but even if it was, the Bank's legal department construed it in the Applicant's favor at the time, and she and her supervisors within the Bank acted in reliance upon this construction at the time of her separation from the Bank. The Respondent offers no explanation why the Tribunal should ignore these compelling facts so long after the event.

28. It is therefore the conclusion of the Tribunal that the Respondent's failure to consider the Applicant in the management-selection round of the Reorganization constituted a non-observance of the Applicant's contract of employment as a staff member, in that it violated the Staff Rules governing the Reorganization. It remains to determine whether the Applicant suffered any compensable injury as a result of this non-observance, and if so what the proper remedy should be.

29. It cannot be concluded with any assurance whether the Applicant would have been assigned to a managerial position had she been timely considered in the Reorganization process. It is, however, rather significant that the three identifiable positions into which her previous position as Data Administrator were distributed were graded at levels 25, 25 and 26, and that the persons assigned to those positions in the Reorganization had previously served in positions graded at levels 24, 26, and 26, respectively. In other words, the Applicant—whose grade level was determined properly to have been 25—was at a grade level similar to those actually retained to do comparable work after the Reorganization. More important, her work was graded

after the Reorganization at levels of 25 and 26, and her previous performance reviews unequivocally demonstrated that she was able to perform such work in a highly satisfactory manner.

30. There is thus every probability that the Applicant would have been given serious consideration for assignment to a comparable position as 'manager' in the Reorganization had she been properly considered by the Bank in the management-selection round. It is appropriate to place the burden on the Respondent to demonstrate otherwise, given the fact that it was the Bank's failure so to consider her that constituted a violation of the Applicant's rights in the case at hand.

31. The Respondent contends, however, that the Applicant's failure to accept a staff position offered her at grade level 24, after she had opted to leave the Bank with Package B, warrants denying her any compensatory remedy. In effect, the Respondent contends that the termination of the Applicant's service with the Bank resulted not from any improper non-selection in the management-selection round but rather from her own decision to remove herself from consideration in the later staff-wide selection rounds and to choose instead separation with Package B.

32. The Tribunal does not share this view. It is true that the Applicant could have chosen to keep herself in consideration for other assignments through the staff-selection process. It appears that there would have been available positions at her then grade level and even managerial positions that had not been filled in the management-selection round. The fact remains, however, that the Bank had improperly and without explanation excluded her from being considered for a suitable managerial position in the management-selection round, and that she was reasonably concerned about her prospects for such a suitable position thereafter, particularly in view of the fact that at the time of the staff-wide selection process her current position was still being graded by the Bank at level 24 and had not yet been upgraded as a result of administrative review.

In choosing Package B under these circumstances, a choice that was indisputably available to her under pertinent Staff Rules, the Applicant ought not fairly to be regarded as eliminating thereby her claim against the Respondent for her earlier non-selection.

33. In determining the relief which the Applicant may properly claim for the non-observance of her contract of employment, the Tribunal is mindful that the Applicant must show that the compensation to which she is entitled for the injury suffered is 'demonstrably in excess' of the contractual increment received by her under Package B when compared with the pay and benefits ordinarily payable under Section 8 of Staff Rule 7.01 upon termination in usual cases of redundancy: *Harrison*, Decision No. 53 [1987], para. 30.

34. The Respondent contends, apparently without challenge by the Applicant, that such increment is approximately $52,632. The Applicant seeks compensation in the amount of three years' net salary, along with costs and attorneys' fees. She claims that by having to seek part-time employment elsewhere since her departure from the Bank, the Applicant has suffered, among other things, from uncertainties as to her future income, loss of pension rights, and the need to provide for her own health and old-age insurance. She also claims that compensation for these additional burdens 'exceeds by far the differential between Package B and what she would have received under Staff Rule 7.01 Section 8.' (*Harrison (No. 2)*, Decision No. 91 [1990] paras. 26–34)

vi. 24. The evidence adduced by the Applicant in support of this contention is no more than circumstantial and consists principally of the fact that the post was newly created, that the job description was precisely tailored to suit his qualifications and that, after he declined it, the post was not offered to anyone else. However, apart from the procedural irregularity that the Tribunal already found (question (I) above), the only real evidence on the point is the statement in a memorandum from Mr. Dyck to the Applicant: 'of course . . . the Region was also cognizant of Senior Management's desire to place as many qualified staff as possible at their level before the end of Round 2'. This observation must be read in its context, as following a sentence describing the objective justification for offering the post to the Applicant: '. . . the Region offered him this position by virtue of his past experience and expertise as a Project Specialist (and his knowledge of technical assistance) including but not limited to the human resources section.'

25. Even if it were true that the Bank was in difficulty in dealing with all the Enhanced Separation payments within the limits of its budget, the Tribunal cannot see that fact as by itself supporting the allegation that, if otherwise correct, an act of the Bank was improperly motivated. Nor is there, in itself, any evident impropriety in the Bank tailoring a position to meet the circumstances of an officer of experience and quality whose services the Bank understandably wished to retain. (*Lindsay*, Decision No. 92 [1990], paras. 24, 25)

vii. 43. The Applicant's complaints refer separately to the procedures followed in Rounds 1 and 2 of the Reorganization. As to Round 1, the Applicant contends that the Bank did not comply with assurances to the effect that support staff, prior to stating their preferences, should be informed of where their most recent colleagues would be working. In particular, he complains that the selection of Section Chief was not communicated to the Staff of S-3 before all the staff had submitted their Round 1 statements of preferences for available positions and that this denied him the opportunity to make an informed choice. This grievance relates to the Applicant's dissatisfaction with the selection of his immediate supervisor—the new Section Chief—and his preference for the former incumbent. But the Tribunal does not find this allegation to be relevant, because no harm was caused to the Applicant by the fact that he learned only on July 28 of the name of the new Section Chief. As the sequence of actions shows, the Applicant had prior cognizance of the name of his new Section Chief and had time to consider that fact before deciding on August 3 to reject the position offered to him. Moreover, the fact that he signed a preference form before learning of the new supervisor had no damaging effect, since he retained the possibility of changing his mind and refusing the offer, as he in fact did.

44. In explaining his reasons for rejecting the offer the Applicant asserted that the new Section Chief 'and I have not seen eye to eye on things over the years, which suggests future conflicts in our relationship'. On the other hand, he recognized that her selection was 'a logical one'. But his disagreements with the new Chief and his preference for the former supervisor are not grounds for making the offer not bona fide or justifying his refusal to continue in his current position. Likewise, it is not a valid ground for justifying the Applicant's refusal or altering the bona fide nature of the offer that he was concerned that 'the doubling of the Region size, as well as changes in its institutional structure and functions, would impose unprecedented operation problems' for which he would be almost solely responsible. Nor is it a valid ground for his concern that, as a consequence, 'his experience and technical skills might be exploited without proper compensation'. These fears and concerns might be justifiable grounds for declining the job offered, but not for claiming additional compensation after having refused to perform the additional tasks. . . .

46. With respect to Round 2 procedures, the Applicant alleges that he was deprived of opportunities to find a suitable position by reason of the failure of the Respondent to furnish him the assistance required by the applicable provisions concerning alternative placements in Round 2, in particular, the alleged failure to communicate vacancies for which he was eligible. The Applicant asserts that he 'was never personally contacted by any member of the Personnel team from August 10 to September 29'. However, the record shows that he had a

meeting with the Chief Personnel Officer for Asia on September 22. Besides, obtaining new placements in the Bank-wide roster for Round 2 did not depend exclusively on the initiative of Personnel Officers. It has to be seen as a two-way effort, in which the staff member was expected to take a leading role. In a Model Memorandum addressed by the Bank to staff members participating in Round 2 they were advised as follows:

> When you identify a position or positions in which you are interested and for which you are qualified or could become qualified with training, you should check with the personnel team for the appropriate vice-presidential unit to verify that they are aware of your interest and potential candidacy.

47. The Applicant deliberately decided to reject his former position in order, in his own words, 'to look for something better in Round 2', believing that 'Round 2 offers the opportunity to market my organizing, analytical and report-writing, as well as my technical and training skills'. However, the record shows that the Applicant did not pursue the search for alternative positions with the required dedication and urgency. He sent off applications for other positions only after the end of August despite having decided to market his technical skills on August 3. For various reasons, some of them legitimate, he was absent from the Bank in the final crucial days in the Round 2 exercise, at the end of September. Taking into account all the circumstances, the Tribunal concludes that the lack of response or interest in selecting the Applicant cannot be attributed to a defective assistance by the Personnel services, nor to the absence of a correct telephone connection. As the Appeals Committee found, this latter fact alone 'should not have prevented the Appellant from looking for other jobs'.

48. In any event, the Applicant was not properly qualified for the vacancy he identified in his reply as the one that should have been communicated to him by Personnel, since he lacked the required secretarial skills. This lack of secretarial skills could not be

remedied by training, because he did not qualify for receiving secretarial training. Staff Rule 5.09 speaks of training only for those without the requisite skills (para. 1.06 *c*). The fact that he was twice offered a position is in itself evidence that he possessed skills for which the Bank had a continuing need and which did not require additional training. (*Pavesich*, Decision No. 94 [1990], paras. 43–4, 46–8]

viii. 49. As the Tribunal observed in *Apkarian*, Decision No. 58 [1988], para 48:

> [I]n the operations of a large and complex enterprise [the Bank] will predictably, on occasion, commit an oversight.

Moreover, it is the Tribunal's view that the Applicant should have discovered this omission and had it immediately rectified, by means of a corrigendum, instead of allowing it to be repeated for two weeks. As the Tribunal has stated in *Pavesich*, Decision No. 94 [1990], para 46:

> obtaining new placements in the Bank-wide roster for Round 2 did not depend exclusively on the initiative of Personnel Officers. It has to be seen as a two-way effort, in which the staff member was expected to take a leading role.

50. The Tribunal is satisfied that the Bank corrected the oversight within a reasonable time, thus curing its negative effect. This claim is dismissed. (*Kassab*, Decision No. 97 [1990], paras. 49, 50)

ix. 30. The Applicant contends that the Respondent failed to observe the terms of his appointment and the conditions of his employment by:

1. Demoting him without cause from the post of a Division Chief at Grade 26 which he occupied prior to the 1987 Reorganization to that of a Principal Economist at Grade 25, thus violating his right to security in employment which he considers to be an essential element of his conditions of employment.
2. Creating an inaccurate and baseless performance evaluation which resulted in his non-selection for a

Division Chief position or for any other grade 26 positions.

31. The essence of the first contention is that paragraph 5.03 of Staff Rule 5.09 should be invalidated because it undermines an essential element of staff member conditions of employment in that it permits 'individual staff members identified by the VPP as ready for promotion to be selected.' The Applicant contends that the Articles of Agreement, the Principles of Staff Employment and the Staff Rules promulgated thereunder, and the past practice of the Bank, all create an obligation on the part of the Bank to secure to each staff member continued employment at his grade level, unless there is some fault on the part of the staff member which renders him unfit for continued service.

32. In *Fernandes*, Decision No. 90 [1990], the Applicant invoked Principle 2.1 (*d*) of the Principles of Staff Employment providing that the Bank shall 'provide staff members security in their employment consistent with the terms of the appointment, their satisfactory performance and conduct, and the efficient administration of the Bank,' and Principle 6.1 providing that 'the basic objectives of the [Bank's] compensation policy shall be to . . . enable the [Bank] to recruit staff of the highest caliber appropriate to job requirements,' which the Applicant also invokes in this case. The Tribunal there concluded:

> . . . these two principles do not justify inferring a staff right to priority of assignment over a lower graded staff member, when in the course of a comprehensive reorganization the Bank, within the range of its allowable discretion, determines that the promotable employee is in fact more qualified to perform the job (para. 28).

33. In application of the decision in *Fernandes* the Tribunal concludes that by eventually selecting a lower grade staff member to occupy positions at the level of the Applicant's previous position, but after first considering the Applicant for those positions, the Respondent had acted within the requirements of all pertinent

Principles and Staff Rules. Para. 1.06 (6) of Staff Rule 5.09 cannot properly be invoked to question the validity of the Applicant's non-selection. Para. 1.06 provides that in the selection process, candidates occupying positions graded at a level higher than that of the position to be filled are to be 'considered' first; it does not provide that such candidates are also to be 'offered' the positions in preference to lower graded promotable staff members. It, therefore, becomes unnecessary to determine whether any such right should properly be regarded as an 'essential element' of the conditions of employment, as claimed by the Applicant.

34. The Tribunal, therefore, concludes that the selection of a lower grade staff member to occupy a position graded at level 26 in preference to the Applicant, and the non-selection of the Applicant to a level 26 position, do not violate his conditions of employment.

35. The second contention of the Applicant goes to the circumstances surrounding his non-selection during the first stage of the Reorganization. He attributed his initial non-selection for a Division Chief position, which eventually resulted in his non-selection for any level 26 position, to the unfounded negative written comment made on the Applicant's PPR by his previous supervisor, the then Vice President, South Asia Region (SAR).

36. The Respondent tries to minimize the impact of that negative comment on the selection for a Division Chief position, by referring to the collegial nature of the selection process, and by insisting that the managerial skills of the Applicant were the subject of doubt on the part of his supervisors during the preceding years. The Respondent also maintains that the Vice President, SAR, informed his successor of his changed conclusion as to the Applicant's management capabilities, and that such correction took place before the Region finalized its list of tentative selection.

37. The Tribunal does not share the Respondent's view of the impact of the negative written comments by the Vice President, SAR, and though corrected

subsequently, such correction was never recorded in writing and made available to those making the selection for Division Chief positions. Those negative comments were made at the very time when the selection process was at its first stage. Moreover, as noted by the Appeals Committee report of January 21, 1989, when decisions about Division Chiefs for the new Asia Region were about to be made (by June 4, 1987), 'Appellant's immediate supervisors who could have given some balance to the Vice President's comments, were not available.' Equally important is the fact that information of the modification of the Vice President, SAR's, initial negative evaluation of the Applicant's capabilities as Division Chief was only made orally to the new Vice President; no written modification on the file occurred until June 9, 1987, several days after the selection process for Division Chief was concluded, by which time much of the damage had been done.

38. The Tribunal concludes that, although the strongly worded negative comments by the previous Vice President may have only been one of several negative aspects in the Applicant's file, and although it is impossible to ascertain that had it not been for that negative comment, the Applicant would have been selected for the post of a Division Chief, the Tribunal infers that the strong negative comment must have had considerable influence in shaping the impression of the selecting individuals as to the Applicant's capabilities and qualifications, and must have contributed to his non-selection at the initial stage of the Reorganization. Moreover, the Respondent did not act reasonably when it failed to record the Vice President, SAR's, modified evaluation of the Applicant in due time and to make it fully and immediately available to all the selecting individuals. The impact of such a negative comment is considerably magnified when it is made at the time when the Applicant's capabilities and qualifications are being measured against the capabilities of other who are equally considered for selection to the same positions. As the

Tribunal said in *Robinson*, Decision No. 78 [1989] 'when the Bank owes a duty to a staff member, it must act reasonably in the circumstances.' . . .

40. The Applicant also claims that once he is not selected for a position at his previous grade level, and is demoted to a lower level position without a fault of his own, he becomes eligible to be permanently grandfathered and to receive on an indefinite basis the compensation and related benefits of his former higher grade. The Applicant argues, in particular, that the effect of his downgrading on his salary is not eliminated by the fact his present salary does not exceed the ceiling of his new grade. He maintains that, because he is much higher in his new grade than in his previous grade, his salary adjustments will be smaller in terms of percentage than they otherwise would be. To substantiate this claim the Applicant cites the Tribunal decision in *Pinto*, Decision No. 56, [1988].

41. The Tribunal does not find the *Pinto* holding to be controlling in the Applicant's case. Under *de Merode*, Decision No. 1 [1981], and *Pinto*, Decision No. 56 [1988] the staff member is entitled to periodic adjustments of his salary. He is not guaranteed a certain percentage of increase in salary. The Tribunal notes, however, that in order to secure some financial remedy both to staff members whose position was downgraded as a result of a job evaluation and to staff members assigned to a lower level position in the Reorganization, as informed by the Respondent, the Executive Directors on August 3, 1989 approved certain salary protection arrangements to be applicable beginning with the 1990 salary review. In consequence, even when a staff member's salary at the end of the grandfathering period is above the range of the grade of his position, he will, nevertheless, be eligible for the minimum increase available to fully satisfactory staff members. His salary will not be frozen in violation of the right to periodic adjustments. (*Klaus Berg (No. 2)*, Decision No. 99, [1990] paras. 30–8, 40–1]

x. 30. As the Tribunal has often stated, a decision by the Bank to select a staff member for a particular position rests within the Bank's discretion, and may be overturned by the Tribunal only when it concludes that this discretion has been abused. 'The Administration's appraisal in that respect is final, unless the decision constitutes an abuse of discretion, being arbitrary, discriminatory, improperly motivated or carried out in violation of a fair and reasonable procedure,' *Suntharalingam*, Decision No. 6 [1981], para. 24. The Tribunal will not set aside a decision of the Bank unless it was 'reached in an arbitrary manner, involving, for example, unfairness, failure to allow the Applicant to state his case, or other departures from established procedures, bias, prejudice, the taking into consideration of irrelevant factors or manifest unreasonableness,' *de Raet*, Decision No. 85 [1989], para. 67. This standard of scrutiny has been applied by the Tribunal in cases arising from the 1987 Reorganization, in which staff members have been displaced from their previous positions on the ground of redundancy as a result of the redefinition of job duties or the reduction in the number of departmental positions.

31. In earlier cases arising from the Reorganization, the Tribunal has been confronted with claims that an applicant was improperly denied selection to a position that the Bank in fact gave to another staff member. This is the first case before the Tribunal in which an applicant claims to be qualified to serve in a post-Reorganization position that was left vacant. In such a case, a finding of redundancy must turn upon a conclusion that the content of the position was so defined as to render its previous occupant no longer qualified to discharge its responsibilities. Unsatisfactory performance by a staff member in his or her position prior to the Reorganization cannot alone furnish a basis for terminating service with the Bank on the ground of redundancy. To do so would be an improper use of the Reorganization procedures in order to avoid the protection otherwise afforded by the Bank's governing

documents—Staff Rule 7.01 in particular—for termination of employment, and would therefore constitute *détournement de pouvoir*, subject to reversal by the Tribunal. . . .

34. The Respondent, on several occasions in its pleadings, insists that 'the responsibilities of Applicant's position were changed as a result of the reorganization,' that 'Applicant was found to be unqualified for the new position,' that 'the skills requirements of [the audit analyst position] were altered, and generally new priorities were adopted,' and that 'changes were made and the requirements for positions were enlarged.' Yet the Respondent fails altogether to go beyond these general assertions to state with any particularity the respects in which the audit analyst position was changed in the course of the Reorganization. It was surely contemplated that in the Reorganization certain positions would be changed in their job content such that, for example, new technical skills (such as in macroeconomics or computers) would henceforth be required. The Bank might well, in such circumstances, reasonably conclude that the present occupant of that position lacked the requisite skills for the position as redefined, and indeed that such skills could not be acquired after a reasonable period of training. Non-selection by virtue of redundancy might then be appropriate even though that position would remain vacant for lack of any other qualified staff member. But the Respondent has failed to provide any specific information that would warrant a conclusion that the audit analyst position was redefined in so substantial a manner . . .

55. The negative views of the Applicant's qualifications held by the most influential participant in the selection process were altogether without support in the Applicant's prior annual evaluation reports, and also fundamentally and clearly failed to reflect the positive views of the three senior auditors who were consulted by the Acting Director and who were fully familiar with the Applicant's work. The Bank's decision that the

Applicant was unfit for a level 20 audit analyst position is found to be lacking in any evidentiary support and is therefore an abuse of discretion. . . .

57. The Applicant, while serving previously in a level 19 position, had been unqualifiedly praised and recommended (even by the person who ultimately became the Acting Director) for a promotion, and three senior auditors had stated in May 1987 that his performance was fully within, and in some respects beyond, what was expected of a level 20 audit analyst. There is thus no rational basis whatever for concluding that the Applicant could not perform at a level 19 position after the Reorganization—even accepting the Respondent's vague assertions that all audit analyst positions had taken on more rigorous qualifications. . . .

59. The Respondent claims that the Selection Committee's decisions not to select the Applicant for a level 19 position, or for further training, were justified by the Applicant's written statement shortly before the selection process that he wished to be selected for a position outside IAD, or indeed that he preferred to leave the Bank altogether with the special financial benefits contained in the Enhanced Separation Package (Package B). There is considerable factual dispute about the Applicant's stated preferences in this regard. Suffice it to say that the formal minutes of the Selection Committee state that the Applicant's 'request not to be selected into IAD was taken into account. However, he did not meet the selection criteria.' It therefore appears that the principal basis, if not the exclusive basis, for the Committee's decision not to select the Applicant was his lack of qualifications rather than his preferences regarding assignment. It is that decision that the Tribunal concludes to have been an abuse of discretion. (*Jassal*, Decision No. 100 [1991], paras. 30, 31, 34, 55, 57, 59)

xi. 31. As the Tribunal has often stated, a decision by the Bank to select a staff member for a particular position rests within the Bank's discretion, and may be overturned by the Tribunal only when it concludes that this discretion has been abused. 'The Administration's appraisal in that respect is final, unless the decision constitutes an abuse of discretion, being arbitrary, discriminatory, improperly motivated or carried out in violation of a fair and reasonable procedure,' *Suntharalingam*, Decision No. 6 [1981], para. 24. The Tribunal will not set aside a decision of the Bank unless it was 'reached in an arbitrary manner, involving, for example, unfairness, failure to allow the Applicant to state his case, or other departures from established procedures, bias, prejudice, the taking into consideration of irrelevant factors or manifest unreasonableness,' *de Raet*, Decision No. 85 [1989], para. 67. This standard of scrutiny has been applied by the Tribunal in cases arising from the 1987 Reorganization, in which staff members have been displaced from their previous positions on the ground of redundancy as a result of the redefinition of job duties or the reduction in the number of departmental positions.

32. In earlier cases arising from the Reorganization, the Tribunal has been confronted with claims that an applicant was improperly denied selection to a position that the Bank in fact gave to another staff member. This case, along with *Jassal*, Decision No. 100 [1991], appear to be the only cases before the Tribunal in which an applicant claims to be qualified to serve in a post-Reorganization position that was left vacant. As the Tribunal stated in *Jassal*, at para. 31:

> In such a case, a finding of redundancy must turn upon a conclusion that the content of the position was so defined as to render its previous occupant no longer qualified to discharge its responsibilities. Unsatisfactory performance by a staff member in his or her position prior to the Reorganization cannot furnish a basis for terminating service with the Bank on the ground of redundancy. To do so would be an improper use of the Reorganization procedures in order to avoid the protections otherwise afforded by the Bank's governing documents—Staff Rule 7.01 in particular—for the termination of employment, and would therefore constitute *détournement de pouvoir*, subject to reversal by the Tribunal. . . .

35. The Respondent in its pleadings insists that 'the responsibilities of Applicant's position were changed as a result of the reorganization,' and that 'the responsibilities of the position she occupied had changed so that Applicant was not qualified to fill it.' Yet the Respondent fails altogether to go beyond these general assertions to state with any particularity the respects in which the audit-analyst position was changed in the course of the Reorganization. It was surely contemplated that in the Reorganization certain positions would be changed in their job content such that, for example, new technical skills (such as in macroeconomics or computers) would henceforth be required. The Bank might well, in such circumstances, reasonably conclude that the present occupant of that position lacked the requisite skills for the position as redefined, and indeed that such skills could not be acquired after a reasonable period of training. Non-selection by virtue of redundancy might then be appropriate even though that position would remain vacant for lack of any other qualified staff member. But the Respondent has failed to provide any specific information that would warrant a conclusion that the audit-analyst position was redefined in so substantial a manner. . . .

38. It is not for the Tribunal, in assessing the validity of the selection or non-selection of a staff member, to undertake its own examination of that staff member's record, or a criterion-by-criterion assessment of his or her qualifications. That is for the Bank to do in the first instance, subject to review by the Tribunal only for abuse of discretion. But the Tribunal is charged with determining whether the Bank's decision was the product of bias, prejudice, arbitrariness, manifest unreasonableness, or unfair or improper procedure. Thus, if the Bank's conclusion regarding the Applicant's qualifications for selection as audit analyst altogether lacks support in factual evidence or reasonable inference, or was the product of an improper procedure, that conclusion must be found to be an abuse of discretion. The Tribunal will now consider whether such is the case here. . . .

44. It is therefore indisputable that whatever shortfall there might have been in the Applicant's performance of the auditing responsibilities of a level 19 audit analyst, they were attributable to the assignments given her by her supervisors in previous years. Moreover, it must be inferred there was inadequate opportunity from the time of her Spring 1987 PPR until the selection round of the Reorganization—no matter how conscientious and motivated the Applicant might have been—for the Bank to provide appropriate assignments, monitoring and counseling so as to permit her to improve her auditing skills. In the judgment of the Tribunal, it was manifestly unreasonable for the Bank to conclude that the Applicant was unfit (as distinguished from being less fit than some other staff member competing for the same job vacancy) for selection into a post-Reorganization audit analyst position that has not been shown by the Bank to be different in any material respect from the position that the Applicant was already holding. If the Applicant's Manager was prepared to concede that any weaknesses in her work as an audit analyst were the result of supervisory decisions rather than of the Applicant's own inadequacies, the same attribution of responsibility may fairly be made with respect to the Applicant's non-selection for any one of the three audit analyst positions left vacant after the Reorganization.

45. It is particularly to be noted that the flaws identified by the Applicant's Manager in the 1986–87 PPR related to excessive time spent on work and to inadequate planning and organizational skills. The fact that he attributed these to her conscientiousness and her prior absence from audit work clearly indicates that he thought that these could be rectified with time and with counseling. The Respondent, however, asserts in its answer that the Selection Committee concluded not only that the Applicant fell short of the requirements of a level 19 audit analyst position but also that 'in light of Applicant's past experience and her limited potential for professional growth, neither retraining nor the offer of a position at a lower level constituted suitable

alternatives.' Putting aside the question whether the record warrants this assertion as to what the reasons of the Selection Committee actually were, the record requires the Tribunal to conclude that the failure of the Committee to offer the Applicant an audit analyst position at level 18, one level below the grade she presently held, and its failure to offer her the opportunity for further training—comparable to that extended to her by her Manager (and, by then, the Acting Director of IAD) only approximately one week before—were manifestly unreasonable. . . .

47. The Tribunal does not find substantiated in the record the Applicant's charge that the Acting Director discriminated against her because of her knowledge of alleged mismanagement on his part and because she was a vocal critic of him within the IAD. But the Tribunal does conclude that it is highly likely that the negative appraisal on the part of the Acting Director was controlling within the Selection Committee, and that neither he nor the Committee gave any weight to the Applicant's amenability to training or to the Bank's own responsibility for retarding the professional development of the Applicant.

48. The Tribunal also finds that the selection process was likely tainted by a serious procedural irregularity. The Respondent asserts in its answer that the Acting Director and the other members of the Selection Committee had before them the Applicant's career file and that the Acting Director supplemented this with highly critical comments that had been previously related to him by the Applicant's supervisor in EDP; these critical comments were later (on November 5, 1997) put into writing by that supervisor. The Tribunal gives no weight to this memorandum. First, it must be noted that the November 5, 1987 memorandum was prepared at the explicit request of the Acting Director, who was the subject of an investigation by an impartial panel appointed slightly more than one week before, in light of charges of mismanagement that had been leveled by staff members against him; its preparation

under these circumstances and long after the selection decisions were made in July 1987 cast grave doubt upon the credibility of its contents. Moreover, the negative comments set forth in the November 1987 memorandum and assertedly communicated orally as well to the Selection Committee some months before are flatly contradictory to the very positive evaluations contemporaneously made by that same supervisor in several previous annual evaluation reports.

49. The Tribunal for the same reason concludes that the Selection Committee ought not to have given weight to such strongly negative evaluations when considering the Applicant for the audit analyst position. There is not the slightest suggestion that these critical views of November 1987 were ever called to the attention of the Applicant or of any other staff member at any time before; indeed, even the Acting Director in the Applicant's 1987 PPR noted the praise given to the Applicant by her previous supervisor.

50. The Tribunal therefore concludes that the non-selection of the Applicant for the level 19 position of audit analyst in IAD, at a time when three such positions were left vacant after the Reorganization, constituted an abuse of discretion. (*Fabara-Nunez*, Decision No. 101 [1991], paras. 31, 32, 35, 38, 44, 45, 47–50)

3. Separation package

[See also Sect. 4, 'Release Agreements', 2.i–iii; Sect. 12, 'Substantive Irregularity', 1.vi; Sect. 16, 'Classification', 17.i; Sect. 17, 'Recruitment', 2.i; Sect. 23, 'Promotion and Demotion', 1.i; Sect. 28, 'Reorganization', 1.ii; Sect. 29, 'Remedies', 1.iii.]

i. 29. On October 31, 1987 the Applicant left the service of the Bank, and in connection with her departure she received the Enhanced Separation Package (Package B) of severance pay and benefits. The Applicant's departure took place one month after the expiration of the two-year grandfathering period. During that month no salary review took place, and consequently the Applicant did not incur any financial loss as a result of the expiration of the limited grandfathering period. On March 18, 1988 the Respondent informed the Tribunal of the Applicant's separation from service, and of its contention that, as a result of these developments, the Applicant was not entitled to any further compensation. Although the Applicant was duly notified, she did not respond to that contention.

30. In light of the above the application has become moot. (*Kaplan*, Decision No. 65 [1988], paras. 29–30)

ii. 37. Although the case was listed as ready for hearing on July 22, 1987, the Respondent on March 18, 1988 informed the Tribunal that the Applicant had left the service of the Bank on November 20, 1987, having received the Enhanced Separation Package (Package B) of severance pay and benefits. It follows that, apart from the relevance of any possible increase in the salaries of staff that might have become effective during the two-month period September 30–November 30, 1987, none of the remedies sought by the Applicant remains relevant. As to that two-month period following September 30, 1987, no salary review took place and consequently the Applicant did not incur any financial loss as a result of the expiration of the limited grandfathering period.

38. A copy of the Respondent's letter of March 18, 1988 was sent to counsel for the Respondent who, being unable to make contact with the Applicant, in a letter dated March 25, 1988, contended, by reference to the Rules of the Tribunal, that the letter should not be made part of the record. The Tribunal rejects this contention, bearing in mind particularly that under Article XIII of the Statute of the Tribunal it is the facts as known to the Tribunal at the date of the judgment that are material to its decision. Since the Tribunal is now aware of the fact that the Applicant has left the Bank's service, there is no point in giving effect to a purely formal objection to the admissibility of the Respondent's letter of March 18, 1988. The Tribunal

has therefore made both the letters of March 18 and 25, 1988 part of the record.

39. In light of the above, the application has become moot. (*Tucker*, Decision No. 68 [1988], paras. 37–9)

iii. 21. The Applicant has requested compensation in the amount of three years salary or more for violation of his rights and for loss of his tenured professorship given up in order to join the Bank. He has also requested that the Tribunal order the payment of reasonable legal fees. Upon his non-selection to a level-26 position in the reorganization, the Applicant chose—as Bank regulations expressly permitted him to do—to leave the Bank with the Enhanced Separation Package (Package B). The Respondent estimates that by doing so, the Applicant received between $30,000 and $63,000 more than he would have received had he separated from the Bank under the usual terms provided in Staff Rule 7.01. The Respondent correctly points out that, under the Tribunal's decision in *Harrison*, Decision No. 53 [1987], this increment must be taken into account in any calculation of damages, such that an applicant must demonstrate that the injury suffered is in excess of that increment.

22. The Tribunal concludes that such a demonstration has been made. The Tribunal considers that, in the calculation of damages, weight should be given to the Applicant's extended service as a consultant to the Bank before he joined the staff full time, a factor that accounted for the Bank's waiver of the Applicant's initial probationary period and his quick rise to a position as division chief. Taking that factor into account, and taking into account the Tribunal's conclusion that the Bank has not demonstrated that the Applicant's non-selection in the management-selection round was consistent with his conditions of employment, and also considering the rule set down in *Harrison*, it is the conclusion of the Tribunal that the Respondent should pay the Applicant damages in the amount of $80,000 net of tax. The Applicant's additional request for attorney's

fees is denied. The Applicant prepared his application without the assistance of counsel, and counsel did not enter the case until the preparation and attempted filing of the reply, which the Tribunal has not accepted because of its untimeliness. (*Bertrand*, Decision No. 81 [1989], paras. 21, 22)

iv. 36. It is the conclusion of the Tribunal that the above-quoted language of Rule 5.09, para. 7.06 is not ambiguous as pertains to this case, and by its terms the Applicant is not eligible for the Enhanced Separation Package. During the reorganization, the Staff Assistant position offered to her in the Latin America Technical Department, Human Resources Division, was graded at level 15. We therefore conclude that under para. 7.06 the Applicant had been 'selected for a position at [her] current or higher grade level.' Having been offered this position, the Applicant was no longer eligible for the Enhanced Separation Package, so that the Respondent's insistence upon standard separation terms did not constitute a violation of the Applicant's contract of employment.

37. The Applicant contends that the above-quoted language from Staff Rule 5.09 is ambiguous, and that it could be construed to require that the Bank should have offered the Applicant a position graded at level 16, on the theory either that that was then her salary level (by virtue of the two-year 'salary grandfathering' after her previous downgrading from level G to level 15) or that most of her service in TAP was in level-16 positions such as Administrative Secretary. The Tribunal considers that neither of these constructions is reasonable or intended.

38. Staff Rule 5.09, para. 7.06 does not contemplate that the Enhanced Separation Package will be awarded absent selection to a position that offers a Salary range equal to or greater than the salary currently being paid to the staff member. The text of the rule makes no reference, express or implied, to salary. It speaks of selection to a position at a current or higher grade level.

The Applicant was in fact offered a level-15 position at a time when she was holding a level-15 position.

39. Equally unconvincing is the contention that para. 7.06 requires, before the Applicant would lose her claim to the Enhanced Separation Package, an offer of a position at a level comparable to the level of positions to which she was currently being temporarily assigned in the TAP program. The Applicant contends (although the Respondent takes issue) that almost all of her service in TAP was in level-16 positions and that therefore the Bank's offer of a Staff Assistant position at level 15 did not comport with para. 7.06. The Tribunal gives the pertinent language its obvious meaning: that 'a position at [the Applicant's] current . . . grade level' means a level-15 position. The principal document establishing the terms of the TAP program—Pers. /11/81, dated June 30, 1981—reinforces this conclusion in its provision to the effect that 'When staff members join the Temporary Assignment Program, they will retain their salary and level.' Level 15 is indisputably the grade level given to the Applicant's position in TAP (as it was the grade of her previous position), and this is evidenced by the unambiguous reference to Level 15 in all of the Applicant's pertinent personnel documents.

40. Even apart from its clear language, para. 7.06 should be read as the Respondent contends lest the current grade level of a staff member working in TAP constantly vacillate, depending upon the temporary work assignment at any given time. It is not likely that the separation rights of staff members were intended to be left in such an unsettled state, one which could just as easily redound to the serious detriment of a staff member (if temporarily working in a lower graded position) as to his or her benefit.

41. Although the Applicant relies upon some colorable supportive language in a document dated February 10, 1986, from the Assistant Director, PMD, to another supervisor in the department, that is too slender a reed upon which to rest the Applicant's claim. First, it is not explained how this memorandum could supersede the

clear language of Pers./11/81. Nor is there any evidence that the memorandum or the personnel manual circular was applied with respect to any other staff member so as to vary the grade level of TAP positions from time to time. Finally, the memorandum of the Assistant Director, PMD continued as follows: 'In future the following provisions apply: a staff member who joins TAP will carry the grade of their [*sic*] previous regular assignment on a personal basis for up to two years and will be given assignments appropriate to their grade to the extent possible.' In other words, staff members in TAP were to have their grade level fixed, with temporary assignments to be made consistently therewith—not, as the Applicant contends, the other way around, with grade level being temporarily determined by work assignments.

42. It is pertinent to note that at the time of the reorganization and the offer to her of a position graded at her then-current 15 level, the Applicant's principal grievance was directed at her downgrading from level G to level 15, a grading decision that was made some two years before and that the Applicant admittedly failed to challenge in a timely way. The core of her case before the Tribunal, in substance, is that her work in TAP and her skills used there warranted a grade higher than level 15—so that the offer of a grade-15 position in September 1987 was effectively a demotion. The Tribunal cannot countenance at this time what is in effect an untimely challenge to the Applicant's grading decision of years before. Her application must be dismissed. (*Montesa*, Decision No. 82 [1989], paras. 36–42)

v. 58. On September 30, 1987 the Applicant was informed of the terms proposed by the Respondent for an agreed separation from the service of the Bank. These terms included special leave through November 30, 1987, the lump sum equivalent of six months net pay, and a release of claims provision. On October 9, 1987 the Applicant maintained his claim to a Standard Separation Package or alternatively to reach an agreement under the terms of an Enhanced Separation Package, on the ground that he had not been offered a position comparable to his former position. He proposed certain amendments to the separation terms concerning educational benefits and medical insurance. The Respondent did not accept these amendments.

59. On November 16, 1987 the Applicant filed an appeal with the Appeals Committee requesting as relief (*a*) Package B or (*b*) Package A or (*c*) the opportunity to negotiate the terms of a separation package 'appropriate to the circumstances of his own case'.

60. The Appeals Committee dismissed the appeal in respect of (*a*) and (*b*) and in respect of (*c*) recommended that the Bank make a more generous offer than those made to the Applicant on September 30, 1987. The Senior Vice President, External Affairs and Administration, indicated that he could not accept the Appeal Committee's recommendation on a more generous offer, since the Applicant had already been offered negotiated terms of separation but chose to resign and retain his right of appeal.

61. The decision of the Respondent to deny the Applicant's request for Package A was, for the reasons given, consistent with the provisions of Staff Rule 5.09.

62. As the Applicant had unsuccessfully applied for Package A and had been offered two positions at his current level, he could not subsequently apply for Package B, and it is, therefore, difficult to see how he can base his claim for compensation on Package B. As he had rejected the terms of the separation agreement he was offered by the Bank on September 30, 1987, he cannot now get the Tribunal to order the Bank to accept amended terms put forward by him. (*Apergis*, Decision No. 83 [1989], paras. 58–62)

vi. 46. On the other hand, the Tribunal notes that the commitment assumed by the Respondent in its letter of November 14, 1988, to the effect that the Applicant 'may apply for suitable openings through the Bank's VIS system and will be given consideration similar to staff on active duty', is in force and will continue to be in force until September 30, 1990. While deliberating on the case, the Tribunal was informed by the Respondent that the Senior Operations Adviser, Latin America and the Caribbean Regional Office, had selected the Applicant for a position as Operations Assistant, Level 20. The Respondent further advised the Tribunal that before the Applicant's reemployment can be finalized the question of appropriate restitution for the benefits received under Package B will need to be settled, The Respondent pointed out that this is its first occasion to determine the extent of the restitution appropriate in a case where an offer of a position is made to a former staff member who had previously accepted a separation package, adding that, while the conclusion will be tailored to the particular circumstances, guidelines have not yet been adopted. The Tribunal takes notice of this development which ensures that the time and effort spent by the Applicant on an education selected by the Staff Training Division with a Bank career in mind, and the money invested by the Respondent in subsidizing that education, would not be completely lost.

47. While the Respondent suggested that the Tribunal may wish to consider deferring consideration of the case until its next session in view of this recent development, the Applicant has expressed the view that there is no reason to postpone consideration of the case. The Tribunal is of the view that to pronounce on this application will define and clarify the obligations between the parties and thus assist them in settling the question of restitution. The present proceedings have enabled the Tribunal to dispel a misinterpretation of the Applicant regarding the meaning of the proviso at the end of the letter of November 14, 1988 where it is stated that in the event of the Applicant being offered and accepting a position in the Bank, her 'entitlement to the enhanced separation benefits under Rule 5.09 would be canceled and appropriate restitution would be made for the benefits received'. This proviso does not signify that the Applicant must work without pay, if she accepts a new

position and, consequently, it does not constitute a penalty, nor a misuse or abuse of power. The Respondent made it clear, in the course of the proceedings that the term 'appropriate restitution' is designed to cover all possible situations where, in the absence of some restitution there would be unjust enrichment, such as resettlement benefits when the occasion for resettlement was obviated by reappointment. (*Sukkar*, Decision No. 84 [1989], paras. 46–7)

vii. 30. The applicant also invokes Principle 7.1 (*b*) of the *Principles of Staff Employment*. That Principle deals with separation from service that is initiated by the Bank, and provides that such separation 'shall be based on the needs for efficient administration and for upholding the standards of the [Bank]. Staff members separated at the initiative of the [Bank] have the right to be notified in writing of the decision and the reason for it, which shall be based on the following . . . :

> (iii) when the [Bank] determine(s) that a position or positions are no longer necessary, or that the responsibilities of a position have changed so that the staff member is not qualified to fill it, provided that no vacant position in the same type of appointment exists for which the [Bank] determine(s) that the staff member is eligible and has the required qualifications or for which he or she can be retrained in a reasonable period of time.

The Applicant asserts that under this principle he should not have been denied appointment to a level 26 position in which he was actually or potentially qualified to serve and which was awarded to a lower graded staff member. He also claims that the Bank failed to provide him with a specific reason for his non-selection, contrary to the terms of Principle 7.1 (*b*).

31. The Respondent, in its pleadings, appears to view the Applicant's invocation of this Principle of Employment as bearing only upon his non-selection for one of the four Division Chief positions that remained in EMENA after the Reorganization. As to that decision by

the Bank, the Applicant was indeed rendered redundant with respect to his previous position; and the Applicant appears not to be challenging that decision. The Applicant invokes that Principle not with regard to his former Division Chief position but rather with regard to all remaining level 26 positions for which he contends he was qualified.

32. The Tribunal concludes that Principle 7.1 (*b*) does not support the Applicant's contention. That Principle deals with the situation in which it is the Bank that initiates a staff member's separation from service. In this case, however, it was the Applicant who initiated his separation from the Bank, by opting to leave with the Enhanced Separation Package at a time when he could have attempted to remain in the Bank's employ. Although the Applicant claims that, had he remained in consideration for the staff-at-large selection rounds, he would have forfeited his right to Package B and that he was therefore effectively forced to separate from the Bank after his unsuccessful managerial-selection round, this claim is unfounded. Under Staff Rule 5.09, staff members who remained in the staff-at-large selection rounds but who were not selected to a position were entitled to Package B upon leaving the Bank. (*Fernandes*, Decision No. 90 [1990], paras. 30–2)

viii. 23. The Applicant questions the motivation of the Respondent in offering him the position of PTCO, contending that it 'reflected the Respondent's hope of avoiding its obligation to offer the Applicant separation under the terms of the Enhanced Separation Package, as a result of constraints on available resources for such purpose.'

24. The evidence adduced by the Applicant in support of this contention is no more than circumstantial and consists principally of the fact that the post was newly created, that the job description was precisely tailored to suit his qualifications and that, after he declined it, the post was not offered to anyone else. However, apart from the procedural irregularity that the Tribunal already

found (question (I) above), the only real evidence on the point is the statement in a memorandum from Mr. Dyck to the Applicant: 'of course . . . the Region was also cognizant of Senior Management's desire to place as many qualified staff as possible at their level before the end of Round 2'. This observation must be read in its context, as following a sentence describing the objective justification for offering the post to the Applicant: '. . . the Region offered him this position by virtue of his past experience and expertise as a Project Specialist (and his knowledge of technical assistance) including but not limited to the human resources section.'

25. Even if it were true that the Bank was in difficulty in dealing with all the Enhanced Separation payments within the limits of its budget, the Tribunal cannot see that fact as by itself supporting the allegation that, if otherwise correct, an act of the Bank was improperly motivated. Nor is there, in itself, any evident impropriety in the Bank tailoring a position to meet the circumstances of an officer of experience and quality whose services the Bank understandably wished to retain. . . .

33. Lastly, the Applicant makes an issue of the manner in which his Separation Agreement was concluded, saying that he was tendered a memorandum the contents of which he was not permitted to negotiate and that he had no viable choice but to accept its terms. However, provided that the consensual will is present (as it was here), an agreement is no less an agreement because it follows a form established and even insisted on by one of the parties. The adverb 'mutually' that qualifies the verb 'agreed', and to which the Applicant appears to attach importance, really adds nothing to the verb. Every agreement is 'mutually' agreed. A non-mutually agreed agreement is a juridical impossibility. The Applicant does not, it may be noted, argue that he was subject to any duress in the conclusion of the separation agreement; any such argument could not, on the facts of this case, have been supported. (*Lindsay*, Decision No. 92 [1990], paras. 23–5, 33)

ix. 50. Yet, the next day, September 25, the Applicant received from his supervisor, the Section Chief, the offer to retain his prior position at grade 15. The Applicant complains that the offer was communicated to him by the Section Chief and not personally by the Chief Administrative Officer. This is not a valid reason for not having answered. On September 29 the Chief Personnel Officer for the Asia Section called the Applicant by telephone at his home to urge him to accept the position which had been offered to him a second time. The Applicant was advised that in order to avoid being without a job, he should accept that offer even if he chose later to apply for other positions through the Vacancy Listing Service. His answer was to ask about separation benefits, and he was advised that at that time no provision had been made for severance payments to staff members who had been offered but had not accepted a position at their level.

51. Despite not being required by Rule 7.01, the Bank subsequently decided to offer six months compensation to staff in the Applicant's situation. Those were the conditions offered to the Applicant by close of business on September 30 and he accepted the offer, signing the Separation Agreement in October 1987. There was no duress in that mutual separation agreement, because the situation in which the Applicant found himself was of his own choosing. (*Pavesich*, Decision No. 94 [1990], paras. 50–1)

4. Erroneous conclusions

[See Sect. 28, 'Reorganization', 2.x.]

5. Grandfathering

[See also Sect. 29, 'Remedies', 1.vii.]

i. 40. The Applicant also claims that once he is not selected for a position at his previous grade level, and is demoted to a lower level position without a fault of his own, he becomes eligible to be permanently grandfathered and to receive on an indefinite basis the compensation and related benefits of his former higher grade. The Applicant argues, in particular, that the effect of his downgrading on his salary is not eliminated by the fact that his present salary does not exceed the ceiling of his new grade. He maintains that, because he is much higher in his new grade than in his previous grade, his salary adjustments will be smaller in terms of percentage than they otherwise would be. To substantiate this claim the Applicant cites the Tribunal decision in *Pinto*, Decision No. 56 [1988].

41. The Tribunal does not find the *Pinto* holding to be controlling in the Applicant's case. Under *de Merode*, Decision No. 1 [1981], and *Pinto*, Decision No. 56 [1988], the staff member is entitled to periodic adjustments of his salary. He is not guaranteed a certain percentage of increase in salary. The Tribunal notes, moreover, that in order to secure some financial remedy both to staff members whose position was downgraded as a result of a job evaluation and to staff members assigned to a lower level position in the Reorganization, as informed by the Respondent, the Executive Directors on August 3, 1989 approved certain salary protection arrangements to be applicable beginning with the 1990 salary review. In consequence, even when a staff member's salary at the end of the grandfathering period is above the range of the grade of his position, he will, nevertheless, be eligible for the minimum increase available to fully satisfactory staff members. His salary will not be frozen in violation of the right to periodic adjustments. (*Klaus Berg (No. 2)*, Decision No. 99 [1990], paras. 40, 41)

29. REMEDIES

1. Compensation

[See also Sect. 4, 'Release Agreements', 2.i, iii; Sect. 16, 'Classification', 16.i and ii; Sect. 18, 'Benefits', 1.i; Sect. 25, 'Salary', 2.i, 4.iii; Sect. 28, 'Reorganization', 2.v, 3.i–iii, vi; Sect. 29, 'Remedies', 3.ii and iii, 4.i and ii.]

i. *Decision*:

For the above reasons the Tribunal unanimously decides that:

1. the Respondent shall pay the Applicant a sum equivalent to two months net base salary; . . . (*Alan Berg*, Decision No. 73 [1988], Decision (1))

ii. *Decision*:

2. the Respondent shall pay to the Applicant an amount equivalent to four months net salary; . . . (*Rae*, Decision No. 74 [1988], Decision (2))

iii. 74. The question of the effect of the adverse APR for 1985–86 and of the determination of redundancy upon the Applicant's prospects in the Reorganization involves a degree of speculation into which it is inappropriate for the Tribunal to enter. Even if managers of other divisions were aware of the emerging 1985–86 APR and of the redundancy notice, it does not follow that their rejections of the Applicant's requests were determined by that knowledge. The same goes for the allegation of bias that plays so prominent a role in the Applicant's case. The allegation rests at best on coincidence. There is no direct or circumstantial evidence to support it.

75. The injury done to the Applicant by the wrongful determination of redundancy has in all the circumstances been sufficiently compensated by the increment in separation benefits that the Applicant received under

Package B. (*de Raet*, Decision No. 85 [1989], paras. 74–5)

iv. 31. The Respondent contends, however, that the Applicant's failure to accept a staff position offered her at grade level 24, after she had opted to leave the Bank with Package B, warrants denying her any compensatory remedy. In effect, the Respondent contends that the termination of the Applicant's service with the Bank resulted not from any improper non-selection in the management-selection round but rather from her own decision to remove herself from consideration in the later staff-wide selection rounds and to choose instead separation with Package B. . . .

33. In determining the relief which the Applicant may properly claim for the non-observance of her contract of employment, the Tribunal is mindful that the Applicant must show that the compensation to which she is entitled for the injury suffered is 'demonstrably in excess' of the contractual increment received by her under Package B when compared with the pay and benefits ordinarily payable under Section 8 of Staff Rule 7.01 upon termination in usual cases of redundancy: *Harrison*, Decision No. 53 [1987], para. 30.

34. The Respondent contends, apparently without challenge by the Applicant, that such increment is approximately $52,632. The Applicant seeks compensation in the amount of three years' net salary, along with costs and attorneys' fees. She claims that by having to seek part-time employment elsewhere since her departure from the Bank, the Applicant has suffered, among other things, from uncertainties as to her future income, loss of pension rights, and the need to provide for her own health and old-age insurance. She also claims that compensation for these additional burdens 'exceeds by far the differential between Package B and what she would have received under Staff Rule 7.01 Section 8.'

35. The Tribunal is convinced that the injuries sustained by the Applicant as a result of the Respondent's failure to consider her in the management-

selection round are tangible and substantial, and that they exceed the 'Package B increment'. Accordingly, it orders that the Respondent pay to the Applicant seven months' net salary as compensation and $6,000 in costs.

Decision:

The Tribunal unanimously decides that:

(i) the Applicant be paid seven months' net salary as compensation; . . . (*Harrison (No. 2)*, Decision No. 91 [1990], paras. 31, 33–5, Decision (i))

v. *Decision:*

For the above reasons, the Tribunal unanimously decides that:

(i) the Respondent shall pay the Applicant compensation equal to three months' net salary; . . . (*Lindsay*, Decision No. 92 [1990], Decision (i))

vi. 32. The present proceedings have been brought with a view to securing a determination that the Bank's original decision, communicated to the Applicant on July 1, 1986, not to reemploy her was wrong and entitles her to compensation. The other relief sought by the Applicant in the proceedings before the Appeals Committee was, in effect, given by the Bank when, on March 12, 1990 the Bank reemployed the Applicant as a regular employee. . . .

44. The Applicant also seeks compensation under three heads: (*a*) $7,000 said to represent three and a half months' vacation pay to which she would have been entitled if she had been hired as permanent staff in July 1986; (*b*) attorney's fees in the amount of $2,000; and (*c*) $20,000 for emotional and mental distress that she has suffered as a result of the Bank's action. The Tribunal notes that the Applicant has made no reference to the fact that at the time of her illness the Bank gave her an additional 62 days of sick leave which the Bank ultimately wrote off. While the amount thus waived by the Bank was not large, it was, at the same time, not negligible. Taking into consideration all the circum-

stances of the case, the Tribunal will order the payment to the Applicant of compensation equitably assessed at $6,000. . . .

Decision:

(i) the Respondent shall pay to the Applicant the amount of $6,000 net of tax; . . . (*Arellano*, Decision No. 98 [1990], paras. 32, 44, Decision (i))

vii. 39. Since in the circumstances rescission of the decisions contested or specific performance of the obligation invoked is not a remedy appropriate to the injury done, the Tribunal will order the payment to the Applicant of compensation which it equitably assesses at ten months net salary.

40. The Applicant also claims that once he is not selected for a position at his previous grade level, and is demoted to a lower level position without a fault of his own, he becomes eligible to be permanently grandfathered and to receive on an indefinite basis the compensation and related benefits of his former higher grade. The Applicant argues, in particular, that the effect of his downgrading on his salary is not eliminated by the fact that his present salary does not exceed the ceiling of his new grade. He maintains that, because he is much higher in his new grade than in his previous grade, his salary adjustments will be smaller in terms of percentage than they otherwise would be. To substantiate this claim the Applicant cites the Tribunal decision in *Pinto*, Decision No. 56 [1988]. . . .

Decision:

For the above reasons the Tribunal unanimously decides that:

(i) the Respondent shall pay to the Applicant an amount equivalent to ten months net base salary; . . . (*Klaus Berg (No. 2)*, Decision No. 99 [1990], paras, 39, 40, Decision (i))

viii. 62. Fully to achieve this objective, it is also necessary to compensate the Applicant for any injury suffered by him from the date of his improper non-selection and his separation from the Bank until the date of his reinstatement. Because, upon his separation from the Bank in late 1987 the Applicant was paid cash benefits under the Enhanced Separation Package (Package B), which the record indicates to have been the equivalent of approximately three years' salary, the Respondent is correct in asserting that this amount should be credited toward any monetary award due the Applicant for this interim period.

63. One component of such an award is the amount of earnings that the Applicant would have received from his employment with the Bank had it continued throughout this interim period. Another component is an amount to compensate the Applicant for the intangible injury resulting from the Bank's wrongful decision and the aggravating circumstances in which that decision was taken. The Tribunal concludes that these two components taken together approximate the cash payments already made to the Applicant under the Enhanced Separation Package. The Tribunal also notes that it would be unfair to require that the Applicant, as a condition of his return to Bank employment, pay back a substantial amount of money that he has received, and on which he has had to sustain himself, over a period of years since his separation.

64. Should the President of the Bank decide under Article XII (i) of the Statute of the Tribunal, that the Applicant should be compensated without further action being taken in the case, the Tribunal decides that the Applicant should be awarded compensation beyond that which has been noted in the preceding paragraph and already paid to the Applicant under Package B. The Tribunal sets this compensation, which should embrace his lost future earnings from Bank employment, in an amount equal to two years' net salary as of the date of the Applicant's separation from the Bank.

Decision:
For the above reasons, the Tribunal unanimously decides that:

(i) the decision not to select the Applicant for the position of audit analyst at level 20 be rescinded; the Respondent reinstate the Applicant to that (or an equivalent) position; and the amounts already paid by the Respondent to the Applicant upon his separation from the Bank under the Enhanced Separation Package may be retained by the Applicant as compensation for the injuries sustained by him by virtue of the non-selection decision;

(ii) should the President of the Respondent, within thirty days of the notification of the judgment, decide in the interest of the Respondent that the Applicant be compensated without further action being taken in the case, then the Respondent pay the Applicant (in addition to the payment ordered under paragraph (i) of this decision) a sum equal to two years' net salary; . . . (*Jassal*, Decision No. 100 [1991], paras. 62–4, Decision (i), (ii))

[For a similar statement see *Fabara-Núñez*, Decision No. 101 [1991], paras. 52–4, Decision (i), (ii).]

2. Rescission/specific performance

[See also Sect. 10, '*Détournement de Pourvoir*', 1.i; Sect. 13, 'Procedural Irregularity', 6.i; Sect. 14, 'Performance', 1.ii; Sect. 16, 'Classification', 8.i, 14.i; Sect. 17, 'Recruitment', 1.i; Sect. 29, 'Remedies', 1.v–viii, 7.i.]

i. *Decision:*
For the above reasons the Tribunal unanimously decides that the decision of the Vice President, PA, of September 18, 1987 is rescinded so far as it does not provide for the payment to the Applicant, as from September 30, 1987 of the periodic salary review increases approved by the

Respondent for staff members in grade 16. (*Gavidia*, Decision No. 66 [1988], Decision)

ii. 41. For these reasons, the Tribunal concludes that the treatment of the Applicant fell short of the required standards and this has effectively caused him harm. However, the decision adopted by the Respondent in 1985 assigning grade 26 to the position occupied by the Applicant is not disputed. Moreover, the Tribunal considers the suppression of personal grades to be one of the legitimate purposes of the Job Grading exercise. Consequently, rescission of that 1985 decision is not a remedy appropriate to the intangible injury done. In these circumstances the Tribunal will order the payment to the Applicant of compensation which it equitably assesses at two months net base salary.

Decision:

2. . . . the decision of the Vice President, PA, of May 11, 1987 is rescinded so far as it does not provide for the payment to the Applicant, as from September 30, 1987, of the periodic salary review increases approved by the Respondent for staff members in grade 27; . . . (*Alan Berg*, Decision No. 73 [1988], para. 41, Decision (2))

iii. *Decision:*

For the above reasons the Tribunal unanimously decides that:

1. the decision of the Respondent, dated March 23, 1987, confirming the grading of the Applicant's position at level 17 is quashed and the case is remanded to the Respondent for reconsideration according to prescribed rules and proper procedures; . . . (*Rae*, Decision No. 74 [1988], Decision (1))

iv. 34. The Tribunal has determined in paragraph 22 above that the Respondent did not follow the procedure prescribed in Staff Rule 5.09, Section 8, for the grading of the new position, but has rejected the other grounds of the Applicant's complaint. The first determination does not necessarily lead to a finding that the decision reached by the Respondent after failing to follow the prescribed procedure is a nullity. As the Tribunal recalled in its decision in *Broemser* (Decision No. 27 [1985], para. 40):

> There have been a number of cases in which the Tribunal, though finding that there has been a procedural irregularity in the Bank's treatment of a staff member, has concluded that the rescission of the decision contested or specific performance of the obligation invoked was not a remedy appropriate to the injury done . . . Instead, the Tribunal has ordered the payment to the staff member of compensation for the intangible injury thus suffered.

(*Lindsay*, Decision No. 92 [1990], para. 34)

v. 43. The Applicant seeks rescission of the original decision of the Bank not to employ her in a permanent position. Such rescission is unnecessary because she has already been given a permanent position. (*Arellano*, Decision No. 98 [1990], para. 43)

vi. 39. Since in the circumstances rescission of the decisions contested or specific performance of the obligation invoked is not a remedy appropriate to the injury done, the Tribunal will order the payment to the Applicant of compensation which it equitably assesses at ten months net salary. (*Klaus Berg (No. 2)*, Decision No. 99 [1990], para. 39)

3. Material injury

[See also Sect. 13, 'Procedural Irregularity', 1.ii; Sect. 16, 'Classification', 13.iii; Sect. 28, 'Reorganization', 3.iii; Sect. 29, 'Remedies', 1.ii, iv, vi, and viii.]

i. 52. In the light of the above the Tribunal concludes that the Respondent's decision to grade the Applicant's position at level 17 and to reject the recommendation of the JGAB was taken as a result of a series of measures carried out in violation of fair and reasonable procedures. As a result of these measures the Applicant was deprived of her right effectively to participate in the grading exercise and to be notified in good time of the measures, communications and decisions taken affecting different aspects of her employment with the Respondent. Consequently, in these circumstances the decision should be quashed and remanded to the Respondent, and compensation should be granted to the Applicant for the tangible injury suffered by the Applicant as a result of the irregular procedure followed in determining the grade of her position. (*Rae*, Decision No. 74 [1988], para. 52)

ii. 48. It is, however, possible to measure the financial injury caused by the unexpected taxation of a substantial proportion of the Applicant's commuted pension payments in November and December 1986. The Applicant estimates her 'commutation tax loss' as in excess of $15,000, the amount paid by her in 1986 taxes. But this neglects to take into account that even under the revised tax law, there is to be no tax upon pension payments equal to her earlier pension contributions, and that the only difference is in the timing of the exclusion from tax. Under the previous law, the exclusion would have been total in late 1986 and later pension payments would have been fully taxable to the Applicant as income, whereas under the revised law, the exclusion will continue with respect to a portion of the Applicant's pension receipts throughout the remainder of her life. This tax exclusion in 1987 and in later years has not been reflected in the Applicant's claims for 'commutation tax loss'. Taking that exclusion into account, the Respondent calculates that the actual financial injury incurred by the Applicant is approximately $4,700. The Tribunal endorses the approach taken by the Respondent to the calculation of the commutation tax loss, but the pleadings presently before it do not permit of a full and accurate calculation of the precise amount of that loss. This amount should also take into account the payment of interest beginning with the date on which the Applicant made the tax payments in question. The Tribunal is confident that such details can be determined by the parties to this proceeding, and relegates the question to them, subject to recourse to the Tribunal in the unlikely event that such will be necessary to resolve the matter.

Decision:
For these reasons, the Tribunal unanimously decides:

(i) that the Respondent shall pay the Applicant a sum equal to the difference between the Applicant's federal and state tax liability on her pension receipts as calculated according to the cost-recovery and exclusion-ratio methods, with interest; . . . (*Robinson*, Decision No. 78 [1989], para. 48, Decision (i))

iii. 28. It is therefore the conclusion of the Tribunal that the Respondent's failure to consider the Applicant in the management-selection round of the Reorganization constituted a non-observance of the Applicant's contract of employment as a staff member, in that it violated the Staff Rules governing the Reorganization. It remains to determine whether the Applicant suffered any compensable injury as a result of this non-observance, and if so what the proper remedy should be. . . .

33. In determining the relief which the Applicant may properly claim for the non-observance of her contract of employment, the Tribunal is mindful that the Applicant must show that the compensation to which she is entitled for the injury suffered is 'demonstrably in excess' of the contractual increment received by her under Package B when compared with the pay and benefits ordinarily payable under Section 8 of Staff Rule 7.01 upon termination in usual cases of redundancy: *Harrison*, Decision No. 53 [1987], para. 30. . . .

35. The Tribunal is convinced that the injuries sustained by the Applicant as a result of the Respondent's failure to consider her in the management-selection

round are tangible and substantial, and that they exceed the 'Package B increment'. Accordingly, it orders that the Respondent pay to the Applicant seven months' net salary as compensation and $6,000 in costs. . . . (*Harrison (No. 2)*, Decision No. 91 [1990], paras. 28, 33, 35)

4. Moral injury

[See also Sect. 13, 'Procedural Irregularity', 1.ii and iv; Sect. 16, 'Classification', 13.iii; Sect. 29, 'Remedies', 1.ii, iv, and v, 2.ii.]

i. 52. In the light of the above the Tribunal concludes that the Respondent's decision to grade the Applicant's position at level 17 and to reject the recommendation of the JGAB was taken as a result of a series of measures carried out in violation of fair and reasonable procedures. As a result of these measures the Applicant was deprived of her right effectively to participate in the grading exercise and to be notified in good time of the measures, communications and decisions taken affecting different aspects of her employment with the Respondent. Consequently, in these circumstances the decision should be quashed and remanded to the Respondent, and compensation should be granted to the Applicant for the tangible and intangible injury suffered by the Applicant as a result of the irregular procedure followed in determining the grade of her position. (*Rae*, Decision No. 74 [1988], para. 52)

ii. 36. In these circumstances the Tribunal considers it appropriate to award compensation in respect of the intangible injury suffered by the Applicant from the non-observance by the Respondent of the procedure for grading laid down in Staff Rule 5.09, Section 8.

Decision:
For the above reasons, the Tribunal unanimously decides that:

(i) the Respondent shall pay the Applicant compensation equal to three months' net salary; . . .

(*Lindsay*, Decision No. 92 [1990], para. 36, Decision (i))

5. Restitution

[See Sect. 28, 'Reorganization', 3.v; Sect. 30, 'Procedure before Tribunal', 11.i; Sect. 32, 'Miscellaneous', 5.i.]

6. Reinstatement

[See also Sect. 12, 'Substantive Irregularity', 1.xii; Sect. 28, 'Reorganization', 2.x.]

i. 61. Because the Tribunal has concluded that the non-selection of the Applicant for the level 20 position of audit analyst in IAD constituted an abuse of discretion, and because the record indicates that three audit analyst positions were left vacant at the conclusion of the Reorganization, the appropriate remedy is to order the Respondent to reinstate the Applicant to such a position. Such an order would help to place the Applicant in the position he would be in, had the Respondent not violated his contract of employment. . . .

Decision:
For the above reasons, the Tribunal unanimously decides that:

(i) the decision not to select the Applicant for the position of audit analyst at level 20 be rescinded; the Respondent reinstate the Applicant to that (or an equivalent) position; and the amounts already paid by the Respondent to the Applicant upon his separation from the Bank under the Enhanced Separation Package may be retained by the Applicant as compensation for the injuries sustained by him by virtue of the non-selection decision; . . . (*Jassal*, Decision No. 100 [1991], para. 61, Decision (i))

[For a similar Statement see *Fabara-Nunez*, Decision No. 101 [1991], para. 50, Decision (i).]

7. Removal from file

i. *Decision:*

For the above reasons the Tribunal unanimously decides that:

(i) the undated manuscript memorandum referred to in paragraph 64 above and the redundancy notice given to the Applicant on January 7, 1986 shall be removed from the Applicant's personnel file; . . . (*de Raet*, Decision No. 85 [1989], Decision (i))

8. Remand

[See also Sect. 6, 'Administrative Review', 1.iii; Sect. 8, 'Sources of Law', 1 (*b*) i; Sect. 13, 'Procedural Irregularity', 5.iii; Sect. 16, 'Classification', 15.i; Sect. 25, 'Salary', 2.i; Sect. 29, 'Remedies', 2.iii.]

i. 27. It is not certain, however, that even had the Bank awarded Hay points to the Applicant's position for the required bilingual skills, this would have resulted in an increase in the grade level of that position. Therefore, the Tribunal quashes the decision to assign the Applicant's position to level 15 and remands the case to the Respondent so that a new decision on the grade of the Applicant's position may be taken. . . .

29. The Applicant's main contention is that his salary review increases after the effective date of the job regrading should not be limited by the two-year grandfathering requirement. The paragraph of Staff Rule 5.06 which provides for this reads:

> A staff member whose position is graded at a lower level as a result of a formal job evaluation assumes the lower grade upon the effective date of the evaluation. However, for a period of 24 months thereafter, he will be eligible for increases as if the salary range formerly applicable to the position, adjusted for any increases in the salary structure, had remained in effect. . . . If after 24 months the staff member has not been selected for a position at his previous or a higher level, future increases in his salary will be administered within the range of his new grade. If

at this time the staff member's salary exceeds the maximum of the salary range of the position occupied, the salary will remain unchanged until the maximum of the range exceeds that amount.

In his reply, the Applicant invokes, in support of his claim, para. 5 (1) f of the Principles of Staff Employment, which states that the Respondent shall

> establish procedures and conditions under which staff members may be assigned to positions graded at various levels, while providing reasonable measures to alleviate adverse effects on staff members assigned to positions graded or regraded at a lower level.

The Applicant contends, on the basis of the above Principle, that he should be grandfathered in his previous salary level. He also contends that by freezing his salary the Bank would deny him a 'fundamental element in Applicant's conditions of employment which the Bank does not have the right to change unilaterally,' namely, the right as embodied in *de Merode* (Decision No. 1 [1981], para. 112) to benefit from 'periodic adjustments reflecting changes in the cost of living and other factors.'

30. In *de Merode* (Decision No. 1 [1981], paras. 111 and 112) the Tribunal found 'that a consistent practice of periodic adjustment has been established, and that the Bank makes these adjustments out of the conviction that it is legally obliged to do so'. The Tribunal concluded:

> [I]n consequence . . . the Bank is obliged to carry out periodic reviews of salaries, taking into account various relevant factors. . . . [T]he established practice, and statements confirming that practice, have created a legal obligation to make periodic adjustments reflecting changes in the cost of living and other factors. In the opinion of the Tribunal such an obligation is a fundamental element in the Applicant's conditions of employment which the Bank does not have the right to change unilaterally.

In *Pinto* (Decision No. 56 [1988], para. 40), where the same contention was raised as has been raised in this case, the Tribunal held:

The Tribunal concludes that the freezing of the Applicant's salary, from September 30, 1987, would deprive her, without justifiable cause, of the right to benefit from periodic adjustments reflecting changes in the cost of living and other factors, which the Tribunal has found to be a fundamental element in the Applicant's conditions of employment which the Bank does not have the right to change unilaterally. This is not to suggest that a staff member may under no circumstances have his or her grade reduced or salary frozen, for example, when this is done for cause as for disciplinary action. In the present case, however, the downgrading of the Applicant and her position was done not because of her misconduct but because of the organizational needs of the Bank; in such circumstance, the staff member is reasonably entitled to more equitable treatment, as appears to be contemplated by Staff Principle 5 (1) f.

The Tribunal will apply the same ruling in this case and decides that the Applicant should, as from September 30, 1987, receive the periodic salary review increases approved by the Respondent for staff members in grade 16, the grade in which he was before his position was regraded.

Decision:

(i) the decision of the Respondent of November 24, 1986 insofar as it assigns a grade level 15 to the Applicant's position be quashed and remanded to the Respondent so that a new decision may be taken; and

(ii) in the event that after the remand the Applicant's position is graded at level 15, the Respondent provide for the payment to the Applicant, as from September 30, 1987 of the periodic salary review increases approved by the Respondent for staff members in grade 16. (*Chakra*, Decision No. 70 [1988], paras. 27, 29–30, Decision (i), (ii))

For similar statements see *Cardenas*, Decision No. 71 [1988], paras. 28, 30–1, Decision (i) and (ii).]

ii. 42. The Applicant also contends that she did not receive a fair trial before the Appeals Committee. For this reason she requests the Tribunal to order that the case be remanded to the Bank's administration in accordance with Article XII (2) of the Statute of the Tribunal. In support of that request the Applicant refers to what she considers to be three procedural defects: (*a*) that she did not get adequate expert assistance before and during the hearing; (*b*) that the hearing panel was weighted in favor of Management; and (*c*) that the Respondent made certain unfair and prejudicial attacks against her motives in acquiring U.S. citizenship and in eventually considering renouncing it. The Tribunal cannot find any ground for these contentions. The principles contained in Staff Rule 9.03 on the Appeals Committee have been respected by the Respondent and none of the Applicant's procedural guarantees under this rule or the general principles of law has been violated. (*Wahie*, Decision No. 93 [1990], para. 42)

iii. *Decision:*
For these reasons the Tribunal unanimously decides that the case is remanded to the Respondent for pursuit of the internal procedure validly initiated by the Applicant's request for administrative review. (*Ramorasoavina*, Decision No. 95 [1990], Decision)

9. Nullity of decision

[See Sect. 12, 'Substantive Irregularity', 1.viii.]

i. 34. The Tribunal has determined in paragraph 22 above that the Respondent did not follow the procedure prescribed in Staff Rule 5.09, Section 8, for the grading of the new position, but has rejected the other grounds of the Applicant's complaint. The first determination does not necessarily lead to a finding that the decision reached by the Respondent after failing to follow the prescribed procedure is a nullity. As the Tribunal recalled in its decision in *Broemser* (Decision No. 27 [1985], para. 40):

> There have been a number of cases in which the Tribunal, though finding that there has been a procedural irregularity in the Bank's

treatment of a staff member, has concluded that the rescission of the decision contested or specific performance of the obligation invoked was not a remedy appropriate to the injury done . . . Instead, the Tribunal has ordered the payment to the staff member of compensation for the intangible injury thus suffered. (*Lindsay*, Decision No. 92 [1990], para. 34)

10. Costs

[See also Sect. 5, 'Review of Judgments', 1.i.; Sect. 8, 'Sources of Law', 5 (*b*) ii; Sect. 28, 'Reorganization', 3.i; Sect. 29, 'Remedies', 1.iv and vi, 2.ii.]

i. 45. While the Applicant has made a request for costs he has not submitted to the Tribunal an itemized statement of costs at the conclusion of the proceedings. In these circumstances the Tribunal decides to award the Applicant costs in the amount of $1,000. . . .

Decision:

3. the Respondent shall pay the Applicant costs in the amount of $1,000; . . . (*Alan Berg*, Decision No. 73 [1988], para. 45, Decision (3))

ii. 32. When the Tribunal decided to dismiss the applications in Decisions 41–54, it also decided to dismiss by implication all the pleas contained in each application, including the claims for costs. If the Tribunal had wanted to adopt the unusual course of awarding costs to the losing parties it would have expressly so stated. In the jurisprudence of the Tribunal, only those claims for costs or attorneys' fees which are accepted by the Tribunal are expressly mentioned in the judgment; and silence means rejection. In so acting the Tribunal has followed a dictum of the International Court of Justice in its advisory opinion of July 12, 1973, concerning the review of Judgment No. 158 of the United Nations Administrative Tribunal. In that case the Court said:

Account must also be taken of the basic principle regarding the question of costs in contentious proceedings before international tribunals, to the effect that each party shall bear its own in the absence of a specific decision of the tribunal awarding costs (cf. Article 64 of the Statute of the Court) . . . the decision merely to allow the general principle to apply does not necessarily require detailed reasoning, and may even be adopted by implication. (1973 ICJ Reports, para. 98, p. 212)

(*Agodo et al.*, Decision No. 76 [1989], para. 32)

iii. 49. The Applicant also requests that the Tribunal award her attorney's fees and costs. It is the decision of the Tribunal that the Respondent pay the Applicant $1,000 in such fees and costs.

Decision:

(ii) . . . hat the Respondent shall pay the Applicant the sum of $1,000 for attorneys' fees and costs; . . . (*Robinson*, Decision No. 78 [1989], para. 49, Decision)

iv. 22. The Tribunal concludes that such a demonstration has been made. The Tribunal considers that, in the calculation of damages, weight should be given to the Applicant's extended service as a consultant to the Bank before he joined the Staff full time, a factor that accounted for the Bank's waiver of the Applicant's initial probationary period and his quick rise to a position as division chief. Taking that factor into account, and taking into account the Tribunal's conclusion that the Bank has not demonstrated that the Applicant's non-selection in the management-selection round was consistent with his conditions of employment, and also considering the rule set down in *Harrison*, it is the conclusion of the Tribunal that the Respondent should pay the Applicant damages in the amount of $80,000 net of tax. The Applicant's additional request for attorney's fees is denied. The Applicant prepared his application without assistance of counsel, and counsel did not enter the case until the preparation and attempted filing of the reply, which the Tribunal has not accepted because of its untimeliness. [*Bertrand*, Decision No. 81 [1989], para. 22)

v. 14. In Decision No. 73, dated November 7, 1988, the Tribunal ruled in favor of the Applicant on the merits of his claim. As regards costs, the Tribunal observed, among other things, in paragraph 45:

> While the Applicant has made a request for costs he had not submitted to the Tribunal an itemized statement of costs at the conclusion of the proceedings. In these circumstances the Tribunal decides to award the Applicant costs in the amount of $1,000.

These words have been interpreted by the Applicant as an invitation to submit reasons—detailed in paragraphs 4 to 9 above—why the Tribunal should award him an additional sum of $6,121 to cover attorney's fees and costs.

15. The Applicant has misunderstood the nature of the Tribunal's observation. The Applicant made a request for costs and the Tribunal did not make an interim decision on his request, postponing a final decision and inviting him to submit further particulars to enable it to make a final decision. On the contrary the Tribunal did make a final decision—awarding him costs in the amount of $1,000 which was intended to include attorney's fees. This decision makes the award *res judicata*, as is confirmed by Article XI (1) of the Tribunal's Statute, which declares its judgments 'final and without appeal'. Thus, clearly the Tribunal cannot reopen Decision No. 73 by way of appeal. As was stated in *Van Gent (No. 2)*, Decision No. 13 [1983], para. 21:

> No party to a dispute before the Tribunal may bring his case back to the Tribunal for a second round of litigation, no matter how dissatisfied he may be with the pronouncement of the Tribunal or its considerations. The Tribunal's judgment is meant to be the last step along the path of settling disputes arising between the Bank and the members of its staff.

(*Alan Berg (No. 2)*, Decision No. 87 [1990], paras. 14, 15)

vi. 35. The Tribunal is convinced that the injuries sustained by the Applicant as a result of the Respondent's failure to consider her in the management-selection round are tangible and substantial, and that they exceed the 'Package B increment'. Accordingly, it orders that the Respondent pay to the Applicant seven months' net salary as compensation and $6,000 in costs.

Decision:

(ii) . . . the Applicant be paid $6,000 in costs; . . . (*Harrison (No. 2)*, Decision No. 91 [1990], para. 35, Decision (ii))

vii. *Decision:*

(ii) . . . the Respondent shall pay the Applicant costs in the amount of $3,000; . . . (*Lindsay*, Decision No. 92 [1990], Decision (ii))

viii. 44. The Applicant also seeks compensation under three heads: (*a*) $7,000 said to represent three and a half months' vacation pay to which she would have been entitled if she had been hired as permanent staff in July 1986; (*b*) attorney's fees in the amount of $2,000; and (*c*) $20,000 for emotional and mental distress that she has suffered as a result of the Bank's action. The Tribunal notes that the Applicant has made no reference to the fact that at the time of her illness the Bank gave her an additional 62 days of sick leave which the Bank ultimately wrote off. While the amount thus waived by the Bank was not large, it was, at the same time, not negligible. Taking into consideration all the circumstances of the case, the Tribunal will order the payment to the Applicant of compensation equitably assessed at $6,000.

Decision:

(ii) . . . the Respondent shall pay to the Applicant costs in the amount of $1,000; . . . (*Arellano*, Decision No. 98 [1990], para. 44, Decision (ii))

ix. *Decision:*

(ii) . . . the Respondent shall pay to the Applicant as costs the amount of $3,000; . . . (*Klaus Berg (No. 2)*, Decision No. 99 [1990], Decision (ii))

x. *Decision:*

(iii) . . . the Respondent pay the Applicant costs in the amount of $10,000; . . . (*Jassal*, Decision No. 100 [1991], Decision (iii))

[For a similar statement see *Fabara-Núñez*, Decision No. 101 [1991], Decision (iii).]

30. PROCEDURE BEFORE TRIBUNAL

1. Discovery of documents

[See also Sect. 28, 'Reorganization', 2.iii, 3.v; Sect. 32, 'Miscellaneous', 5.i.]

i. 1. The Tribunal rejected the Applicant's request for discovery of certain documents and for hearing of witnesses. (*Sebastian, (No. 2)* Decision No. 57 [1988], para. 1)

ii. 1. . . . The Tribunal rejected the Applicant's request for discovery of certain documents. (*Rae*, Decision No. 74 [1988], para. 1)

iii. 1. . . . At the Applicant's request the Respondent produced a requested document. (*Robinson*, Decision No. 78 [1989], para. 1)

iv. 1. The Tribunal rejected the Applicant's request for production of certain documents. (*Sukkar*, Decision No. 84 [1989], para. 1)

v. 1. The Tribunal rejected the Applicant's request for production of documents and inquiry. (*de Raet*, Decision No. 85 [1989], para. 1)

vi. 6. In its Document Request No. 1, the Applicant requests that for each post-reorganization position listed by the Respondent in response to Interrogatory No. 1, the Respondent produce the pertinent 'statements of responsibility and selection criteria' prepared for use in the management-selection process. Because the Tribunal considers that any such documents might prove to be relevant to the Tribunal's decision on the merits of this case, it concludes that the Respondent should produce them. The Respondent in its Answer appears to assert that there are no such documents for it to produce. If the Respondent reasserts that contention in response to the Applicant's Document Request No. 1, then the Respondent should produce any pertinent job description for the specified post-reorganization positions, should identify the pertinent position grade levels, and should identify the stage of the reorganization process when these positions were filled by decision of the Bank's representatives.

7. In its Document Request No. 2, the Applicant requests that for each pre-reorganization position listed by the Respondent in response to Interrogatory No. 2, the Respondent produce the 'last written job description for that position.' Because the Tribunal considers that any such documents might prove to be relevant to the Tribunal's decision on the merits of this case, it concludes that the Respondent should produce them. (*Harrison (No. 2)*, Order [1989], paras. 6, 7)

vii. 1. The Tribunal ordered the Respondent to produce certain documents and to answer interrogatories. (*Fernandes*, Decision No. 90 [1990], para. 1)

viii. 1. The Tribunal ordered the Respondent to produce certain documents and to answer interrogatories. (*Harrison (No. 2)*, Decision No. 91 [1990], para. 1)

ix. 1. The Tribunal rejected the Applicant's request for certain preliminary measures, including the production of documents. (*Klaus Berg (No. 2)*, Decision No. 99 [1990], para. 1)

x. 2. The Applicant has also requested, in his letter dated October 10, 1989, prepared after the Respondent's filing of its answer, that the Tribunal order the Respondent to 'produce the "IAD Panel" report under conditions to be specified by the Tribunal.'

3. The Tribunal notes that the Respondent made use of this report in its answer and its letter dated October 20, 1989, and reproduced an extract therefrom in an annex to its answer. The Respondent also made reference to the confidential nature of this document.

4. Rule 17 of the Rules of the Tribunal provides:

> The Tribunal may at any state of the proceedings call for the production of documents or of such other evidence as may be required. It may arrange for any measures of inquiry as may be necessary.

5. The Tribunal orders that the Respondent shall within ten days of the receipt of this Order produce for examination by the Tribunal the IAD Investigative Panel Report referred to in the Respondent's answer and letter.

6. The confidential character of the document will, so far as appropriate, be respected. The Tribunal does not accept the contention of the Respondent, advanced in its letter dated October 20, 1989, to the effect that even material parts of the document shall not be released to the Applicant. The determination of what parts, if any, of the document shall be considered relevant to the case and released to the Applicant will be made later.

Order:

For the reasons stated, the Tribunal orders that the Respondent shall comply with the directive contained in para. 5 above, and that the time period for submission of the reply should cease to be suspended upon the Applicant's receipt of any portions of the requested document or upon receipt of a further order of the Tribunal. (*Fabara-Núñez*, Order [1990], paras. 2–6 and Order)

[For identical statements see *Jassal*, Order [1990], paras. 2–6 and Order.]

xi. 1. Consequent upon a request made by the Applicant the Tribunal ordered the Respondent to provide the Applicant with a copy of the 'IAD Investigative Panel Report' abridged under the supervision of the Tribunal. The Tribunal decided not to grant the Applicant's other request for documents and answers to interrogatories. (*Jassal*, Decision No. 100 [1991], para. 1)

[For an identical statement see *Fabara-Núñez*, Decision No. 101 [1991], para. 1.]

2. Additional statements

[See also Sect. 30, 'Procedure before Tribunal', 1.vi, vii, viii, xi.]

i. 1. . . . The Applicant filed an additional statement which the President made part of the record. (*Apkarian*, Decision No. 58 [1988], para. 1)

[Similar statements admitting additional statements were made in the following cases:

Benner, Decision No. 59 [1988], para. 1
Dosik, Decision No. 60 [1988], para. 1
Hovsepian, Decision No. 61 [1988], para. 1
Hunger, Decision No. 62 [1988], para. 1
Papinchak, Decision No. 63 [1988], para. 1
Witty, Decision No. 64 [1988], para. 1.]

ii. 1. . . . On March 18, 1988 the Respondent filed an additional statement which the Tribunal made part of the record. (*Kaplan*, Decision No. 65 [1988], para. 1)

iii. 1. . . . On March 18, 1988 and March 25, 1988 respectively the Respondent and the Applicant filed additional statements. (*Tucker*, Decision No. 68 [1988], para. 1)

iv. 1. . . . The Tribunal decided to make part of the record the additional statements filed by the parties. (*de Jong*, Decision No. 89 [1990], para. 1)

v. 1. . . . The President of the Tribunal rejected the Applicant's request for *additional documents*, and, because the time limit for filing the Reply had expired, asked the parties to file additional written statements in order to complete the proceedings, so that the Tribunal could reach an informed decision. (*Lindsay*, Decision No. 92 [1990], para. 1)

vi. 1. . . . The parties filed additional written statements which the Tribunal decided to make part of the record. (*Georgiev*, Decision No. 96 [1990], para. 1)

3. Evidence

(*a*) *General*

[See also Sect. 7, 'Appeals Committee', 1.i; Sect. 8, 'Sources of Law', 3 (*a*) i; Sect. 11, 'Prejudice/Discrimination', 2.iv; Sect. 12, 'Substantive Irregularity', 1.xii; Sect. 13, 'Procedural Irregularity', 1.iv; Sect. 28, 'Reorganization', 3.iv and viii; Sect. 30, 'Procedure before Tribunal', 19.i.]

i. 41. Although the Applicant relies upon some colorably supportive language in a document dated February 10, 1986, from the Assistant Director, PMD, to another supervisor in the Department, that is too slender a reed upon which to rest the Applicant's claim. First, it is not explained how this memorandum could supersede the clear language of Pers./11/81. Nor is there any evidence that the memorandum or the personnel manual circular was applied with respect to any other staff member so as to vary the grade level of TAP positions from time to time. Finally, the memorandum of the Assistant Director, PMD, continued as follows: 'In future the following provisions apply: a staff member who joins TAP will carry the grade of their [*sic*] previous regular assignment on a personal basis for up to two years and will be given assignments . . .' (*Montesa*, Decision No. 82 [1989], para. 41)

ii. 54. . . . The report of the Committee is never regarded as 'the basis' upon which this Tribunal deals with cases and is in no way binding upon it. The Tribunal is the only body within the Bank that deals with complaints judicially and it does so only on the basis of the evidence before it. . . .

62. There is also a risk that, in the absence of such explicit redefinition or job content, Bank management may too readily fall into the error of terminating on redundancy grounds the services of a staff member whose superiors are in reality moved by the poor quality of his performance rather than by his lack of the skills newly incorporated in a 'redesigned' position; there is, indeed, some evidence that precisely this error may have occurred in the initial decision to terminate the Applicant on the basis of redundancy. If this view is correct, the requirements of subsection (*c*) were not met and the procedure followed in relation to the Applicant must be found not to have been correct. (*de Raet*, Decision No. 85 [1989], paras. 54, 62)

iii. 21. . . . The Tribunal will not interfere with the exercise of such discretion 'unless the decision constitutes an abuse of discretion, being arbitrary, discriminatory, improperly motivated or carried out in violation of a fair and reasonable procedure.' (*Saberi*, Decision No. 5 [1982], para. 24; *Suntharalingam*, Decision No. 6 [1982], para. 27, *Thompson*, Decision No. 30 [1986], para. 24; *Pinto*, Decision No. 56 [1988], para. 36). In this case there is no evidence of the operation of any of these vitiating factors. (*Klempin*, Decision No. 88 [1990], para. 21)

iv. 41. There is no evidence before the Tribunal to substantiate any such finding in this case. Indeed, the Applicant's challenge to the Bank's selection of level 25 staff members to level 26 positions is based not on the particular qualifications of the former group of employees but rather upon a claim that 'the selection of a lower level staff member into positions for which Applicant was qualified is *per se* a violation of his essential employment rights.' (*Fernandes*, Decision No. 90 [1990], para. 41)

v. 24. The evidence adduced by the Applicant in support of this contention is no more than circumstantial and consists principally of the fact that the post was newly created, that the job description was precisely tailored to suit his qualifications and that, after he declined it, the post was not offered to anyone else. However, apart from the procedural irregularity that the Tribunal already found (question (I) above), the only real evidence on the point is the statement in a memorandum from Mr. Dyck to the Applicant: 'of course . . . the Region was also cognizant of Senior Management's desire to place as many qualified staff as possible at their level before the end of Round 2'. This observation must be read in its context, as following a sentence describing the objective justification for offering the post to the Applicant: '. . . the Region offered him this position by virtue of his past experience and expertise as a Project Specialist (and his knowledge of technical assistance) including but not limited to the human resources section.' [*Lindsay*, Decision No. 92 [1990], para. 24)

vi. 37. It is not for the Tribunal, in assessing the validity of the selection or non-selection of a staff member, to undertake its own examination of that staff member's record, or a criterion-by-criterion assessment of his or her qualifications. That is for the Bank to do in the first instance, subject to review by the Tribunal only for abuse of discretion. But the Tribunal is charged with determining whether the Bank's decision was the product of bias, prejudice, arbitrariness, manifest unreasonableness, or unfair or improper procedure. Thus, if the Bank's conclusion regarding the Applicant's qualifications for selection as audit analyst altogether lacks support in factual evidence or reasonable inference, that conclusion must be found to be an abuse of discretion. The Tribunal will now consider whether such is the case here . . .

55. The negative views of the Applicant's qualifications held by the most influential participant in the selection process were altogether without support in the

Applicant's prior annual evaluation reports, and also fundamentally and clearly failed to reflect the positive views of the three senior auditors who were consulted by the Acting Director and who were fully familiar with the Applicant's work. The Bank's decision that the Applicant was unfit for a level 20 audit analyst position is found to be lacking in any evidentiary support and is therefore an abuse of discretion. (*Jassal*, Decision No. 100 [1991], paras. 37, 55)

For similar statements see *Fabara-Núñez*, Decision No. 101 [1991], paras. 38, 45.]

vii. 32. Although the Applicant challenges the Respondent's evaluation of his performance as being discriminatory and motivated by a general hostile attitude on the part of the VPCOF towards the Applicant, the Tribunal does not find in the record any evidence that substantiates that contention. (*Mathew*, Decision No. 103 [1991], para. 32)

(*b*) *Burden of proof*

[See also Sect. 11, 'Prejudice/Discrimination', 2.iii; Sect. 28, 'Reorganization', 2.v.]

i. 16. The question in this case is whether there is evidence of the operation of any of these vitiating factors. There is evidence that the Applicant and his director disagreed strongly over certain substantive policy issues and that the Applicant sharply criticized him. There is also evidence that the director on occasion praised the Applicant. . . .

20. The Tribunal concludes, in light of all of these factors, including the detailed allegations and factual support presented by the Applicant in his pleas, that his case should properly be treated as one in which the burden of proof moved to the Respondent to show that Bank management acted fairly to the Applicant, rather than resting upon the Applicant the burden to show that the Bank acted unfairly. In the typical case in which the Applicant points to specific reasons for casting serious doubt upon the fairness of the Bank's selection process,

it is for the Bank to dissipate this doubt by providing the facts that are readily available to it in order to show no more than that its discretion has been fairly exercised. The Bank has not attempted to discharge this burden, other than with conclusory statements relating to the content and manner of assertion of the Applicant's policy views, and the perceived superiority of other candidates for managerial positions. The Tribunal believes that these statements are insufficiently detailed to discharge the Respondent's burden of demonstrating that its decision-making process was based upon giving no more than their due weight to legitimate factors. (*Bertrand*, Decision No. 81 [1989], paras. 16, 20)

ii. 30. There is thus every probability that the Applicant would have been given serious consideration for assignment to a comparable position as 'manager' in the Reorganization had she been properly considered by the Bank in the management-selection round. It is appropriate to place the burden on the Respondent to demonstrate otherwise, given the fact that it was the Bank's failure so to consider her that constituted a violation of the Applicant's rights in the case at hand. (*Harrison (No. 2)*, Decision No. 91 [1990], para. 30)

(*c*) *Witnesses*

[See Sect. 3, 'Inadmissibility for Other Reasons', 1.i, iii; Sect. 30, 'Procedure before Tribunal', 1.i.]

4. Intervention

i. 1. . . . An application to intervene was filed by a present member of the Bank staff on August 20, 1990. The principal proceedings were suspended and pleadings relating to the intervention were exchanged among the staff member and the parties. . . .

66. A staff member of the Bank sought to intervene in this proceeding in order to protect his asserted right to confidentiality of the contents of a report prepared in late 1987 by a committee especially appointed to look into

charges of mismanagement in IAD. He claims that on a number of occasions the Bank gave him explicit assurances that the contents of the report would not be disclosed, and the Respondent has in fact acknowledged its confidential nature. Because the Tribunal has taken steps to preserve such confidentiality in connection with its earlier Order to make an abridged copy of the report available to the Applicant, and has otherwise satisfied the interest of the petitioning staff member to the degree it deems proper and possible, the Tribunal without ruling on the issue of admissibility, decides that the application for intervention is in any event without object. (*Jassal*, Decision No. 100 [1991], paras. 1, 66)

[For identical statements see *Fabara-Núñez*, Decision No. 101 [1991], paras. 1, 56.]

5. *Amicus curiae*/staff association

i. 1. The President made the following procedural decisions: (i) under Rule 23 para. 2, he allowed the representatives of the World Bank Staff Association to participate in the proceedings as a friend-of-the-court; (ii) under Rule 25 he decided to permit cross-referencing for legal arguments and annexes and that the memorandum filed by the Staff Association be incorporated in the Application; (iii) under Rule 25 on the Respondent's request for summary dismissal of the application he decided not to stay the proceedings and that the parties should proceed to an exchange of pleadings in accordance with shortened time limits as set by him. The Tribunal decided that the fourteen applications be decided upon together. (*Agodo et al.*, Decision No. 76 [1989], para. 1)

ii. 1. The Tribunal decided that the Staff Association could participate in the proceedings as an *amicus curiae*. The usual exchange of pleadings took place. The cases were listed on August 11, 1989. The Tribunal decided to consolidate the cases. (*Hammond et al.*, Decision No. 86 [1989], para. 1)

6. Summary dismissal

[See Sect. 30, 'Procedure before Tribunal', 5.i.]

7. Stay of proceedings

[See Sect. 30, 'Procedure before Tribunal', 5.i.]

8. Cross referencing of legal arguments

[See Sect. 30, 'Procedure before Tribunal', 5.i.]

9. Consolidation

[See Sect. 30, 'Procedure before Tribunal', 5.i and ii.]

10. Suspension of principal proceedings

[See Sect. 30, 'Procedure before Tribunal', 4.i.]

11. Deferral of consideration

[See also Sect. 28, 'Reorganization', 3.vi; Sect. 32, 'Miscellaneous', 5.i.]

i. 47. While the Respondent suggested that the Tribunal may wish to consider deferring consideration of the case until its next session in view of this recent development, the Applicant has expressed the view that there is no reason to postpone consideration of the case. The Tribunal is of the view that to pronounce on this application will define and clarify the obligations between the parties and thus assist them in settling the question of restitution. The present proceedings have enabled the Tribunal to dispel a misinterpretation of the Applicant regarding the meaning of the proviso at the end of the letter of November 14, 1988, where it is stated that in the event of the Applicant being offered and accepting a position in the Bank, her 'entitlement to the enhanced separation benefits under Rule 5.09 would be canceled and appropriate restitution would be made for the benefits received'. This proviso does not signify that the Applicant must work without pay, if she accepts a new position and, consequently, it does not constitute a penalty, nor a misuse or abuse of power. The Respondent made it clear, in the course of the proceedings that the term 'appropriate restitution' is designed to cover all possible situations where, in the absence of some restitution there would be unjust enrichment, such as resettlement benefits when the occasion for resettlement was obviated by reappointment. (*Sukkar*, Decision No. 84 [1989], para. 47)

12. Interrogatories

[See also Sect. 30, 'Procedure before Tribunal', 1. vi, vii, viii, xi.]

i. 3. The Tribunal held, in its Order in *Harrison* (No. 2) of this date, that Rules 7 (3) (*a*) and 17 clearly grant to it the power to order a party to produce documents or to answer interrogatories when they are 'potentially material and useful in deciding upon the issues before it.'

4. In its interrogatory and document request, the Applicant seeks information relating to 'positions graded at level 16 which were filled during the reorganization selection process by persons who prior to their selection held positions graded at a lower level.' Because the Tribunal considers that any such information might prove to be relevant to the Tribunal's decision on the merits of this case, it concludes that the Respondent should be directed to respond to the interrogatory posed and produce any related documents as requested. (*Fernandes*, Order [1989], paras. 3, 4)

ii. 3. The Tribunal concludes that there is no requirement in the Rules of the Tribunal that there be an 'exceptional case' before the Tribunal may direct a party to produce documents or to answer interrogatories. Rules 7 (3) (*a*) and 17 clearly grant the Tribunal these powers whenever the Tribunal considers that any such document or information is potentially material and useful in deciding upon the issues before it.

4. In its Interrogatory No. 1, the Applicant requests that the Respondent furnish a list of 'the post-reorganization positions assigned the duties performed by Applicant prior to the reorganization.' The Bank has purported to furnish this information in the pleas and annexes in its Answer. At this time, this appears to be an adequate response to Interrogatory No. 1. The Applicant's request for this preliminary measure is therefore denied.

5. In its Interrogatory No. 2, the Applicant requests that for each position listed by the Respondent in response to Interrogatory 1, it also list the 'pre-reorganization position and grade of the staff member who was selected' for that post-reorganization position. Because the Tribunal considers that this information (but not the names of the staff members) might prove to be relevant to the Tribunal's decision on the merits of this case, it concludes that the Respondent should respond to Interrogatory No. 2. (*Harrison (No. 2)*, Order [1989], paras. 3, 4, 5)

iii. 1. In her application, the Applicant has requested that the Tribunal order the Respondent to answer an interrogatory, and to produce a document, regarding Level 19 positions to which staff members were promoted from Level 18 positions in the course of the 1987 Reorganization. The Tribunal has determined that such information is not material to the disposition of this case, and therefore denies these requests: *Fernandes*, Decision No. 90 [1990]. (*Fabara-Núñez*, Order [1990], para. 1)

[For an identical statement see *Jassal*, Order [1990], para. 1.]

13. Inquiry

[See Sect. 30, 'Procedure before Tribunal', 1.v and x.]

14. Preliminary measures

[See also Sect. 30, 'Procedure before Tribunal', 1.ix, 12.ii.]

i. 5. The Respondent should comply with these preliminary measures within 30 days from the transmission of this Order. The suspension of the time period provided in Rule 9 for the filing by the Applicant of a reply shall cease on the date on which the information and documents furnished by the Respondent pursuant to this order are transmitted to the Applicant. (*Fernandes*, Order [1989], para. 5)

[For an identical statement see *Harrison (No. 2)*, Order [1989], para. 5.]

15. Suspension of time limits

[See also Sect. 30, 'Procedure before Tribunal', 4.i.]

i. *Order:*
For the above reasons, the Tribunal orders that the Respondent shall comply with the directives contained in paras. 4 and 5 above and that the time period for submission of the reply should cease to be suspended as stated in para. 5 above. (*Fernandes*, Order [1989], Order)

[For a similar statement see *Harrison (No. 2)*, Order [1989], Order.]

ii. 5. The Tribunal orders that the Respondent shall within ten days of the receipt of this Order produce for examination by the Tribunal the IAD Investigative Panel Report referred to in the Respondent's answer and letter . . .

Order:
For the reasons stated, the Tribunal orders that the Respondent shall comply with the directive contained in para. 5 above, and that the time period for submission of the reply should cease to be suspended upon the Applicant's receipt of any portions of the requested document or upon receipt of a further order of the Tribunal. (*Fabara-Núñez*, Order [1990], para. 5, Order)

16. Separation of jurisdictional issues from merits

i. 1. The Respondent filed a request, which was granted, to separate jurisdictional issues from the merits, and to file an answer limited to the jurisdictional issues. Thereafter the usual pleadings were exchanged on the jurisdictional issues. (*Steinke*, Decision No. 79 [1989], para. 1)

ii. 1. . . . The Respondent filed a request, which was granted, to separate jurisdictional issues from the merits, and to file an answer limited to the jurisdictional issues. Thereafter the usual pleadings were exchanged on the jurisdictional issues. The case was listed on January 17, 1990. . . .

28. Against this application the Respondent has raised a jurisdictional issue, based on the alleged non-compliance by the Applicant with the statutory requirement of exhaustion of internal remedies. The Respondent's request to separate the jurisdictional issue from the merits having been granted, the present judgment will address this issue without going into the merits. (*de Jong*, Decision No. 89 [1990], paras. 1, 28)

iii. 1. . . . The Respondent filed a request, which was granted, to separate the jurisdictional issues from the merits, and to file an answer limited to the jurisdictional issue. Thereafter the Respondent submitted an answer on the jurisdictional issue. (*Ramorasoavina*, Decision No. 95 [1990], para. 1)

17. Oral proceedings

i. 1. . . . The Applicant's subsequent request for oral proceedings was denied by the Tribunal, which decided that such proceedings were unnecessary. (*Bertrand*, Decision No. 81 [1989], para. 1)

ii. 1. . . . The Tribunal rejected the Applicant's request for oral proceedings as unnecessary. (*Wahie*, Decision No. 93 [1990], para. 1)

iii. 1. . . . The Tribunal rejected the Applicant's request for oral proceedings as unnecessary. (*Mathew*, Decision No. 103 [1991], para. 1)

18. Amended pleadings

i. 1. . . . After the Respondent filed its answer the Applicant requested that he be permitted to withdraw the application but later asked that he be permitted to proceed with the case on the basis of amended pleadings. The Tribunal ordered that the case proceed. (*Spier*, Decision No. 77 [1989], para. 1)

19. Rules of procedure

[See also Sect. 30, 'Procedure before Tribunal', 1.x, 12.i.]

i. 4. Rule 17 of the Rules of the Tribunal provides:

> The Tribunal may at any stage of the proceedings call for the production of documents or of such other evidence as may be required. It may arrange for any measures of inquiry as may be necessary. (*Fabara-Núñez*, Order [1990], para. 4)

[For a similar statement see *Jassal*, Order [1990], para. 4.]

20. Confidentiality

i. 3. The Tribunal notes that the Respondent made use of this report in its answer and its letter dated October 20, 1989, and reproduced an extract therefrom in an annex to its answer. The Respondent also made reference to the confidential nature of this document. . . .

6. The confidential character of the document will, so far as appropriate, be respected. The Tribunal does not accept the contention of the Respondent, advanced in its letter dated October 20, 1989, to the effect that even the material parts of the documents shall not be released to the Applicant. The determination of what parts, if any, of the document shall be considered relevant to the case and released to the Applicant will be made later. (*Fabara-Núñez*, Order [1990], paras. 3, 6)

[For identical statements see *Jassal*, Order [1990], paras. 3, 6.]

21. Withdrawal of application

i. *Decision*:
Considering that the applications have been withdrawn, the Tribunal unanimously decides to record the withdrawal of the applications. (*Sopher and Staples*, Decision No. 67 [1988], Decision)

[For identical statements see:

Buyten (No. 2), Decision No. 80 [1989], Decision
Verdier, Decision No. 102 [1991], Decision.]

31. JUDGMENT

1. Mootness

[See also Sect. 16, 'Classification', 16.i and ii; Sect. 28, 'Reorganization', 3.i and ii.]

i. 59. In the light of the Tribunal's conclusions above this request has become moot. (*Kassab*, Decision No. 97 [1990], para. 59)

32. MISCELLANEOUS

1. Right of confidentiality

[See also Sect. 30, 'Procedure before Tribunal', 4.i.]

i. 66. A staff member of the Bank sought to intervene in this proceeding in order to protect his asserted right to confidentiality of the contents of a report prepared in late 1987 by a committee especially appointed to look into charges of mismanagement in IAD. He claims that on a number of occasions the Bank gave him explicit assurances that the contents of the report would not be disclosed, and the Respondent has in fact acknowledged its confidential nature. Because the Tribunal has taken steps to preserve such confidentiality in connection with its earlier Order to make an abridged copy of the report available to the Applicant, and has otherwise satisfied the interest of the petitioning staff member to the degree it deems proper and possible, the Tribunal, without ruling on the issue of admissibility, decides that the application for intervention is in any event without object. (*Jassal*, Decision No. 100 [1991], para. 66)

[For a similar statement see *Fabara-Núñez*, Decision No. 101 [1991], para. 56.]

2. Medical examination

i. 34. The relevant provision of the Staff manual was Staff Rule 4.01 which provides in Section 4.04 as follows:

> Before an appointment to the staff of the Bank becomes effective, the Director, Medical or a physician assigned to the Health Room or retained by the Bank Group, shall have cleared the person for appointment under the following conditions:
>
> (*a*) In the case of candidates selected for all appointments except as provided in subparagraph (*b*) below, based on the results of a complete medical examination.
>
> (*b*) In the case of candidates selected for Temporary; Local Temporary; Consultant; and Local Consultant appointments of a specified duration of more than one month, but less than six months, whose positions do not require international travel, after they have submitted a certificate from their personal physician indicating that they are in good health and have no communicable diseases, and have provided any pertinent medical information which may be needed in case of a medical emergency.

The exception in sub-paragraph (*b*) relates to prospective temporary staff and consultants, into neither of which categories did the appointment offered to the Applicant fall, and is therefore not pertinent. . . .

36. As can be seen, the Bank is, in effect, saying that although medical clearance is a condition precedent to an appointment, and the giving of that clearance is a matter for the Medical Department, that Department is not under an obligation to perform a complete medical examination before denying appointment for medical reasons to an otherwise qualified applicant. The Tribunal does not see how this approach can be reconciled with the plain words of para. 4.04 of the Staff Rules, namely, that there shall have been a complete medical examination. That is what the Rule prescribes and it is to that that the Applicant is entitled. The right reserved by the Bank to reject an otherwise acceptable individual after medical examination necessarily implies an obligation upon the Bank not to reject such an individual without conducting a medical examination.

37. The attempt by the Bank to support its approach by saying that no purpose would have been served by an examination 'in the case of candidates that are otherwise unfit, as in the Applicant's case, due to an uncontested prior illness' is not convincing. What matters is not whether in the particular case an examination may medically 'serve any purpose' but the fact that the relevant Staff Rule prescribes that there shall be a complete medical examination. The requirement is mandatory. If the Bank had intended that the conduct of an examination should be a matter for the discretion of the medical staff in the light of the medical history of any candidate for employment it could have expressed Section 4.04 of Staff Rule 4.01 in terms which would have permitted the medical staff to base their clearance 'either on the results of a complete medical examination or on their assessment of the candidate's medical history.' But the Staff Rule does not say this and it is not open to the Bank to interpret the existing words in this way.

38. The Bank also argues that even if a medical examination had taken place at the time of assessment, 'under the Bank's policy, medical clearance could not have been given until that five-year period had expired.' The Bank goes on to say that the refusal of medical clearance to the

Applicant was 'a reasoned, deliberate application of established policy.' The Tribunal sees two objections to this argument. . . .

41. The Tribunal sees a second objection to the Bank's invocation of the 'application of an established policy' of which the UN Guidelines appear to form a significant part. While, in principle, the adoption by the Bank medical staff of a policy contained in the UN Guidelines or any other internal guidelines, cannot be questioned, it is essential that the application of the policy should be fully consistent with the provisions of the Staff Regulations which require a complete medical examination.

42. This is enough to dispose of the substance of the case. The Applicant should have been medically examined and she was not. It is unnecessary, therefore, to consider her other contentions. (*Arellano*, Decision No. 98 [1990], paras. 34, 36–8, 41–2)

3. Nationality

i. 36. In ruling upon the application the Tribunal will have to interpret the controlling Staff Rule. As to the Applicant's first argument in para. 34 above, the Tribunal concludes that the second sentence in Staff Rules 6.13 and 6.14, para. 2.01, is applicable to the Applicant. That sentence, by virtue of its punctuation and purpose, distinguishes between staff members who become U.S. citizens and those who become permanent residents. It is only with respect to the latter group—which does not include the Applicant—that any application filing date becomes pertinent. . . .

39. In reaching this conclusion the Tribunal has borne in mind its understanding of the rationale behind the whole system of expatriate benefits and the proper approach to citizenship as a reflection of allegiance to and connection with a particular State. To provide for the reacquisition of certain economic benefits when a staff member renounces his or her nationality might encourage a casual approach to the responsibilities and

implications of citizenship. The Applicant does not conceal the real purpose of her decisions first to acquire U.S. citizenship and then to consider renouncing it. In her application before the Tribunal she 'affirms that she took U.S. citizenship because of rumors that the Bank was planning a reduction in force and if deprived of a job she felt that she would stand a better chance of finding another one in the U.S. market if she had U.S. citizenship'. She equally admits that her desire to renounce U.S. citizenship stems, partly at least, from her realization that her decision to take U.S. citizenship had cost her her eligibility for expatriate benefits.

40. The Tribunal does not accept the Applicant's contention that by denying her re-eligibility for expatriate benefits if she renounces her U.S. citizenship the Respondent would be interfering with the right of staff members freely to acquire and reassume their citizenship. The Applicant remains free to renounce her previously acquired U.S. citizenship and to revert to the G-4 visa status, but she cannot use that freedom as the basis for requiring the Respondent to grant her certain benefits. The Respondent's regulation of eligibility for expatriate benefits is a proper exercise of its power to regulate the rights and obligations of staff members. (*Wahie*, Decision No. 93 [1990], paras. 36, 39, 40)

4. Retroactivity

[See Sect. 16, 'Classification', 13.iii; Sect. 26, 'Taxation', 1.i.]

5. Resettlement

[See also Sect. 8, 'Sources of Law', 2 (*c*) iii; Sect. 30, 'Procedure before Tribunal', 1.iv; Sect. 32, 'Miscellaneous', 6.i.]

i. 39. The Applicant asserts that an implied obligation on the part of the Respondent results from the fact that she had assumed, on her part, the obligation to stay with the Bank for a specified period of time. This, in the Applicant's contention, created a bilateral contract establishing mutual obligations regarding service to the Bank. This argument refers to the fact that the Bank, in subsidizing full-time external training, requires from the staff member the undertaking to remain in the service of the Bank for at least three years upon completion of the full-time study program. If the beneficiary leaves the Bank within three years for any reason, he is required to repay the Bank a prorated portion of the costs it incurred. Such a commitment was obtained from the Applicant, although she continued working in the Bank on a part time basis. However, this 'bonding', as it is called, does not signify the existence of a corresponding, mutual obligation on the part of the Bank to retain for a period of time the services of the beneficiary of a full time external program. There is no indication that the Bank has given up its power of declaring a position redundant. This is confirmed by the letter of September 23, 1985 approving the Applicant's study program, where reference is made to the possibility of a termination grant and of resettlement upon termination. In any event, the 'mutuality' sought by the Applicant in her bilateral contract was already amply provided when the Bank paid a substantial portion of her educational expenses. . . .

47. While the Respondent suggested that the Tribunal may wish to consider deferring consideration of the case until its next session in view of this recent development, the Applicant has expressed the view that there is no reason to postpone consideration of the case. The Tribunal is of the view that to pronounce on this application will define and clarify the obligations between the parties and thus assist them in settling the question of restitution. The present proceedings have enabled the Tribunal to dispel a misinterpretation of the Applicant regarding the meaning of the proviso at the end of the letter of November 14, 1988, where it is stated that in the event of the Applicant being offered and accepting a position in the Bank, her 'entitlement to the enhanced separation benefits under Rule 5.09 would be canceled and appropriate restitution would be made for the benefits received'. This proviso does not signify that the Applicant

must work without pay, if she accepts a new position and, consequently, it does not constitute a penalty, nor a misuse or abuse of power. The Respondent made it clear, in the course of the proceedings that the term 'appropriate restitution' is designed to cover all possible situations where, in the absence of some restitution there would be unjust enrichment, such as resettlement benefits when the occasion for resettlement was obviated by reappointment. (*Sukkar*, Decision No. 84 [1989], paras. 39, 47)

6. Training

[See also Sect. 8, 'Sources of Law', 2 (*c*) iii, Sect. 22, 'Transfer and Reassignment', 1.iii; Sect. 28, 'Reorganization', 1.iii, 2.vii and x; Sect. 32, 'Miscellaneous', 5.i.]

i. 38. In support of her contentions the Applicant invokes Principle 5 (*d*) of the Principles of Staff Employment, which provides that the Respondent shall 'establish programs and arrangements for staff training and development for the purpose of updating and improving staff skills to meet the needs of the Organization'. The Applicant further invokes in support of her claims Personnel Manual Statement (PMS) 4.03, Section 1 which reads as follows:

> The World Bank's long term effectiveness in providing assistance to its member countries is largely dependent upon the professional excellence of its staff.
>
> Professional excellence, however, cannot be assumed to be self-sustaining in a context where standards of performance, the state of knowledge and the range of Bank Group activities are steadily evolving. It must be systematically maintained and renewed through suitable training programs.

These statements merely describe the Bank's policy to encourage and support staff members to develop further their own education and skills through a partially subsidized program. But neither Principle 5 (*d*) nor PMS 4.03 creates for the Respondent the legal obligations claimed by the Applicant (see *de Merode*, Decision No. 1 [1981], para. 22).

39. The Applicant asserts that an implied obligation on the part of the Respondent results from the fact that she had assumed, on her part, the obligation to stay with the bank for a specified period of time. This, in the Applicant's contention, created a bilateral contract establishing mutual obligations regarding service to the Bank. This argument refers to the fact that the Bank, in subsidizing full-time external training, requires from the staff member the undertaking to remain in the service of the Bank for at least three years upon completion of the full-time study program. If the beneficiary leaves the Bank within three years for any reason, he is required to repay the Bank a prorated portion of the costs it incurred. Such a commitment was obtained from the Applicant, although she continued working in the Bank on a part time basis. However, this 'bonding', as it is called, does not signify the existence of a corresponding, mutual obligation on the part of the Bank to retain for a period of time the services of the beneficiary of a full time external program. There is no indication that the Bank has given up its power of declaring a position redundant. This is confirmed by the letter of September 23, 1985 approving the Applicant's study program, where reference is made to the possibility of a termination grant and of resettlement upon termination. In any event, the 'mutuality' sought by the Applicant in her bilateral contract was already amply provided hen the Bank paid a substantial portion of her educational expenses. (*Sukkar*, Decision No. 84 [1989], paras. 38, 39)

ii. 48. In any event, the Applicant was not properly qualified for the vacancy he identified in his reply as the one that should have been communicated to him by Personnel, since he lacked the required secretarial skills. This lack of secretarial skills could not be remedied by training, because he did not qualify for receiving secretarial training. Staff Rule 5.09 speaks of training only for those without the requisite skills (para. 1.06 *c*). The fact that he was twice offered a position is in itself evidence that he possessed skills for which the Bank had a conntinuing need and which did not require additional training. (*Pavesich*, Decision No. 94 [1990], para. 48)

iii. 34. The Respondent, on several occasions in its pleadings, insists that 'the responsibilities of Applicant's position were changed as a result of the reorganization,' that 'Applicant was found to be unqualified for the new position,' that 'the skills requirements of [the audit analyst position] were altered, and generally new priorities were adopted,' and that 'changes were made and the requirements for positions were enlarged.' Yet the Respondent fails altogether to go beyond these general assertions to state with any particularity the respects in which the audit analyst position was changed in the course of the Reorganization. It was surely contemplated that in the Reorganization certain positions would be changed in their job content such that, for example, new technical skills (such as in macro-economics or computers) would henceforth be required. The Bank might well, in such circumstances, reasonably conclude that the present occupant of that position lacked the requisite skills for the position as redefined, and indeed that such skills could not be acquired after a reasonable period of training. Non-selection by virtue of redundancy might then be appropriate even though that position would remain vacant for lack of any other qualified staff member. But the Respondent has failed to provide any specific information that would warrant a conclusion that the audit analyst position was redefined in so substantial a manner. . . .

56. For all of the above reasons, the Tribunal reaches the same conclusion with even greater confidence concerning the Bank's decisions that the Applicant was unfit for a level 19 position and that further training would not cure his weaknesses. . . .

58. The conclusion of the Selection Committee that any shortfall in the Applicant's qualifications could not be addressed by additional counseling and training is also arbitrary and manifestly without rational basis. The few references in earlier PPRs to the Applicant's amenability

to training all support the conclusion that he was indeed receptive to training. The record before the Selection Committee would have shown that the Applicant's prior experience with the Bank had been characterized by a failure on the part of his supervisors to recommend or provide training opportunities. As the Appeals Committee concluded:

> In spite of favorable performance evaluations, there was reportedly some dissatisfaction with several aspects of his performance, and yet he seems to have received minimal—if any—feedback, counselling, career development assignments, or training. In this situation, it is hard to understand how the Bank could have rejected the training/retraining program for the Appellant.

Moreover, the principal criticism of the Applicant that was set forth by the Acting Director in the 1986–87 PPR, prepared by him initially in draft form in the same week as the Reorganization selections were made—that he 'need[s] to sharpen his focus on the broad and important implications of his findings'—is (to the extent it can be understood) of the sort that does not appear to defy correction through counseling and training. (*Jassal*, Decision No. 100 [1991], paras. 34, 56, 58)

iv. 45. It is particularly to be noted that the flaws identified by the Applicant's Manager in the 1986–87 PPR related to excessive time spent on work and to inadequate planning and organizational skills. The fact that he attributed these to her conscientiousness and her prior absence from audit work clearly indicates that he thought that these could be rectified with time and with counseling. The Respondent, however, asserts in its answer that the Selection Committee concluded not only that the Applicant fell short of the requirements of a level 19 audit analyst position but also that 'in light of Applicant's past experience and her limited potential for professional growth, neither retraining nor the offer of a position at a lower level constituted suitable alternatives.' Putting aside the question whether the record warrants this assertion as to what the reasons of the Selection

Committee actually were, the record requires the Tribunal to conclude that the failure of the Committee to offer the Applicant an audit analyst position at level 18, one level below the grade she presently held, and its failure to offer her the opportunity for further training—comparable to that extended to her by her Manager (and, by then, the Acting Director of IAD) only approximately one week before—were manifestly unreasonable. . . .

47. The Tribunal does not find substantiated in the record the Applicant's charge that the Acting Director discriminated against her because of her knowledge of alleged mismanagement on his part and because she was a vocal critic of him within the IAD. But the Tribunal does conclude that it is highly likely that the negative appraisal on the part of the Acting Director was controlling within the Selection Committee, and that neither he nor the Committee gave any weight to the Applicant's amenability to training or to the Bank's own responsibility for retarding the professional development of the Applicant. (*Fabara-Núñez*, Decision No. 101 [1991], para. 45, 47)

INDEX

The manufacturer's authorised representative in the EU for product safety is Oxford University Press España S.A. of el Parque Empresarial San Fernando de Henares, Avenida de Castilla, 2 – 28830 Madrid (www.oup.es/en or product.safety@oup.com). OUP España S.A. also acts as importer into Spain of products made by the manufacturer.

www.ingramcontent.com/pod-product-compliance
Lightning Source LLC
LaVergne TN
LVHW101442200926
848483LV00001B/27
9780198258193